INTERNATIONAL PERSPECTIVES IN THE EARLY YEARS

The Critical Issues in the Early Years Series

This series provides both national (UK-wide) and international perspectives on critical issues within the field of early years education and care.

The quality of early childhood education and care (ECEC) has remained a high priority on government agendas in recent years (OECD, 2006). This series reflects this developing early childhood context which includes professionalizing, and up-skilling, the early childhood workforce. In particular, the series brings a critical perspective to the developing knowledge and understanding of early years practitioners at various stages of their professional development, to encourage reflection on practice and to bring to their attention key themes and issues in the field of early childhood.

Series Editor

Linda Miller is Emeritus Professor, Early Years at The Open University. She has worked both with and for young children throughout her professional life as a practitioner, teacher trainer and university lecturer. She has been involved in national consultations on the workforce strategy and professionalization agenda in England. International work includes contributing to a European study on Competence Requirements in Early Childhood (CoRE, 2011) and a review of teacher education in England, with Claire Cameron, for the University of Bremen (2011). After chairing the Sector Endorsed Foundation Degrees in Early Years National Network from 2003 to 2008, she is now an honorary life member. Linda is a member of the Editorial Board of the *International Journal of Early Years Education* (Routledge) and former Book Reviews editor for that journal. She has published widely, in co-edited and single authored books and in national and international journals.

References

CoRE (2011) Competence Requirements in Early Childhood and Care: A Study for the European Commission Directorate-General for Education and Culture. Available at: http://ec.europa.eu/education/more-information/doc/2011/core_en.pdf

Miller, L. and Cameron, C. (2011) The integrated qualifications framework and the early years professional status: a shift towards a graduate-led workforce. Unpublished report for CORE project, University of Bremen.

Miller, L. and Cameron, C. (2011) Training of teachers who work in the field of early childhood education in England. Unpublished report for the University of Bremen.

Organisation for Economic Co-operation and Development (OECD) (2006) *Starting Strong II: Early Childhood Education and Care*. Paris: OECD.

Titles in the series

Miller and Cable, *Professionalization, Leadership and Management in the Early Years*
Miller and Hevey, *Policy Issues in the Early Years*
Miller and Pound, *Theories and Approaches to Learning in the Early Years*

INTERNATIONAL PERSPECTIVES IN THE EARLY YEARS

Edited by
Linda Miller and Claire Cameron

Los Angeles | London | New Delhi
Singapore | Washington DC

Los Angeles | London | New Delhi
Singapore | Washington DC

SAGE Publications Ltd
1 Oliver's Yard
55 City Road
London EC1Y 1SP

SAGE Publications Inc.
2455 Teller Road
Thousand Oaks, California 91320

SAGE Publications India Pvt Ltd
B 1/I 1 Mohan Cooperative Industrial Area
Mathura Road
New Delhi 110 044

SAGE Publications Asia-Pacific Pte Ltd
3 Church Street
#10-04 Samsung Hub
Singapore 049483

Editor: Jude Bowen
Assistant editor: Miriam Davey
Project manager/copyeditor: Sharon Cawood
Production editor: Thea Watson
Proofreader: Rosemary Campbell
Indexer: Catriona Armit
Marketing manager: Lorna Patkai
Cover designer: Wendy Scott
Typeset by: C&M Digitals (P) Ltd, Chennai, India
Printed in India by Replika Press Pvt Ltd

Editorial arrangement, Chapter 1 and Chapter 11 © Linda Miller
and Claire Cameron 2014
Chapter 2 © Pamela Oberhuemer 2014
Chapter 3 © Yoshie Kaga 2014
Chapter 4 © Tullia Musatti, Donatella Giovannini, Susanna
Mayer and Group Nido LagoMago 2014
Chapter 5 © Anne-Marie Doucet-Dahlgren 2014
Chapter 6 © John Bennett 2014
Chapter 7 © Margaret Kernan and Kathia Loyzaga 2014
Chapter 8 © Bronwen Cohen and Wenche Rønning 2014
Chapter 9 © Claire Cameron 2014
Chapter 10 © Roger Hancock, Ann Cameron and Ayshe
Talay-Ongan 2014

First published 2014

Library of Congress Control Number: 2013937252

British Library Cataloguing in Publication data

A catalogue record for this book is available from
the British Library

ISBN 978-1-4462-5536-0
ISBN 978-1-4462-5537-7 (pbk)

Education at SAGE

SAGE is a leading international publisher of journals, books, and electronic media for academic, educational, and professional markets.

Our education publishing includes:

- accessible and comprehensive texts for aspiring education professionals and practitioners looking to further their careers through continuing professional development

- inspirational advice and guidance for the classroom

- authoritative state of the art reference from the leading authors in the field

Find out more at: **www.sagepub.co.uk/education**

CONTENTS

ABOUT THE EDITORS AND CONTRIBUTORS

Editors

Linda Miller is Emeritus Professor, Early Years at The Open University. She has worked both with and for young children throughout her professional life as a practitioner, teacher trainer and university lecturer. She has been involved in national consultations on the workforce strategy and professionalization agenda in England. Her international work includes contributing to a European study on Competence Requirements in Early Childhood (CoRE, 2011) and a review of teacher education in England, with Claire Cameron, for the University of Bremen (unpublished, 2011). After chairing the Sector Endorsed Foundation Degrees in Early Years National Network from 2003 to 2008, she is now an honorary life member. Linda is a member of the Editorial Board of the *International Journal of Early Years Education* (Routledge) and former Book Reviews editor for that journal. She has published widely, in co-edited and single authored books and in national and international journals.

Claire Cameron is Senior Reader in Education at the Thomas Coram Research Unit, Institute of Education, University of London. She has a long-standing record of research on children's services, including studies of the early childhood care and education workforce. She undertook, with Peter Moss and Charlie Owen, the first comprehensive study of male workers in ECEC services in England (Paul Chapman, 1999), and, with Peter Moss, a study of quality of employment in care work in six countries, *Care Work in Europe* (Routledge, 2007). She contributed to the European study Competence Requirements in Early Childhood (CoRE, 2011) and has a well established record in studies of social pedagogic approaches to children's services in continental Europe and the UK. Most recently, she edited *Social Pedagogy and Working with Children and Young People: Where Care and Education Meet* (with Peter Moss) (Jessica Kingsley, 2011).

Contributors

John Bennett has worked in the early childhood policy field in international early childhood organizations, including UNESCO, UNICEF and the UN Committee on the Rights of the Child. In 1998, he joined the OECD as senior consultant to the Early Childhood Policy Review, where he co-authored two comparative works on early childhood policy in 20 OECD countries. The reports, *Starting Strong: Early Childhood Education and Care,* were published by the OECD in 2001 and 2006. John sits on the editorial boards of the *European Early Childhood Education Research Journal* (Routledge) and the *Journal of Early Childhood Research* (SAGE), and is a contributing editor to the *Early Childhood Development Encyclopaedia* (Centre of Excellence for Early Childhood Development, Montreal). During his career, he has reviewed early childhood policies and services in over 50 countries worldwide. He is currently engaged in researching early childhood policies for Roma and other children from disadvantaged backgrounds in Europe.

Ann Cameron is Honorary Professor in the Psychology Department at the University of British Columbia; Emerita and Honorary Research Professor at the University of New Brunswick; and Adjunct Professor in the School of Child and Youth Care at the University of Victoria, Canada. She conducts cultural research with resilient children and youth in communities around the globe using visual methodologies to afford young people a voice in collaboratively seeking to explore their experiences. Professor Cameron's research also includes: cross-cultural differences in children's moral judgements of truth telling and verbal deception, relations between physiological stress reactivity, attachment, affect and gender with children, youths and their parents; parent–child telephone-mediated communications and emergent literacy; and evaluations of community-based, gender-sensitive violence-prevention interventions. She publishes internationally in these areas.

Bronwen Cohen is Honorary Professor in Social Policy at the University of Edinburgh, with over 30 years of experience in social and educational policy and research at NGO, government and university levels. This included 10 years as the UK representative on the European Commission's Childcare Network, leading on rural childcare and the use of the Structural Funds, and 20 years as Chief Executive of Children in Scotland, the national agency for public, private and voluntary organizations working with children and their families across Scotland. She has published extensively, is a founder member of the magazine *Children in Europe* and directed the EC-funded programme 'Working for Inclusion: The role of the early years workforce in addressing child poverty and promoting social inclusion'. She is currently undertaking research on place-based learning in Alabama, Norway and Scotland with Wenche Rønning and Jack Shelton.

Anne-Marie Doucet-Dahlgren has pursued doctoral studies in France (University of Paris X-Nanterre) and in Sweden (University of Stockholm). She is now a part-time lecturer in the Science of Education and a Research Fellow at the University of Paris

Ouest-Nanterre La Défense, France. She has carried out many studies with parents and children with a particular focus on early childhood and child-rearing practices. She has published in co-edited and single authored books and international journals. Her main interests and publications are in the social and cultural study of children's everyday lives, family education and early intervention within an international perspective. She is currently working on two European projects: a comparative study (France, Italy, Romania) on foster families and a comparative study on the cultural representation of family in picture books (France, Sweden).

Roger Hancock was originally inspired by a physics teacher to want to be an educator. Roger went on to teach in a variety of English educative settings – primary schools, special schools, school advisory services and higher education. For many years he was a lecturer/researcher at The Open University, a distance learning organization in the UK, where he learnt to write in a way that engages readers. Since 2011, he has been semi-retired. In addition to research related to 'A Day in the Life' (see Chapter 10 in this book), he works with doctoral researchers. He now has more time for this form of teaching so he can do it in a way that truly explores the relationship between teaching and learning.

Donatella Giovannini, since 1986, has been a member of the psycho-pedagogical coordination group in the Department of Education, City of Pistoia, Italy. She supervises the organization of all the ECEC services for children under 3 in the city and the in-service training of their personnel. She has participated in numerous in-service training initiatives for ECEC professionals in other Italian cities. She has been involved with international meetings on early childhood education in Europe and in the USA, and is the author of articles in both Italian and non-Italian journals.

Yoshie Kaga is Programme Specialist in early childhood care and education (ECCE) at UNESCO HQ, Paris, and has been involved in ECCE projects in various parts of the world since 1998. Yoshie has supported and participated in national ECCE policy reviews and consultations in a range of countries such as the Dominican Republic, Kenya, Kazakhstan, the Republic of Korea, Tunisia and the United Arab Emirates. From 2006 to 2010, she managed and occasionally authored the UNESCO Policy Brief on Early Childhood series. From 2008 to 2010, she coordinated a research project on the integration of ECCE, which drew on experiences from Belgium (Flanders), Brazil, Finland, France, Hungary, Jamaica, New Zealand, Slovenia and Sweden, and co-authored, with John Bennett and Peter Moss, *Caring and Learning Together: A Cross-national Study on the Integration of ECCE within Education* (UNESCO, 2010). She is co-editor, with Ingrid Pramling Samuelsson, of *The Contribution of Early Childhood Education to a Sustainable Society* (UNESCO, 2008).

Margaret Kernan has been working internationally in the field of early childhood care and education and primary education for more than 25 years as a practitioner, researcher, trainer and consultant. Her specific interests include children's play, rights and diversity issues and policy and curriculum development in early childhood education and care. She is also interested in developing interdisciplinary approaches in researching issues affecting young children's lives. She is coordinator of an interdisciplinary, intergenerational project, TOY: *Together Old and Young*, which is being funded by the European Commission as part of the Grundtvig Life Long Learning Programme (www.toyproject.net). Margaret's current position is Senior Programme Manager in International Child Development Initiatives, in the Child's Rights Home, Leiden, The Netherlands (www.icdi.nl).

Kathia Loyzaga has a degree in Audiovisual Communication from the Universidad Iberoamericana in México City. She was previously head of the Capacity Building Department at Melel Xojobal A.C., a children's human rights NGO located in San Cristóbal de Las Casas, Chiapas. At the same time, she coordinated the Grupo de Trabajo Infancia Indígena y Educación (Indigenous Children and Education Working Group). She has coordinated and participated in various national and international publications regarding children's human rights and indigenous communities in Chiapas. Currently, she is working on a project regarding children involved in criminal justice processes as part of her Master's dissertation.

Susanna Mayer is a researcher at the Institute of Cognitive Sciences and Technologies, National Research Council of Italy. She studies young children's play with objects and communicative development in play contexts among children and between children and adults.

Tullia Musatti was Senior Researcher at the Institute of Cognitive Sciences and Technologies, National Research Council of Italy, until 2012, and is now Associate Researcher at the same Institute. She conducts research on young children's socialization and learning processes and is the author of several books and articles in the field of early childhood development and education. She has participated in numerous working committees and action projects to reorganize social and educational services in collaboration with Italian public administrations.

Nido LagoMago Research Group is based in the Department of Education, City of Pistoia, Italy. The group participated in the action research reported in the study in Chapter 4, and was composed of Armanda Cassaresi, Franca Gualtieri, Gabri Magrini and Simona Petruzzi, educators at the municipal *nido LagoMago*, and Rita Benedetto. Since the 1980s, all the *nido LagoMago* personnel have participated in numerous action-research initiatives and have conducted important innovative experiences in educational practice, in particular learning and social processes among children.

Pamela Oberhuemer is a freelance researcher and early years consultant, having worked for over 30 years at the Munich-based State Institute of Early Childhood Research. She was the lead researcher of the SEEPRO study commissioned by the German Federal Ministry for Family and Youth Affairs on systems of early education and professionalization in the 27 European Union countries, and of a six-country study on the continuing professional development of the early years workforce commissioned by the German Youth Institute (DJI), published in 2012. Currently (2012–2013), she is contributing to an eight-country study on access and quality issues relating to children from disadvantaged backgrounds conducted by The Centre for Analysis of Social Exclusion at the London School of Economics and Political Science. She is one of three academic editors of *Early Years: An International Research Journal*.

Wenche Rønning is Associate Professor at the University of Nordland and Senior Researcher at Nordland Research Institute, both located in Bodø, Norway. Before starting full-time as an educational researcher in 2000, Wenche worked for many years at the National Education Office in Nordland, where she was responsible for a number of development projects involving teachers and school leaders within compulsory education in Norway. Her research has focused on issues concerning school in society, teacher thinking and classroom research, and initiatives such as outdoor education and entrepreneurship in education. In her PhD, she focused on active learning in the Norwegian context historically, but also on how teachers today interpret and view active learning in the current educational context.

Ayshe Talay-Ongan is a Turkish-born author and retired academic from Macquarie University, Sydney. She is an alumnus of Columbia University (NYC, 1975) and is a Speech and Language Pathologist and Developmental Psychologist. Her research interests are in early and preventive intervention; developmental disabilities; and relationships, risk and resilience in young children. Her books include: *Typical and Atypical Development in Early Childhood* (Memo Press, 1999), *Early Development, Risk and Disability: Relational Contexts* (Pearson, 2004) and, with Emily Ap, *Child Development and Teaching Young Children* (Thomson, 2006). She is also the author of *Turquoise: A Love Story* (Sid Harta Publishers, 2012).

CHAPTER 1

INTERNATIONAL PERSPECTIVES: THEMES AND ISSUES

Linda Miller and Claire Cameron

Overview

This book seeks to explore some of the many ways in which early childhood education and care (ECEC)[1] is understood in Europe and beyond. The main objective of the book is to bring critical attention to some key issues from both a national and international perspective relating to the themes of early education and care, intervention in the lives of children and families and the concept of children's spaces. In this chapter, we describe the rationale and organization of the book. The book draws upon international perspectives to 'shine a light' on established practice in the UK and consider how to improve the ways in which services are developed and delivered to best serve all children in a very challenging and uncertain social and economic climate. The chapters reflect these changing and challenging policy agendas and aim to support the professional development of practitioners who work in this field. The book is intentionally research focused and draws on work from renowned academics, researchers and practitioners as co-researchers.

Introduction

We hope this book will offer fresh perspectives at a time of change and uncertainty across Europe and beyond, which is impacting on ECEC services. The economic crisis in particular is having a negative impact on children's health and well-being (Bennett, 2012); European governments question whether spending on ECEC can be justified in stringent economic times. In England, although ECEC services are in theory protected and supported by legislation, the drive to localism is putting services under unprecedented pressure. After a decade or more of investment, we are seeing increased 'marketization' and privatization of services (Lloyd, 2012; see also Woodrow, 2011) and the transfer of funding and decision making to local authorities. The number of children's centres offering full day care nearly halved between 2009 and 2011 (Brind et al., 2011). In 2011, a report into early intervention programmes for young children argued for funding through private investment in what have traditionally been publicly funded services (Allen, 2011). At the time of writing, further changes are proposed to the (de)-regulation of early years provision and to the training and qualifications of staff (DfE, 2013), which we believe could have a negative impact on the quality of early years provision. These developments are cause for concern to those involved in ECEC as economic and political factors can influence both practitioners and parents, so that what is appropriate for young children becomes less clear and less central in public debates. In this context, the book draws attention to a common ECEC agenda: that is the crucial role that early childhood services play in the well-being and learning of children and their families, and in forming democratic societies.

Why international perspectives?

Across the world, governments and non-governmental organizations have recognized the importance of ECEC services in supporting the development of children, and in the economic well-being of societies. The OECD carried out a high impact review of ECEC in 20 'rich' countries and found that integrated early childhood policies underpin significant social and economic policies among OECD countries (OECD, 2006). In particular, early childhood programmes can have a significant role to play in reducing and lessening the impact of child poverty, and investing in children's future at an early age has a higher rate of return than at later ages (OECD, 2006). However, such services alone cannot break the poverty cycle, and what is needed is a 'multi-dimensional approach' involving 'supportive economic and social policies' (Bennett, 2012: 11).

There are many similarities among ECEC services worldwide, but also significant differences. Table 1.1 summarizes key features of the context, including the degree of child poverty and mortality, the ranking in well-being indices, the age compulsory schooling starts, and spending on ECEC services, as well as the degree of access to ECEC that children enjoy. While data collection is far from

Table 1.1 The context for ECEC: a comparison of countries featured in this volume

| | | % children living in households with income lower than 50% of national median[i] | Child mortality rate: probability of dying between birth and age 5, rate per 1,000 live births[ii] | Ranking in UNICEF (2007) child well-being index (1 = high, 18 = low) | Age compulsory education starts[iii] | % GDP spent on EC[iv] | % attend EC services | | Unitary or split ECEC system (split = provision is for children aged 0–3 and 3–6 years; unitary means government responsibility, access, funding, regulation and workforce integrated across all ECEC services)[vii] |
							0–2-year-olds in formal ECEC (group care or family day care)[v]	3+ years in public and private educational institutions[vi]	
EU member states	England	12.1	5	18.2	4–5	.6	33	90	Part unitary
	Scotland								
	France	8.8	4	13	6	1	44.2	100	Split
	Italy	15.9	4	10	6	.6	11.9	94.8	Split
	Norway	6.1	3	8.7	6	.8	61	95.7	Unitary
	Sweden	7.3	3	5	7	1	70	92	Unitary
	Denmark	6.5	4	7.2	6	1.2	63.2	92.3	Unitary
	Hungary	10.3	6	14.5	5	.7	10	82.2	Split
	Czech Republic	7.4	4	12.5	6	.5	20.5	72.5	Split
EU candidate countries	Romania	25.5	14	N/A	7	.8	N/A	77.5 (a)	Split
	Serbia	N/A	7	N/A	7	N/A	N/A	52.3 (a)	N/A
	Macedonia	N/A	12	N/A	7	N/A	N/A	24.1 (a)	Unitary
	Turkey	N/A	18	N/A	6	N/A	N/A	10.3	N/A
Central and Latin American countries	Mexico	N/A	17	N/A	4	N/A	N/A	69.4	N/A
	Peru	N/A	19	N/A	6	N/A	N/A	78.06 (a)	N/A
North America	USA	23.1	8	18	4-6	.4	N/A	59.9	Split at many levels

N/A = not available

Notes:

[i]UNICEF (2007)
[ii]UNICEF (2012)
[iii]OECD (2012)
[iv]Bennett (2006)
[v]Bennett (2006); Oberhuemer et al. (2010); see also UNICEF/Innocenti Social Monitors
[vi]OECD (2012)
[vii]Bennett and Moss (2010); EACEA (2009); UNICEF (2012)

comprehensive, it is clear that certain characteristics go together: low levels of child poverty, high rankings of child well-being, high levels of coverage of ECEC for children under 3 and unitary systems are all features of the three Nordic countries discussed in this book. These differences are complemented by others, prompted by questions such as 'what is our image of the child?' (Moss, 2010) and what is the ECEC system for? Does ECEC primarily prepare children for school? Or is children's citizenship an uppermost concern and educating them for democracy the main focus? Is accessing ECEC seen as a social right for all children or a product of parental 'choice'? Another approach is to see ECEC as a force for community cohesion, so the role of ECEC is as a site for catalysing family and community members in shaping local services. Are the services broadly 'educationist' or 'protectionist' in orientation? Do they hope to 'rescue' some children from the disadvantages of home life or seek to educate all – or both?

The book features two key themes. In Part 1, five chapters explore different aspects of the relationship between care and education and between ECEC and schools and consider the relevance and impact of possible 'schoolification' of ECEC settings in the search for improved 'school readiness'. Chapters 4 and 6 challenge ideas of intervention within ECEC, who it is for and how it is carried out, and consider different examples of early interventions, from community-based solutions to specific programmes. The chapters in Part 2 focus on 'Children's spaces'. This reorients ECEC away from services as meeting the needs of societies and economies and instead considers children's lives within services. Considering children's spaces, both geographic and metaphoric, embracing the physical, cultural and familial, enables us to analyse some relationships between what happens within ECEC settings and what happens outside. ECEC is no longer just about what care and education provide; it is also about what children's families and communities bring to the experience of ECEC settings.

Part 1: Care, education and notions of intervention

An enduring issue in ECEC is that of split and integrated systems of care and education. Split systems are most common worldwide, and at their extreme feature 'care' for children from birth to age 3 and 'education' for children aged 3+, with lower qualified staff in care services and higher educated teachers in education services. Integrated systems, on the other hand, recognize that children's lives are lived as a whole and that care and education are inseparable (Bennett, 2012). The workforce is then educated to match this holistic orientation. Bennett and Moss (2010) argue that integrated systems are also better – more inclusive and more equal.

Pamela Oberhuemer sets the scene for the book in Chapter 2, pointing out the increased awareness in recent years of the advantages of well-resourced systems in ECEC. Her chapter looks at similarities and differences across the 27 member states of the European Union (EU) in relation to three key issues: the dominant vision that countries choose to follow when making decisions about the ECEC system as a whole, the staffing of early childhood services, and cooperation and networking across Europe, where early childhood systems remain 'distinctly diverse'.

In Chapter 3, Yoshie Kaga discusses the relationship between early childhood and primary education and its current importance for early years practices. The chapter reviews three models: the school-readiness model and the ready-school model – for strengthening the linkage between the two sectors; a 'strong and equal partnership' model is then considered as a possible way forward for the future of the two sectors.

Chapter 4 offers a refreshing perspective on early childhood curricula. Lead authors Tullia Musatti, Donatella Giovannini and Susanna Mayer document their work in an Italian *nido* with early childhood practitioners and researchers to answer questions about the nature and culture of ECEC. Linking to the theme of Chapter 3, they discuss the role of educational experiences directly geared to the acquisition of specific skills and knowledge, in contrast with the broader educational goal of supporting and developing children's full potential. They show how it is possible to construct a powerful and detailed curriculum for children in their earliest years.

Two chapters in Part 1, Chapters 5 and 6, focus on the notion of intervention in ECEC services. They raise questions about what intervention might mean. Is it the accessibility of universal services that support all children and their communities? Or is it a specific programme shaping particular outcomes such as those aimed at parents whose children attend centres and which may reduce the risk of undesirable outcomes? This idea can be understood in two ways: first, using services to support the lives of young children and families on a universalist or community basis; and second, more usual in Anglo-American countries, as a specific method to address perceived problems or deficits in a child's upbringing.

Anne-Marie Doucet-Dahlgren in Chapter 5 provides an overview of some of the characteristics of the French approach to ECEC and family support, including specific forms of provision and early intervention. She describes the Service de Protection Maternelle et Infantile (PMI) and considers the ways in which specific groups of parents respond to a 'folk university' parenting initiative. She makes suggestions on how to take some elements of the French experience as a model in an international perspective.

The Roma Early Childhood Inclusion (RECI) Project is the focus of Chapter 6, in which John Bennett describes an initiative to gather data and information in four Central and South-Eastern European (CSEE) countries – the Czech Republic, Macedonia, Romania and Serbia – about the inclusion of young Roma children and their access to public services. The chapter documents the size of the Roma population and the persecution they have had to suffer over the centuries, outlines the main findings from national reports and charts some tentative conclusions.

Part 2: Children's spaces

Recent research has begun to explore new perspectives on children's experience of ECEC. From many possibilities we include: children's understanding of 'place' and 'community' and the relationship with children's well-being, and the concept of children's spaces within the context of the outdoors. The chapters in Part 2 are deliberately diverse in scope: they open up fresh perspectives on actually being in children's services and draw on data gathered in international research projects.

The theme of space and place is the focus of Chapter 7, where Margaret Kernan and Kathia Loyzaga make a case for including spatial and place perspectives when exploring notions of belonging, participation and citizenship in relation to services for young children in urban societies, in particular marginalized and migrant children. Their chapter references two projects of Melel Xojobal, a non-governmental organization working to improve the quality of life of indigenous migrant children and their families in the city of San Cristóbal de Las Casas, Chiapas, Mexico.

Place-based learning is an approach to ECEC that makes use of local economic activities and the unique history, culture, tradition and other community reference points to engage more effectively with children and young people within the context of their lives. In Chapter 8, Bronwen Cohen and Wenche Rønning look at its origins as a pedagogical approach and how it is developing in Norway and Scotland. They explore what we can learn from services which help children to understand and engage with 'place' and 'community' and the use of nature, and how we might use this as a tool for active learning.

ECEC work is a feminized profession and very few men work in ECEC centres. Continuing the theme of using the outdoors, in Chapter 9 Claire Cameron considers the relationship between being outdoors and being a male worker, using data from a study of the views of practitioners and experts in three countries: England, Denmark and Hungary. She cites research that argues that ECEC centres need to promote working outdoors in order to recruit more men. When discussing being outdoors, Cameron argues that there are two main orientations to practice: a care orientation and a pedagogic orientation. She concludes that gendered practice is more likely to be visible in a care orientation to practice.

We conclude with a consideration of well-being and thriving, key themes in Chapter 10. This draws on a study by an international team of researchers of seven young girls from seven countries who were filmed for a day in their lives. Roger Hancock, Ann Cameron and Ayshe Talay-Ongan use four illustrative examples from Peru, Turkey, the UK and the USA, respectively, to examine the ways in which children's agency and well-being are promoted jointly by caregivers and the children themselves, and, in particular, the significance of the 'culture of play'. Linking to the theme of Chapters 3 and 4, they make a plea that early educationalists, and especially those working in schools, do all they can to promote children's personal agency and thus their well-being.

Final thoughts

In this chapter, we have raised questions about the role of ECEC. We have argued that choices made in the development and formation of these services reflect particular country concerns such as the well-being of children, child poverty, the socialization of children into a particular country's culture and values, and issues around 'school readiness' and early intervention. We believe that by taking an inter-national perspective we can bring critical attention to familiar policy, provision and practice.

▢ Summary

- In this chapter, we argue for looking outside the UK to consider the changes and developments in Europe and beyond which are impacting on ECEC services and on the well-being of children and families, and to consider what we might learn from this.
- We have said that globally governments and non-governmental organizations are increasingly recognizing the importance of ECEC services in supporting the development of children, and in the economic well-being of societies.
- We propose that an awareness and understanding of changing and challenging policy agendas, such as those documented in this book, can support the professional development of practitioners who work in ECEC services by enabling them to see the familiar with a fresh and critical eye.

Questions for discussion

1. What might be the value of looking to Europe and beyond in informing policy and practice in the UK?
2. What in your view should be the role of ECEC services, for example to educate, care, protect, rescue?
3. What do you think should be the role of intervention in the lives of young children and families? *(Higher-level question)*

Further reading

Levels 5 and 6

Siraj-Blatchford, I. and Woodhead, M. (eds) (2009) *Effective Early Childhood Programmes*. Milton Keynes: The Open University/The Hague: Bernard van Leer Foundation.

Woodhead, M. and Moss, P. (eds) (2007) *Early Childhood and Primary Education: Transitions in the Lives of Young Children*. Milton Keynes: The Open University/The Hague: Bernard van Leer Foundation.

These two books are from the Early Childhood in Focus Series (M. Woodhead and J. Oates, Series Editors). The books in this series provide clear and accessible views of recent research, information and analysis on key policy issues relating to early childhood in a global context, and are underpinned by a children's rights perspective. The publications have been developed with key experts and researchers in the field.

Levels 6 and 7

Bennett, J. (2012) *A Shared European Approach to Quality in Early Childhood Services*. Brussels: Eurochild.
This background paper highlights the need to improve quality ECEC services across European countries and underlines three policy strands deemed to be essential in order to achieve this goal, including children's rights and a multi-dimensional approach to attacking poverty.

Moss, P. (ed.) (2012) *Early Childhood and Compulsory Education: Reconceptualising the Relationship*. London: Routledge.
This book raises an important question about the relationship between pre-school and compulsory education. The book contests the 'readying for school' relationship and explores some alternative relationships, including a strong and equal partnership and the vision of a meeting place.

Website

www.childrenineurope.org
This website, featuring the *Children in Europe* publication, offers up-to-date information on European policies, research and good practice for those working with children from birth to 10.

Note

1. Early childhood education and care is a term generally used in Europe and beyond and reflects the historical and separate development of early childhood services under a two-tier organization emphasizing childcare for children up to age 3 and 'pre-primary education' for 3–6-year-olds (OECD, 2006). In England, 'childcare' covers the 'care' oriented services such as childminders, full day care and sessional care, while 'early years' covers the maintained sector – nursery schools and nursery and reception classes in primary schools (Brind et al., 2011). In all the books within the *Critical Issues in the Early Years Series*, we take the view that it should be impossible to educate without caring, or care without developing and promoting children's learning. We also use the term *she* when referring to individuals of both genders, which seems appropriate in a heavily gendered workforce.

References

Allen, G. (2011) Early Intervention: The Next Steps. An Independent Report to her Majesty's Government. Available at: http://www.preventionaction.org/prevention-news/allens-early-intervention-next-steps/5476 (accessed 20 January 2011).
Bennett, J. (2006) Early Childhood Care and Education Regional Report: Europe and North America. Available at: http://unesdoc.unesco.org/images/0018/001892/189211E.pdf

Bennett, J. (2012) *A Shared European Approach to Quality in Early Childhood Services*. Brussels: Eurochild.

Bennett, J. and Moss, P. (2010) Working for Inclusion: An Overview of European Union Early Years Services and their Workforce. Available at: http://www.childreninscotland.org.uk/docs/WFI_Researchoverviewreport_Jan10.pdf

Brind, R., Norden, O., McGinigal, S., Oseman, D., Simon, A. and La Valle, I. (2011) Childcare and Early Years Providers Survey 2011. Available at: https://www.education.gov.uk/publications/eOrderingDownload/DFE-RR240.pdf

Department for Education (DfE) (2013) More Great Childcare: Raising Quality and Giving Choice to Parents. Available at: http://www.education.gov.uk/publications/eOrderingDownload/More%20Great%20Childcare%20v2.pdf (accessed 11/02/2013).

Education, Audiovisual and Culture Executive Agency (EACEA) (2009) Tackling Social and Cultural Inequalities through Early Childhood Education and Care in Europe. Available at: http://eacea.ec.europa.eu/about/eurydice/documents/098EN.pdf

Lloyd, E. (2012) The marketization of early years education and childcare in England. In: L. Miller and D. Hevey (eds) *Policy Issues in the Early Years*. London: SAGE, pp. 107–121.

Moss, P. (2010) What is Your Image of the Child? UNESCO Policy Brief on Early Childhood No. 47. Available at: http://www.waece.org/contenidoingles/notas/47eng.pdf

Oberhuemer, P., Schreyer, I. and Neuman, M. (2010) *Professionals in Early Childhood Education and Care Systems: European Profiles and Perspectives*. Opladen: Barbara Budrich.

Organisation for Economic Co-operation and Development (OECD) (2006) *Starting Strong II: Early Childhood Education and Care*. Paris: OECD.

Organisation for Economic Co-operation and Development (OECD) (2012) *Education at a Glance*. Paris: OECD.

UNICEF (2007) An Overview of Child Well-being in Rich Countries: A Comprehensive Assessment of the Lives and Well-being of Children and Adolescents in the Economically Advanced Nations. Innocenti Report Card 7. Available at: http://www.unicef-irc.org/publications/pdf/rc7_eng.pdf

UNICEF (2012) The State of the World's Children 2012: Children in an Urban World. Available at: http://www.unicef.org/sowc/files/SOWC_2012-Main_Report_EN_21Dec2011.pdf

Woodrow, C. (2011) Challenging identities: a case for leadership, in L. Miller and D. Hevey (eds) *Professionalisation, Leadership and Management in the Early Years*. London: SAGE, pp. 29–46.

PART 1

CARE, EDUCATION AND NOTIONS OF INTERVENTION

CHAPTER 2

SEEING EARLY CHILDHOOD ISSUES THROUGH A EUROPEAN LENS

Pamela Oberhuemer

Overview

Driven by demographic, economic and social pressures, policy makers across Europe have become increasingly aware in recent years of the advantages of well-resourced systems of early childhood education and care (ECEC). Beneficial effects are seen in terms of family and employment policies, long-term education policy, social inclusion and anti-poverty policies, and also economic policy. Despite this common recognition across countries, the format of early childhood systems in Europe remains distinctly diverse. What can we learn from these different approaches? This chapter explores three key issues. The first focuses on the dominant vision that countries choose to follow when making decisions about the ECEC system as a whole. How do these decisions affect the structure, regulation and profiles of early childhood services? The second revolves around the staffing of early childhood services. What overall vision of the workforce do staffing

(Continued)

(Continued)

policies reveal? The third issue is that of European cooperation and networking. How can we learn more by exchanging views and approaches and deliberating and co-constructing alternatives? In outlining and analysing these issues, the chapter looks at similarities and differences across the 27 member states of the European Union (EU) and raises questions for critical discussion.

Common goals but different strategies in national policy making

Systems of early childhood education and care across Europe have many similarly formulated goals and aspirations, and yet the ways in which countries seek to achieve these goals may differ considerably. These varying approaches towards educating and caring for the youngest in society are embedded in specific historical, socio-political and geo-political contexts and relate strongly to the status of women's and children's rights in a particular country. The following sections will examine similarities and differences between ECEC systems in EU countries, which will be grouped according to their geographic location in northern, southern, eastern or western Europe. This regional lens will be the backdrop for examining common and divergent features among countries, followed by a focus on current issues in two selected countries. The regional classification follows the definition used by the United Nations Statistics Division (UNSD, 2011) and does not necessarily reflect former political groupings in 'East' or 'West' Europe.

Northern Europe

According to the UNSD definition of northern Europe, the EU countries in this group are Denmark, Estonia, Finland, Ireland, Latvia, Lithuania and Sweden, together with the United Kingdom of Great Britain and Northern Ireland (UK). Classified another way, these countries could be referred to as the Baltic States, the Nordic EU countries, and the British Isles.

Systemic similarities and differences in northern European countries

The Baltic and Nordic countries share a number of common features regarding the way early childhood education and care is organized. For example, they all have unitary systems under the auspices of a single ministry at the national level. In most cases, this is now the Education ministry, as in a small but steadily growing number of countries in different parts of the world (Bennett and Kaga, 2010). The decision to envision and organize early childhood services in this coherent and equitable way has led to a unitary form of provision across the 1–6 age range in Finland and Sweden, whereas in Estonia, Denmark, Latvia and Lithuania centre-based provision includes a variety of institutional forms, some age-integrated (0–6) and some age-segregated (0–3; 3–6). In most countries, there is some kind of transition class into school. In Finland, Lithuania and Sweden, where compulsory schooling begins at age 7, this is a one-year non-mandatory pre-school class located either in an early childhood centre or in school, whereas in Estonia and Latvia, where children also start school at age 7, such preparatory classes are compulsory (in Latvia for the two years preceding school entry). In all countries, provision is largely publicly funded or subsidised, and the number of private for-profit services is negligible.

The ECEC systems in Ireland and the UK (England, Wales, Scotland and Northern Ireland) represent a very different basic model. Despite moves towards a more coordinated vision at the national level under education administrations, the actual landscape of funding, staffing and regulatory requirements for provision for children below statutory school age – which in the UK is much lower than in the other northern European countries – continues to reflect historically ingrained divisions between the education and welfare/care sectors.

While the Nordic countries have chosen to invest in a solid and largely publicly funded infrastructure of ECEC provision, in the UK and Ireland, private provision and a market concept are dominating forces and parents share a considerable proportion of costs. In England, for example, the childcare market is financed by a mixture of funding streams, but private individuals continue to shoulder the burden, and nursery fees are among the highest in Europe (Moss, 2012). Such a strong reliance on market-driven childcare provision generates considerable limitations and risks, particularly if it is not flanked with effective, comprehensive and multi-level regulation. Ball (1998: 124), referring to the education system as a whole, uses the term 'policy magic' to describe the belief in a simplified formula for solving educational problems, according to which social markets/institutional devolution = raising standards/educational performance = increased international competitiveness. According to Penn (2012: 34), who refers directly to early childhood education and care, this 'commodity view' seriously 'undermines equity and quality'. It certainly represents a very different vision of ECEC compared with that in the Nordic countries, where early childhood education is considered to be a basic entitlement and a public good, accessible by all children from a very early age, regardless of their family background.

Current issues in England and Sweden

Recently, in both England and Sweden, new versions of earlier early childhood curricula have been issued. Why is this? What kinds of changes have been made?

In England, the Early Years Foundation Stage (EYFS), introduced in 2008 for ECEC provision for children from birth to 5, both in the maintained sector and in the much larger private, voluntary and independent sector, was reissued under the centre-right coalition government just four years later, in September 2012, in a new format. It is a statutory framework, and the sub-title 'Setting the standards for learning, development and care for children from birth to five' indicates that it is a document of prescribed standards for early years providers (DfE, 2012). Based on recommendations from the government-commissioned Tickell Review (2011), specific changes include an overall reduction in length, a simplification of assessment procedures and a radical cut in the number of Early Learning Goals (ELGs) from 69 to 17. While this could be interpreted as a positive move, the expectations in the ELGs for literacy and number have been raised, making it likely that an increasing number of children will find it challenging to reach this level, particularly those children born in the summer rather than the autumn (Institute for Fiscal Studies, 2012). Three *prime* learning areas are singled out (communication and language; physical development; personal, social and emotional development), to be supported by four *specific* areas: literacy; mathematics; understanding of the world; and expressive arts and design. However, the expectations set for the ELGs in literacy and number could arguably result in a narrowing of this spectrum and an increase in inappropriate pressure on children to achieve.

In Sweden, a new edition of the 1998 pre-school curriculum for 1–5-year-olds came into force in the summer of 2011. The original document, a slim volume of around 15 pages, has been revised to include more specified goals in four areas of learning: language, mathematics, science and technology. Beyond this, the roles of pedagogical staff and centre leaders have been detailed more specifically, particularly in terms of documentation and evaluation (Karlsson Lohmander in Oberhuemer, 2012). The areas chosen for stronger goal specification relate clearly to the assessment priorities in international comparisons of educational achievement such as the PISA, TIMSS and PIRLS[1] studies. This shift is seen by experts as contributing towards elements of 'schoolification' (Pramling Samuelsson and Sheridan, 2010) or 'readying for school' (Moss, 2013) in early childhood settings, which in Sweden have traditionally had strong roots in a holistic, socio-pedagogical approach (see also Chapter 3).

Despite this shift, the goals in Sweden remain goals to strive towards (and not standards to achieve), whereas the English framework explicitly 'promotes teaching and learning to ensure children's "school readiness"' (DfE, 2012: 2). Additionally, and controversially, the English government has prescribed certain reading methods (phonics) to be taught to children in nursery and reception classes, and tested at the end of the first grade at age 6. This 'phonics check' includes children having to decode contextualized 'nonsense' words, i.e. words with no meaning – an approach sharply criticized by major professional organizations.[2]

Southern Europe

Southern Europe as defined by the UNSD includes six EU member states: Greece, Italy, Malta, Portugal, Slovenia and Spain. Cyprus, although not included in the UN classification, is also a southern European country belonging to the EU. Slovenia is the only country in this group to have been part of the post-war Eastern Bloc (within former Yugoslavia) under the influence of the Soviet Union.

Systemic similarities and differences in southern European countries

Spain was the first European country to integrate both the education/care of the under-3s and of 3–6-year-olds into the education system (*educación infantil*), albeit in two age-segregated cycles with different kinds of provision for each age group. This move, made in 1990, was re-endorsed in the 2006 Education Act. However, the only country in this group with a fully unitary system is Slovenia. Following the post-1990 political restructurings, all early childhood education and care provision up to school entry came under Education in 1993. As in Finland and Sweden, early childhood centres are also organized in an integrated way across the 1–6 age group. Although there are no longer transition classes in Slovenia, continuity between the early childhood and school sectors is enhanced through organized collaboration, with an early childhood pedagogue working alongside the class teacher during the first year of schooling.

Compared with the coherently organized system in Slovenia, responsibilities in Cyprus, Greece, Italy and Portugal are multi-layered. In Italy, for example, services for under-3s and 3–6-year-olds are not only assigned to different ministries, but also regulated at different levels (municipal, regional and national), often with little coordination between each level.

Additionally, provision for 3–6-year-olds is split between three main providers: the state, municipalities and church organizations. This makes for a very complex system with significant regional disparities (Oberhuemer et al., 2010). Within this diversified system, the larger municipalities in central and northern Italy are well known – even globally – for their innovative pedagogical practices and approaches towards the continuing professional development of early years staff (Lazzari et al., 2013) (see Chapter 4 for an account of an Italian *nido*). Currently, a common cause for concern among experts in Italy, Portugal and Spain is the growing divide between provision for the under-3s and for the 3–6-year–olds, and the implications for the role and status of the staff working in the different forms of provision.

Otherwise, each country tends to have distinguishing features. In Malta, for example, it is the early school starting age (as from 4 years 9 months) compared with other countries in the region, and the heavy reliance on private provision for under-3s. In Greece and Cyprus, an unusual feature in this region is the parallel split in the organization and regulation of provision, with kindergartens under Education functioning alongside childcare centres under Social Welfare for the 3–5 age group.

Another salient feature of these two countries is the policy of compulsory kindergarten attendance for the year preceding school entry.

Current issues in Italy and Slovenia

Although the early childhood systems in Italy and Slovenia have very different formats, in both countries there are debates under way regarding possible threats to quality in the early childhood field as a result of financial constraints, changes in the working conditions of staff and recent reform proposals.

In Italy, recent central government measures have resulted in a reduction in investments made by municipalities in early childhood services, which pose a threat in particular to the much-needed expansion of provision for under-3s. Municipalities are increasingly contracting out their services to private, non-profit cooperatives in order to reduce management costs. Within the education system, a concern in the *scuole dell'infanzie* for 3–6-year-olds is a recent increase in staff/child ratios and a decrease in posts for support staff, as well as a perceived weakening of the formerly strong pedagogical identity in order to meet curricular demands focusing more on academic learning and school readiness (Lazzari in Oberhuemer, 2012).

In Slovenia, the 2011 White Paper on Education set out wide-reaching proposals for the education system which have precipitated intense debate in the field, some being welcomed and others regarded as problematic. For the early childhood sector, the proposals include (Vonta in Oberhuemer, 2012): extending the opening hours of centres to 12 hours per day; paying special attention in the centres to promoting speech development, pre-literacy and emergent literacy activities; offering foreign language teaching and additional language support for children from socially and culturally disadvantaged backgrounds; maintaining, but not exceeding, 30 groups in free-standing EC centres; reducing the number of groups supervised by a pre-school adviser from 30 to 20; prioritizing access for children with special needs and children from socially and economically less supportive backgrounds; and reducing parental fees for families with more than one child. However, following a change of government in early 2012 and in the current economic climate, it is unclear how many of these proposals will become a reality.

Eastern Europe

Of the 10 countries classified by the UNSD as belonging to eastern Europe, six are members of the European Union: Bulgaria, the Czech Republic, Hungary, Poland, Romania and Slovakia. Whereas other definitions may consider the Czech Republic, Hungary and Slovakia to be part of central Europe and Romania to be part of southeastern Europe, all the states in the UN definition are post-communist nations formerly belonging to the Eastern Bloc.

Systemic similarities and differences in eastern European countries

Romania was the first – and is still the only – country in this group to start integrating services under one ministry (Education) at the national level. This fairly recent move (Law 1/2011) has been combined with the introduction of integrated centres for children from birth to 6 years, although these remain an exception in the overall picture of provision, which is still mainly age-segregated. In the other five countries, at least two ministries are responsible for services up to compulsory school age; in Bulgaria and Hungary, for example, these are the Ministry of Health for provision for under-3s and the Ministry of Education for kindergartens for 3–6/7-year-olds. Most of these countries had well-developed services for the under-3s before the political, economic and socio-cultural changes, but radical cuts in the early 1990s led to a significant reduction in levels of provision; in Slovakia, for example, there is virtually no publicly funded provision for infants and toddlers, and the scarce services available are chiefly the responsibility of local providers (see Oberhuemer et al., 2010). In the meantime, however, most countries are rebuilding this provision in the face of changing family needs, often finding flexible solutions such as lowering the enrolment age in kindergartens. As in the Nordic countries, very little provision in the region is run by private agencies. Nearly all these countries now have a compulsory pre-school year, in effect lowering the school starting age from 7 to 6 (Bulgaria, Poland) or from 6 to 5 (Hungary, Romania, Slovakia).

Current issues in Bulgaria and Hungary

In Bulgaria, approximately one fifth of 3–7-year-olds do not attend kindergarten. This is probably one of the main reasons why there has been a particularly strong move towards introducing compulsory pre-school education (Engels-Kritidis, 2012). Compulsory preparatory groups, located either in kindergartens or schools, were introduced in 2002 for 6-year-olds and in 2012 for 5-year-olds. In new legislation still to be ratified, it is planned to introduce mandatory pre-school education for 4-year-olds as from 2016 (Engels-Kritidis, 2012). However, relatively little attention appears to be focused on provision for the under-3s, whereas in Hungary reforms have been introduced to address the shortage of places for this age group. In small municipalities which cannot afford to maintain separate nursery provision, there has been a move to lower the age of intake into kindergarten, either by integrating 2-year-olds into kindergarten groups for 3-year-olds or by establishing a separate nursery group. A major problem, however, is that current budget cuts in public spending are a real threat to maintaining quality (Korintus in Oberhuemer, 2012).

Western Europe

According to the UNSD definition (2011), six member states of the EU are classified as belonging to western Europe: Austria, Belgium, France, Germany, Luxembourg and the Netherlands. Among them are the only federally organized states in the EU – Germany and Austria, and also Belgium, with its French-speaking, Flemish-speaking and German-speaking communities.

Systemic similarities and differences in western European countries

Belgium, France, Luxembourg and the Netherlands all share a common feature: the ECEC sectors are not organized as a unitary system, as in the Baltic and Nordic countries. Instead, responsibilities are split between different administrations. In France and Belgium, for example, pre-primary provision for 3-, 4- and 5-year-olds comes under the auspices of the national Ministry of Education and is free of charge for parents, whereas centre-based and other provision for younger children under Social Welfare is segmented and fee-paying. Even so, the French childcare system is based on the principle of universality. Compared with the highly centralized education system in France (for 3–6-year-olds), the early childhood sector in Germany (for 0–6-year-olds) is strongly decentralized, as it is in Austria. In Germany, responsibility is shared between the federal level (*Bund*), the 16 regional governments (*Länder*) and the municipalities (*Kommunen*). The latter cooperate with a wide range of state-subsidised non-profit service providers which manage roughly two-thirds of provision overall. As in the Nordic countries, the proportion of for-profit providers (approximately 1.6%) is negligible (Statistisches Bundesamt, 2012).

Current issues in France and Germany

Although the *crèches* for under-3s and particularly the *écoles maternelles* for 3–6-year-olds are well-established institutions in France, a considerable amount of experimentation has been taking place in recent years to introduce more flexible and localized forms of provision. These *multi-accueil* facilities are often attached to the more traditional institutional forms and combine a variety of services which respond to occasional, part-time and regular care needs within the same setting (Oberhuemer et al., 2010). Other innovations include mobile services (*services itinérants*), by means of which staff and learning resources are transported by bus in rural areas, and also regional networks of open-door services (*lieux d'accueil enfants parents*) for parents, children and family day carers (Rayna, 2007) (for further discussion, see Chapter 5).

While France has long had high enrolment levels for under-3s (particularly through registered family day carers), this has not been the case in western Germany. However, since 2009, a radical transformation has been taking place. After decades of political opposition to providing publicly funded places for children under the age of 3, new legislation has pledged to give parents of 1- and 2-year-olds an entitlement to a place either in a centre-based setting or in family day care. A target was first set in 2009 to provide for 35% of this age group (later extended to 37% and then to 39%) by August 2013. Despite a remarkable increase in the number of places available – participation rates have risen from 9% in 2002 to 27.6% in 2012 – the total falls seriously short of government targets, with around 250,000 places still missing just six months before the cut-off date (Oberhuemer, in press). This, of course, is presenting an enormous challenge for the field, not least in terms of finding sufficient personnel with appropriate qualifications. It has been estimated that in the western *Länder* well over 12,000 additional staff will be needed in centre-based settings, as well as up to 29,000 family day carers, if the targets for 2013 are to be achieved (Schilling and Rauschenbach, 2012).

Staff qualifications: What are the main issues?

While the qualifications and working conditions of the staff are widely recognized as perhaps the most significant contributory factors towards achieving and maintaining high quality education and care, they need to be seen in the context of a supportive and 'competent system' (Urban et al., 2012). The SEEPRO (Systems of Early Education and Professionalization) study into qualification requirements across the 27 EU countries revealed a strong link between salient features of the ECEC system overall and staffing patterns (Oberhuemer et al., 2010). And yet, even in those countries with a good track record of investing in provision, the professional pathway requirements for staff vary considerably. Countries with integrated systems tend to have a highly qualified workforce across the early years sector, whereas those with split systems almost invariably have lower qualification requirements for personnel working with under-3s. The following sections examine selected staffing issues across countries.

Is a tertiary-level qualification a *requirement* for core practitioners working with 1–6-year-olds in the EU countries?

In the great majority of countries, the minimum qualification requirement for working as a core practitioner (responsible for a group of children or for the centre) in the *education system* is a Bachelor-level degree, awarded at the end of a full-time course of study of at least three years' duration at a specialized university department or a university college. This means, for example, that core practitioners in the Baltic countries, the Nordic EU countries and Slovenia working with 1- and 2-year-olds have the same higher-level qualifications as those working with 5- and 6-year-olds. Denmark and Finland, both with a unitary system and a long tradition of services under Social Welfare, also have the same qualification standards for core practitioners across the 1–6/7 age range. Conversely, in the UK and Ireland, in Cyprus, Greece, Italy and Malta, in Bulgaria, the Czech Republic, Hungary and Poland, and in Belgium, Luxembourg and the Netherlands, those working with 1- and 2-year-olds have a lower-level qualification, less favourable working conditions and lower wages. In England, for example, the differences can be extreme. Whereas teachers in the state-maintained sector are required to have a higher education qualification of at least three years' duration (level 6 on the National/European Qualifications Framework), those working in the private, voluntary and independent childcare sector may not even be qualified at level 3 (Brind et al., 2012).

Recently, some countries have moved even beyond the Bachelor-level requirement. Alongside the non-EU country Iceland, in both Portugal and Italy a Master's degree is now the requirement for working with children from the age of 3 up to school entry. There are now only five countries in the 27 EU states where a Bachelor degree is not (yet) a *requirement* for working with the 3–6 age group: Austria, the Czech Republic, Germany, Malta and Slovakia, and in the UK it is only a requirement for working in the state-maintained sector (Oberhuemer et al., 2010). However, in all of these countries there have been recent moves to introduce higher education level qualification routes for work in early childhood settings. In Germany, Bachelor qualifications in early childhood or childhood studies have been mushrooming since 2004 and there are now 80 such courses available across the country. However, this was a move initiated by the higher education institutions and not by the federal or regional governments.

As may be expected, the overall proportion of tertiary-level educated staff varies considerably. Whereas in England, only 15% of the early years workforce have a level 6 (or higher) qualification (Brind et al., 2012), in Lithuania approximately 98% have a university or other higher education degree, in Denmark 60%, in Sweden 50% and in Slovenia 35% (Oberhuemer et al., 2010). In Germany, the proportion of staff with a university or university college qualification is particularly low at 4.6% (Statistisches Bundesamt, 2012). In January 2012 a controversial decision was made at the national level (BMBF, 2012) to place the traditional post-secondary vocational qualification on the same level as the Bachelor degree within the National/European Qualifications Framework (level 6). This is considered by academics to be a backward step in the early childhood education professionalization project (see, for example, Stieve and Kägi, 2012).

Do core practitioners working with 1–6-year-olds necessarily have a specialist qualification in early childhood pedagogy?

The answer to this question is a clear 'no'. The countries with an ECEC specialization in early childhood pedagogy for work with children from birth to 6 or 7 years are the Baltic countries, Finland, Slovenia and Sweden. In Sweden, this is the re-introduction of an early childhood focus. For 10 years, from 2001 until 2011, the initial education/training approach was one which combined the professional preparation of early childhood teachers[3] with that of primary school teachers. However, following recruitment problems in the early years sector and national reports about students tending to favour work in primary schools over that in pre-schools, a decision was made to return to the former model of educating and training pre-school teachers separately, and they can now still work in pre-school classes in school but not in compulsory primary school classes (Karlsson Lohmander in Oberhuemer, 2012). In some countries with a split system, the requirement for working with the under-3s is a health/care qualification (e.g. Belgium, Hungary), sometimes without a specific focus on work with very young children. These health/care qualification requirements are also at different formal levels; some are post-secondary awards (Poland, Romania), while others are upper secondary qualifications (Italy, Nether-lands). In a small number of countries, there are no minimum requirements for work-ing with this age group at all. Until very recently, this was the case in Ireland and Malta, both countries with largely market-led private childcare sectors, and also in Belgium (Flanders) for work in private infant–toddler centres. Again, there are moves to change this situation, but without firm conclusions as yet.

In some countries, such as Denmark and Germany, the focus of professional education/training is a broadly conceptualized role as social pedagogue, preparing for work in early childhood settings, but also in a variety of other settings *outside* the school system. Another model is that of the *pre-primary and primary school professional*, i.e. teachers trained for work in primary schools *and* pre-primary set-tings *within* the education sector, such as the *professeur des écoles* in France. The training for work with 3–6-year-olds in Italy and Luxembourg now also follows this model. One inherent problem of this approach is that schools are compulsory and a school-biased professional training curriculum may (and often does) pay too little attention to the non-compulsory pre-school years. Another issue is the enhanced danger of 'schoolification', undermining strong traditions (e.g. in Italy) of independ-ent early childhood approaches to learning (Lazzari in Oberhuemer, 2012) (for further discussion, see Chapters 3 and 4). Other approaches are narrower in empha-sis, focusing either on work with children in the two or three years immediately preceding compulsory schooling (e.g. in Belgium, Greece, Hungary, Malta and Poland) or on pedagogical work with the under-3s (e.g. in Hungary).

In some cases, core practitioners are supported by a fully qualified assistant with an early years specialist focus, as is the case in Slovenia. In other countries (e.g. Cyprus, Greece, Ireland), they work alone with a group of children, without any kind of qualified or non-qualified assistant, except for children with special needs and disabilities. In the Baltic countries, there are few assistants to be found on a daily basis, but regular support is provided by tertiary-level trained specialists in specific areas of learning (e.g. music, physical education).

Are men now part of the workforce?

One of 40 targets formulated by the 12 country experts in the European Commis-sion Network on Childcare nearly two decades ago was that 20% of staff employed in centre-based settings should be men. However, according to the SEEPRO data, the proportion of male workers is still very low. In only 10 of the 27 EU countries is the participation rate higher than 1% (Oberhuemer et al., 2010: 506). Denmark has the highest and a still rising proportion of men in the ECEC workforce. In 2009, male pedagogues accounted for 7% of staff in centres for under-3s, 11% in kindergartens for 3–6-year-olds and 13% in mixed-age centres for children from birth to 6 (see the further discussion in Chapter 10). However, no country has reached the proposed 20%.

In Germany, there are currently moves under way to improve this situation (Cremers et al., 2012). In 2012, men accounted for 4.2% of personnel in early childhood provision (Statistisches Bundesamt, 2012, own calculations), whereas in some metropolitan areas (e.g. in the cities of Bremen and Frankfurt) the proportion can be significantly higher – up to 9%. Research commissioned by the Federal Ministry for Family and Youth Affairs showed that service providers, centre leaders and parents clearly wish to see more men in early childhood provision (Cremers and Krabel, 2012). Within an overall policy framework of equal opportunities, a coordination office and a website have been set up, and a current government initiative (2011–2013) is providing funding to support 16 pilot projects aimed at strengthening regional networking in 13 of the 16 federal states (*Länder*). Some 1300 early childhood centres are involved in these initiatives. Strategic consultancy services are provided to improve the recruitment of men into the early years workforce. Overall, however, apart from one or two exceptions such as initiatives in Belgium and the UK, and particularly in (non-EU) Norway, recruiting men into the workforce has not had significant policy attention. Although 'improving qualifications, training and working conditions' is one of the five main areas considered in the OECD 'quality toolbox' (OECD, 2012: 143 ff.) for policy administrators, no specific reference is made to the recruitment of men (see Chapter 9 for a discussion of recruitment of male workers).

Continuing professional development – some key issues

Within a large-scale workforce initiative in Germany[4] with a focus on the continuing professional development (CPD) of early childhood practitioners, a cross-national study looked at the CPD systems in six European countries: Denmark, England, Hungary, Italy, Slovenia and Sweden (Oberhuemer, 2012). The research focused on the following questions:

Understandings: How is CPD defined and conceptualized?

Main forms: How is CPD predominantly organized?

Framework agreements: Is CPD regulated through a binding and nationally valid framework?

Providers: Who organizes CPD activities and advanced professional studies?

Rights and obligations: Is CPD an optional entitlement or a compulsory duty?

Participation: How high are the chances and how supportive are the working conditions?

Main topics: What is currently in focus – and why?

Credits and career advancement: Are there recognized procedures for the formal endorsement of CPD participation?

Research and monitoring: Are they sufficient?

National and European Qualifications Framework: How do things stand?

The country case studies revealed a number of systemic risks, suggesting that continuing professional development is a major policy challenge across European countries with varying ECEC systems. Some of the main issues include:

- a general lack of framework agreements and regulations with a binding character, particularly for auxiliary staff
- insufficient accreditation requirements and cross-provider quality assurance systems for *all* CPD providers in the field
- a lack of coherence, credit transferability and transparency both *within* formal CPD structures as well as *between* non-formal and formal CPD options
- significant financial constraints regarding funding for CPD leave and supply staff
- equity issues within the workforce in terms of CPD access, leave entitlements, funding – particularly within split systems
- a lack of CPD-related research and monitoring
- in some cases an insufficient balance between macropolitical, reform-driven, centre-related and profession-related CPD topics.

European networking: co-constructing ways forward

The previous two sections have focused on ECEC policy variations between countries in different regions of Europe, looking in particular at aspects of how national systems are organized and how the initial and continuing professional development of those working with young children are conceptualized and implemented. Despite the variations in approach, many of the issues facing ECEC advocates and policy makers are similar. However, in order to develop country-specific strategies, it is necessary not only to have knowledge of different ways of doing things, but also to come closer in terms of understanding *why* various systems are as they are. Even shared terminology can mask significant underlying differences in values. In the recent history of early childhood education and care in Europe, the first two Starting Strong reviews (OECD, 2001, 2006) were pivotal in creating in-depth country profiles as a basis for cross-national analyses and understandings – and in motivating administrators, teacher educators, researchers and practitioners to *find out more*.

In 2011, the European Commission for the first time issued a communication focused solely on early childhood education and care as a comprehensive policy area (European Commission, 2011). Among the proposed issues for cooperation among member states were many of those illustrated in the first two sections of this chapter:

- moving towards ECEC systems which integrate care and education, and improve quality, equity and system efficiency
- widening access to quality ECEC for disadvantaged children, migrants, Roma children (see the further discussion in Chapter 6)
- designing efficient funding models and the right balance of public and private investment
- finding the appropriate balance in the curriculum between cognitive and non-cognitive elements
- promoting the professionalization of ECEC staff: what qualifications are needed for which functions
- developing policies to attract, educate and retain suitably qualified staff to ECEC
- improving the gender balance of ECEC staff.

As a result, the European Commission Directorate-General for Education and Culture set up a Thematic Working Group on ECEC under the 'Strategic Framework for European cooperation in education and training (EU2020)' to support international exchange and to co-construct ways forward on these issues. Somewhat earlier, the OECD also established a Network on ECEC for policy administrators, which meets bi-annually to reflect on issues of ECEC quality in Europe and beyond (see the OECD website: www. oecd.org/education/preschoolandschool/earlychildhoodeducationandcare.htm).

Educational 'policy lending and policy borrowing' is a global issue – one which has long been critiqued by researchers (Ball, 1998). It is highly questionable, if not impossible, to take policies and particularly educational approaches, which are always strongly values-based, from one cultural context to another. The 'Reggio approach', as one popular example, is rooted in local traditions and political movements (Lazzari, 2012), and although certain elements may help to inspire, to question, to rethink, to innovate, they can never be dislodged from one culture and 'implemented' in another. Even within a certain geographical region such as North America, it is a contentious issue as to whether general standards set up by those in 'positional power' can be valid across settings and localities (Manning et al., 2012). However, being challenged to question taken-for-granted assumptions is one of the great benefits of cross-national exchange and discovery.

Summary

- This chapter has outlined just some of the variations across Europe in conceptualizing, organizing, funding, staffing and supporting systems of centre-based early childhood education and care.
- These differences represent varying cultural and political understandings and values. They raise questions related to issues of equality, quality and well-being

in the lives of young children and families. For educators, they presuppose a reflexive and critical stance, relating the needs of settings and the sector to the wider socio-political context.

- While considerable steps forward have been taken, and co-constructive efforts are on the increase, in many countries there remain – even in this second decade of the 21st century – significant conceptual and structural divisions across the early childhood sector. These may seriously hinder the policy enactment of an equitable system of early childhood education and care.

 Questions for discussion

1. Does considering early childhood issues through a European lens help you to critically reflect on the ECEC policies in your country?
2. Are the different staff qualification requirements in many countries for working with older and younger children in the early childhood sector justifiable?
3. What would be your foremost suggestion to policy makers to improve the ECEC system in your country? (*Higher-level question*)

Further reading

Levels 5 and 6

Miller, L., Dalli, C. and Urban, M. (2012) *Early Childhood Grows Up: Towards a Critical Ecology of the Profession*. New York: Springer.
At the heart of this volume are detailed reports of a day in the life of early childhood practitioners in six countries: Australia, England, Finland, Germany, New Zealand and Sweden. These form the basis for examining new 'spaces' emerging from the currently heightened policy attention towards early childhood education and care. A 'new future' for early childhood educators is envisaged, in which critical enquiry is a centrepiece of both professional thinking and transformative agency.

Moss, P. (ed.) (2013) *Early Childhood and Compulsory Education: Reconceptualising the Relationship*. London: Routledge.
Authors from Europe (Belgium, France, Italy, Sweden, Norway) and beyond (New Zealand, the USA) contribute towards a re-examination of the relationship between early childhood education and compulsory schooling in different contexts. 'Readying for school', a 'strong and equal partnership' and 'the vision of a meeting place' are three key concepts used to form the backdrop for a critique of current practices and the elaboration of new visions.

Oberhuemer, P., Schreyer, I. and Neuman, M.J. (2010) *Professionals in Early Childhood Education and Care Systems: European Perspectives and Profiles*. Opladen: Barbara Budrich.
This book gives an overview of early childhood education and care systems in Europe. Its main focus is on the early childhood workforce in the European Union countries. The volume

includes 27 country profiles which provide contextual information on policies and provision, as well as a detailed account of the professional education and training and working conditions of early years staff in each country. Common issues relating to staff professionalization are examined in a cross-national perspective.

Levels 6 and 7

Kjørholt, A.T. and Qvortrup, J. (2012) *The Modern Child and the Flexible Labour Market: Early Childhood Education and Care*. Basingstoke: Palgrave Macmillan.
The contributors to this book are all based in northern European countries. Referring to recent research, they examine the interface between childhoods, education and care policies and the labour market, maintaining that all are influenced by concepts such as flexibility and user-orientation. In particular, they consider how adults and children co-construct new identities in these changing contexts.

Lloyd, E. and Penn, H. (eds) (2012) *Childcare Markets: Can They Deliver an Equitable Service?* Bristol: Policy Press.
This book problematizes a market approach to the provision of early childhood education and care. It assembles contributions by social policy experts, economists and educationalists from countries where childcare markets are the norm: Australia, Canada, Hong Kong, the Netherlands, the UK and the USA. It also includes chapters from New Zealand and Norway and looks at emerging childcare markets in African and post-socialist European countries.

Websites

https://webgate.ec.europa.eu/fpfis/mwikis/eurydice/index.php/Early_Childhood_Education_and_Care
Eurypedia – the European Encyclopedia on National Education Systems – is a resource site with country information on 38 European education systems. It is regularly updated by the Eurydice Network, originally established in 1980, in collaboration with the Eurydice National Units. Since 2011, Eurypedia has also had a section on early childhood education and care.

http://www.oecd.org/education/preschoolandschool/earlychildhoodeducationandcare.htm
The early childhood education and care (ECEC) website of the Organisation for Economic Co-operation and Development (OECD) has information on the OECD Network on ECEC, the Starting Strong publications and the current OECD project on 'Quality Matters in ECEC', with country reports focusing on a chosen area for review. The website also contains invaluable archive materials from the Starting Strong I and II reviews.

http://www.eecera.org/
The European Early Childhood Education Research Association (EECERA) promotes and disseminates multi-disciplinary research on early childhood and its applications to policy and practice. The website gives details of the annual research conferences which take place in a different European country each year, of the association's journal, *EECERJ*, which appears four times a year, and of the Special Interest Groups on key topics in the field of ECEC.

Notes

1. PISA = Programme for International Student Assessment conducted by the OECD (Organisation of Economic Co-operation and Development); TIMSS = Trends in International Mathematics and Science Study conducted by the IEA (International Association for the Evaluation of Educational Achievement); PIRLS = Progress in International Reading Literacy Study, also conducted by the IEA.
2. See, for example, http://www.tactyc.org.uk/pdfs/view-phonicsletter.pdf
3. In official translations published by the Swedish government, core practitioners working with children up to school entry are called 'pre-school teachers' and the early childhood centres for 1–6-year-olds 'pre-schools'.
4. WiFF – *Weiterbildungsinitiative Frühpädagogische Fachräfte* [Professional Development Initiative – Early Childhood Educators], 2009–2014, funded by German Federal Ministry of Education and Research and ESF, coordinated by the German Youth Institute (DJI).

References

Ball, S.J. (1998) Big policies/small world: an introduction to international perspectives in education policy. *Comparative Education*, 34(2): 119–130.

Bennett, J. and Kaga, Y. (2010) The integration of early childhood systems within education. *International Journal of Child Care and Education Policy*, 4(1): 35–43.

Brind, A., Norden, O., McGinigal, S., Oseman, D. and Simon, A. (2012) *Childcare and Early Years Providers Survey 2011*. Research Report DfE RR249. London: Department for Education.

Bundesministerium für Bildung und Forschung (BMBF) (2012) Pressemitteilung: Wichtiger Schritt hin zum Bildungsraum Europa [Press notice: Important step towards a European Education Area]. Available at: http://www.deutscherqualifikationsrahmen.de

Cremers, M. and Krabel, J. (2012) Männer in Kitas: Aktueller Forschungsstand in Deutschland [Men in early childhood settings: the current state of research in Germany]. In: M. Cremers, S. Höyng, J. Krabel and T. Rohrmann (eds) *Männer in Kitas* [Men in early childhood settings]. Opladen: Barbara Budrich, pp. 131–150.

Cremers, M., Höyng, S., Krabel, J. and Rohrmann, T. (eds) (2012) *Männer in Kitas* [Men in early childhood settings]. Opladen: Barbara Budrich.

Department for Education (DfE) (2012) Statutory Framework for the Early Years Foundation Stage: Setting the Standards for Learning, Development and Care for Children from Birth to Five. Available at: https://www.education.gov.uk/publications/standard/AllPublications/Page1/DFE-00023-2012

Engels-Kritidis, R. (2012) Developments in pre-school education in Bulgaria: achievements and challenges. In: T. Papatheodorou (ed.) *Debates on Early Childhood Policies and Practices: Global Snapshots of Pedagogical Thinking and Encounters*. Abingdon: Routledge, pp. 38–50.

European Commission (2011) *Communication from the Commission: ECEC – Providing all Our Children with the Best Start for the World of Tomorrow*. COM(2011)66 final. Brussels: European Commission.

Institute for Fiscal Studies (2012) 'Does when you are born matter?' The impact of month of birth on the development of cognitive and non-cognitive skills throughout childhood project. Presentation to the Institute of Education, 14 March. Available at: http://www.ifs.org.uk/conferences/ioe_born.pdf

Lazzari, A. (2012) The public good: historical and political roots of municipal preschools in Emilia Romagna. *European Journal of Education*, 47(4): 556–568.

Lazzari, A., Picchio, M. and Musatti, T. (2013) Sustaining ECEC quality through continuing professional development: systemic approaches to practitioners' professionalization in the Italian context. *Early Years: An International Research Journal*, 33(2): 133–145.

Manning, J.P., Thirumurthy, V. and Field, H. (2012) Globalization or hegemony? Childcare on the brink: hints from three geographically distant localities in North America. *Contemporary Issues in Early Childhood*, 13(1): 4–16.

Moss, P. (2012) Governed markets and democratic experimentalism: two possibilities for early childhood education and care. In: A.T. Kjørholtand and J. Qvortrup (eds) *The Modern Child and the Flexible Labour Market: Early Childhood Education and Care*. Basingstoke: Palgrave Macmillan, pp. 128–149.

Moss, P. (2013) The relationship between early childhood and compulsory education: a properly political question. In: P. Moss (ed.) *Early Childhood and Compulsory Education: Reconceptualising the Relationship*. London: Routledge, pp. 2–50.

Oberhuemer, P. (in press) Access and quality issues in early childhood education and care: the case of Germany. In: L. Gambaro, K.J. Stewart and J. Waldfogel (eds) *Equal Access to Childcare: Providing Quality Early Education and Childcare to Disadvantaged Families*. Bristol: Policy Press.

Oberhuemer, P. (2012). *Fort- und Weiterbildung frühpädagogischer Fachkräfte im europäischen Vergleich* [Continuing Professional Development of Early Years Educators in Europe: A Cross-national Study]. With D. Hevey, C. Hvorth Weber, M. Karlsson Lohmander, M. Korintus, A. Lazzari and T. Vonta. München: Deutsches Jugendinstitut (WIFF Studien, Band 17).

Oberhuemer, P., Schreyer, I. and Neuman, M.J. (2010) *Professionals in Early Childhood Education and Care Systems: European Profiles and Perspectives*. Opladen and Farmington Hills, MI: Barbara Budrich.

Organisation for Economic Co-operation and Development (OECD) (2001) *Starting Strong I: Early Childhood Education and Care*. Paris: OECD.

Organisation for Economic Co-operation and Development (OECD) (2006) *Starting Strong II: Early Childhood Education and Care*. Paris: OECD.

Organisation for Economic Co-operation and Development (OECD) (2012) *Starting Strong III: A Quality Toolbox for Early Childhood Education and Care*. Paris: OECD.

Penn, H. (2012) Childcare markets: do they work? In: E. Lloyd and H. Penn (eds) *Childcare Markets: Can They Deliver an Equitable Service?* Bristol: Policy Press, pp. 19–42.

Pramling Samuelsson, I. and Sheridan, S. (2010) A turning point or a backward slide? The challenge facing the Swedish preschool today. *Early Years: An International Journal of Research and Development*, 30(3): 219–227.

Rayna, S. (2007) Infant and early childhood education. In: R. New and M. Cochran (eds) *Early Childhood Education: An International Encyclopedia, Vol. 4*. Westport, CT: Praeger, pp. 1089–1092.

Schilling, M. and Rauschenbach, T. (2012) Zu wenig Fachkräfte für unter Dreijährige [Not enough personnel for the under-threes]. *DJI Impulse: Das Bulletin des Deutschen Jugendinstituts*, 2: 8–11.

Statistisches Bundesamt (2012) Statistiken der Kinder- und Jugendhilfe: Kinder und tätige Personen in Tages einrichtungen und in öffentliche förderter Kindertagespflege [Child and youth services statistics: children and workers in centre-based settings and in publicly subsidised family day care]. Available at: www.destatis.de/DE/Publikationen/Thematisch/Soziales/KinderJugendhilfe/TageseinrichtungenKindertagespflege5225402117004.pdf?__blob=publicationFile (accessed 1 March 2012).

Stieve, C. and Kägi, S. (2012) Gleicher Level für Fachschulausbildung und Studium? Der DQR und Rückschritte in der Professionalisierung der Pädagogik der Kindheit [The same level for vocational and academic studies? The German Qualifications Framework and backward steps in the professionalization of childhood education]. *FrüheBildung*, 1(3): 159–162.

Tickell, C. (2011) *The Early Years: Foundations for Life, Health and Learning*. An independent report on the Early Years Foundation Stage to Her Majesty's Government. London: The Stationery Office.

United Nations Statistics Division (UNSD) (2011) *Composition of Macro Geographical (Continental) Regions, Geographical Sub-regions, and Selected Economic and Other Groupings*. Available at: http://unstats.un.org/unsd/methods/m49/m49regin.htm (accessed 3 January 2013).

Urban, M., Vandenbroeck, M., Van Laere, K., Lazzari, A. and Peters, J. (2012) Towards competent systems in early childhood education and care: implications for policy and practice. *European Journal of Education*, 47(4): 508–526.

CHAPTER 3

THE RELATIONSHIP BETWEEN EARLY CHILDHOOD AND PRIMARY EDUCATION

Yoshie Kaga

Overview

First, the chapter aims to define the issue of the relationship between early childhood and primary education, and to show its current importance for early years practices. Second, it highlights the importance of paying attention to historical and structural contexts in understanding the relationship in a given country. It also shows that relating the two sectors can be complex due to their different cultures and traditions and the power relation involved. Third, the chapter reviews two models of relationship – the school-readiness model and the ready-school model – that have been adopted by some countries to strengthen linkage between the sectors. Fourth, it discusses the 'strong and equal partnership' approach as a model for the future of the two sectors, in which they interact as equal partners, encouraging a unified approach to learning, and building on the strengths of each other. The chapter suggests some conditions and measures that may support this direction.

Introduction

Today, an increasing number of young children participate in early childhood education (ECE) services. Just a decade ago, most children in the OECD countries attended
ECE services for at least two years prior to primary schooling (OECD, 2001). In 2010,
on average, 83% of 4-year-olds in OECD countries that are part of the European Union
participated in ECE: Belgium, France, Iceland, Italy, Norway, Spain and Sweden had
more than 90% of their 3-year-olds enrolled in ECE (OECD, 2012). With the great
majority of children now in ECE, how best to design and support children's positive
transition from ECE to primary education is an important issue for professionals and
policy makers concerned with both sectors. Its importance is accentuated by the
growing body of research demonstrating the positive effects of participation in quality
ECE on educational achievement, equity and system efficiency (European Commission, 2011; Eurydice, 2009; Hart and Risely, 1995; Heckman and Masterov, 2004).

The issue is, however, not new, being the object of research, programme and
policy initiatives for some decades (Kagan, 2012). But attention to the issue has
been rather sporadic (Kagan, 2012), considered predominantly an 'operational challenge' needing a 'smoothing out of difficulties' (Bennett, 2012: 60), and generally
limited to a couple of years around primary school entry. It has lacked a broader
perspective that involves a questioning of the purposes, content and methods of the
ECE and primary education sectors and of how these relate to one another. For
example, should ECE provide school learning through environments and pedagogies similar to those used in primary school? Or should primary school be aligned
with ECE to provide for children's all-round development and well-being? Investigating the relationship not only helps improve children's experiences of transition. It
also opens up possibilities for exploring 'the values, goals, concepts, understandings
and practices of education' that could apply across the entire field (Moss, 2012: 2),
which potentially contributes to a realization of the vision of lifelong learning.

This chapter focuses on the relationship between early childhood and primary
education. It uses the term 'early childhood education' (ECE) to broadly include a
range of organized provision for young children below compulsory school age,
regardless of administrative auspices, setting and staffing, and which has an educational component alongside other components relevant to child development. It
employs the term 'primary education' to refer to a designated level within an education system after ECE. Called 'elementary education' or 'basic education' in some
countries, it is usually considered as the first compulsory stage of mass education
(Richards, 2008).

Structural contexts of relationship

As noted above, many children in Europe enter primary school with two- to three-
year experiences of attending organized ECE services. However, their experiences

may differ considerably across countries due to the diverse ways in which ECE and school provision are structured. According to Moss (2008), structural contexts define both certain aspects of the relationship and influence possibilities for change, and include administrative auspice, workforce, compulsory school entry age, provision, curriculum and funding. Below, I give the examples of France and Sweden to illustrate how different children's institutional experiences can depend on structural contexts.

France

In France, early childhood experience before the age of 3 differs to a great extent (see Chapter 5 for further detail): 10% of children under 3 attend day care centres established for children up to the age of 3; 63% of those under 3 stayed at home with one of their parents in 2009 (DREES, 2010); and some attend part-time services. The primary out-of-home provider for the under 3s in France is family day care (18% in 2009). Services for the under-3s are the responsibility of the Ministry of Health but are mainly run by municipalities and non-profit organizations. There is no national curriculum for day care centres (Rayna, 2010). When children turn 3, they attend pre-schools, administered by the Ministry of National Education. Pre-schools are provided in a school environment and are often adjacent to primary schools. Primary schooling is compulsory and begins at the age of 6. Pre-schools and primary schools follow the school calendar, which is 24 hours per week and 36 weeks per year. The average child:teacher ratio of 25.5:1 in pre-schools is considerably different from day care centres that are recommended to have ratios of 5:1 (ages 0–2) and 8:1 (ages 2–3). The children in pre-schools are taught by *professeurs des écoles*, educated at Master's level through a unified initial training for pre-school and primary school teachers – unlike in services for younger children where staff are less educated and lower paid and are qualified as a nurse, childminder or early childhood educator.

Sweden

In Sweden, the Ministry of Education and Research is in charge of all ECE services for children aged 1–6, in addition to compulsory education starting at age 7 (OECD, 2006). ECE services consist of pre-schools, 'pedagogical care' (family day care) and 'open pre-schools' (pre-schools where children are accompanied by a parent or another adult), with the majority of children attending pre-schools: 78.1% of children aged 1–4 and 97.3% of children aged 4–6 attended pre-school activities in 2009 (Eurydice, 2009/2010). Almost all children aged 6–7 are enrolled in a pre-school class, which is voluntary and provided free of charge for at least 525 hours per year within compulsory schools. The Curriculum for the Preschool Lpfö 98, revised in 2010 (Government of Sweden, 2010), promotes, for children aged 1–6, a holistic pedagogy where care, socialization and learning form a coherent whole. This curriculum is conceptually linked with the Curriculum for the Compulsory School, Preschool Class and the Leisure-time Centre 2011 (Government of Sweden, 2011), which together promote a common view of knowledge, learning and development. Initial teacher education for pre-school, pre-school class and compulsory schooling is separate. Swedish pre-schools tend to resemble home environments rather than school classrooms, and children of different ages are often grouped together. The average ratio in pre-schools is 5.6:1 and that in pre-school classes is 13:1 (OECD, 2001). Municipal compulsory schools have a ratio of 8.3 teachers per 100 children (Eurydice, 2009/2010).

Challenges in forging a mutually constructive relationship

Exploring a kind of relationship that equally serves both early childhood and primary education is made complex due to their different traditions and cultures, as well as the power relation between the two sectors that has been nurtured historically. Having become a well-established institution in the 19th century, primary education is conceived and delivered relatively uniformly across countries. ECE, in contrast, generally evolved more slowly, remained in the private sphere until well after the Second World War, and is more diverse in terms of aims, organizations, content and approaches, workforce and funding (OECD, 2006).

Haug (2012) explains that, in Norway, kindergartens and schools were conceived to respond to different needs and to fulfil different societal functions, with differently designed content and methods. The former embodies pedagogy based on free activity, project work and daily routines (e.g. meals, dressing), focusing on the present and centred around the child; and the latter is highly text-oriented, placing importance on the learning of subject content, decided by others, and having a future orientation whereby its worth is determined in later life. Speaking from the US experience, Kagan (2012) states that ECE is rooted in a developmental tradition, upholding an integrated approach to young children's development using a child-centred play method, while compulsory schooling espouses a disciplinary orientation that focuses on the discrete disciplines, delivered through a more scripted and didactic approach to learning. Dahlberg and Lenz Taguchi (1994) argued that a key difference between the Swedish pre-school and school traditions arose from distinct constructions of the child – 'the child as nature' in the former, derived from Rousseau's and Froebel's philosophy and giving importance to children's freedom in expressing ideas, feelings and personalities, the here-and-now and the whole child; and in the latter, 'the child as reproducer of culture and knowledge', influencing organization, content and working methods.

The relationship is very often one-sided (Woodhead and Moss, 2007), with primary education being the dominant partner and exerting influence on the field of ECE. Stronger cooperation between the sectors involves a risk of downward pressure by schools on ECE, bringing a narrow focus on literacy and numeracy at the expense of other important areas of child development, leading ECE 'to adopt the content and methods of the primary school' with a 'detrimental effect on young children's learning' (OECD, 2001: 129). This phenomenon is called the 'schoolification' of ECE by some authors (Bennett, 2006; Moss, 2008, 2012; OECD, 2006; Woodhead and Moss, 2007). For Haddad (2008), the inequality of relationship has been nurtured historically, as evidenced in the trajectory of the respective institutions. Showing a continuous evolution, primary school has been recognized as a 'right' and public good for a longer period of time than ECE, and has clearer objectives and a firm identity; the development of ECE is characterized by 'discontinuity, inconsistencies, contradictions, parallelisms, and overlapping of responsibilities between the social and educational sectors' (Haddad, 2008: 35). Similarly, Kagan (2012: 139) attributes 'ubiquity', 'familiarity' and 'durability' as features that characterize the dominance of schools, in contrast to ECE being 'spotty', 'sporadic', 'inconsistent', 'fragile' and 'mysterious'.

Three models of relationship

This section outlines three models of a possible relationship between early childhood and primary education: (1) school readiness, (2) ready school, and (3) a strong and equal partnership. The first two are rooted in Piaget's proposal of a hierarchical sequence of cognitive developmental stages, their notions arising from the school systems of many Western societies whereby the boundary between ECE and primary schooling coincides with the transition from pre-operational to concrete operational modes of thinking (Blair, 2008). I consider these models as ideal types, with the recognition that situations close to these typologies can be found in particular countries. Acknowledging that these three are among many models that may exist or be conceptualized, I have chosen to present them because the first two models are frequently referred to in ECE literature (e.g. Ackerman and Barnett, 2005; Dowker, 2007; Fabian and Dunlop, 2006; Moss, 2008; Myers and Landers, 1989; OECD, 2006; Shore, 1998), and the third model represents one constructive typology that could be considered for the future of both sectors.

School-readiness model

This model emphasizes the role of ECE in equipping young children with knowledge and skills deemed useful for primary schooling. The research consensus today is that school readiness includes development in five interconnected areas: (1) physical development, (2) socio-emotional development, (3) approaches to learning, (4) language and communication, and (5) cognitive development and general knowledge (UNESCO, 2006). While it provides a benchmark for ECE professionals, the school-readiness model can involve certain risks, such as privileging literacy and numeracy skills over others, placing excessive responsibility on children and their families for school success, and overlooking children's individual differences (Kaga, 2008). Calling this model a 'pre-primary approach to early education', OECD (2006) observes that it is prominent in France, the Netherlands and English-speaking countries except

New Zealand, and that it tends to favour literacy activity, teacher-initiated, large group activities and the adoption of learning standards.

Arguments for supporting this model include the following. First, there is considerable attention paid to economic and labour market rationales, which regard literacy, numeracy and the mastering of technology as key to success in subsequent education and in the job market. This urges ECE services to be mainly concerned with the early acquisition of related skills as their central purpose (Moss, 2008). Second, in contexts where populations have diverse language and cultural backgrounds and levels of inequality are high, a teaching or instructional approach, with a strong focus on the acquisition of basic language skills and general knowledge of the host country, may seem more effective (OECD, 2006). Third, the model appeals to education ministries, keen to see all children start primary school well and equally prepared. Fourth, the model – in its most conservative form – is simple in theory as well as in implementation, requiring the application of 'certain types of human technology' (e.g. developing curricula, training teachers, setting new goals and modes of assessment, introducing incentives and sanctions) to steer ECE towards greater conformity to the demands of primary education (Moss, 2012: 47).

However, in this model, children are likely to find themselves in an over-formalized, school-like situation from an early age, and are 'denied the experience of an appropriate pedagogy where they can follow their own learning paths and learn self-regulation at their own pace' (Bennett, 2007: 40). Research suggests that the narrowing of ECE content does not correspond to the developmental needs of children, and that young children learn best through meaningful interaction using real materials and experiences rather than the teaching of isolated skills (Bodrova, 2008; Elkind, 2007; Marcon, 2002). Research in France, the UK and the USA demonstrates that children from poor and second-language backgrounds tend to do poorly in formal, instructional classrooms compared to children from literate and supportive families, and that they require an environment that can provide more individualized attention and support (Barnett et al., 2004; Blatchford et al., 2002; Piketty and Valdenaire, 2006). Readying children to enter school and achieve predetermined outcomes 'ignores the potential with which children are born, indeed threatens to waste it, and applies a reductionist, fragmented and narrow approach, which is more about taming, controlling and predicting' (Moss, 2012: 41). In the school-readiness formulation, the meaning and value of ECE tends to be defined by what comes next, i.e. ECE as a transitional period for the 'real education' that occurs in primary education; and the image of compulsory school is that which takes the average child as natural, the norm, the one that fits the system (Vandenbroeck et al., 2012).

The ready-school model of relationship

This model stresses the school's adaptation to the child's characteristics and needs, and focuses on the school's accessibility and features of the school environment that can encourage or hinder learning. It recognizes that schools carry a major responsibility for every child's success, and gives attention to aspects such as school leadership and environment, curricula, teacher training and support, and parental and community involvement (Ackerman and Barnett, 2005; Moss, 2008). Vandenbroeck et al. (2012) propose a school readiness premised on welcoming a 'unique' and 'unpredictable' child – and not an 'average' child – who will have similarities and differences with the children primary schools have had so far (2012: 189). Thus, a school being ready for that child 'means being ready for unpredictability and uncertainty and, consequently, being ready to search and to research what ECE may mean for this child and for his family' (2012: 189).

The model favours primary schools reflecting some of the ECE pedagogies, such as attention to well-being, emphasis on the natural learning strategies of the child (e.g. play, active and experiential learning) and avoidance of child measurement and ranking (Bennett, 2006), at least in the first few years of primary schooling. Thus, it advocates an upward influence from early childhood to primary education, which is part of the 'social pedagogical tradition' of linking the two sectors, found in Nordic and central European countries (OECD, 2006). Other examples of ready-school efforts include close collaboration between the 'feeder' nurseries and primary schools to establish curricular and social continuity in Denmark (Broström, 2002, cited in Fabian and Dunlop, 2006: 12). In this initiative, school teachers learned about the interests of individual children through meetings with nursery staff, and facilitated opportunities to make the transition with friends, impacting positively on their emotional well-being and confidence to meet new challenges in new environments. In North Carolina, USA, the State Board of Education, together with various stakeholders, defined 14 items (e.g. the classroom environment, the curriculum, the services offered, collaboration with parents) that can help assess schools' readiness as part of a broad readiness framework (Ackerman and Barnett, 2005).

In the ready-school model of relationship, the image of ECE is not of a subordinate nature, but that of an active collaborator and advisor for primary education. While this model appears more positive for children and their families, there is acknowledgement that ECE's purpose of readying children does not have to be dismissed. Vandenbroeck et al. (2012: 190) state that:

> [f]or some families, this is precisely what they expect. Some immigrant families … do not choose child care as a "home away from home", but precisely because it differs from the home: it is a place for learning the dominant language and for socializing their children, holding out the prospect of integration and social capital.

Moss (2012) argues that ECE's function of readying children for school can be made positive when literacy, numeracy and other icons of school readiness are placed in the wider context of multiple languages – or modes of expression, such as words, drawing, painting, collage, sculpture, movement and music, as promoted by the Reggio Emilia approach (Edwards et al., 1998) – that together contribute to enriched learning; and when space is kept open for movement and experimentation, lines of flight and unexpected directions in the presence of predetermined outcomes that ECE is to pursue. Today, conceptions around the two models increasingly recognize that the readiness of children and that of school systems are two sides of the same coin (Shore, 1998; Woodhead and Moss, 2007). Brown (2010: 137) states that the 'interactionist approach' to defining readiness – constructed from the child's contribution to schooling *and* the school's contribution to the child – is used in the current research in ECE in the USA as well as 'across the globe'.

Strong and equal partnership

Proposed by OECD (2006), based on its review of early childhood policies in 20 countries, this goes beyond the binary models of readying children and readying schools, and is concerned not only with the child–school equation but also the institutional relationship. In this model, the diverse perspectives and methods of early childhood and primary education are brought together, focusing on the strengths of both sectors. Such a partnership is constructed on three elements: (1) ECE as 'a public good', just like primary schooling, and 'an important part of the educational process', with access to quality ECE a right of all children, (2) attention given to children's transition from ECE to school, building bridges across ECE services and schools as well as administrative departments, staff training, regulations and curricula in both sectors, and (3) 'a unified approach to learning' adopted in both ECE and primary education, recognizing the contribution of the early childhood approach to 'fostering key dispositions and attitudes to learning' (OECD, 2006: 59).

A strong and equal partnership seems particularly beneficial for children, parents and professionals. Children would be facilitated to participate in quality ECE services that recognize them as learners and that nurture their learning potential. They would also be supported to make a smooth transition from ECE to primary school through well-conceived connections and a unified approach to learning applied across the sectors. Parents would benefit from facilitated access to quality ECE services for their children. ECE professionals and primary school teachers would be able to enrich their perspectives and capacities through interaction as equal partners and through the cross-fertilization of understanding and experience of young children accumulated in both ECE and primary education. Emphases on parental involvement and social development are examples of strengths in ECE that can contribute positively to enhancing school practices (OECD, 2006).

Bennett (2012), co-author of *Starting Strong I* and *II* (OECD, 2001, 2006), suggests that the four Nordic countries reviewed, i.e. Denmark, Finland, Norway and Sweden, showed characteristics that correspond to the 'strong and equal partnership' conceptualization. These characteristics are: ECE was to nurture child well-being, self-actualization, socialization and playful learning; pre-school classes for 6-year-olds were instituted to offer a mix of ECE and school-like activities before starting compulsory schooling; and ECE professionals respected the natural learning strategies of young children. Conditions that favoured such partnership in these countries include: a strong and coherent identity and a tradition of ECE from birth to compulsory school, governed by a single ministry; a positive public opinion of ECE; and a highly educated workforce in both sectors influencing research (Bennett, 2012; Moss, 2012).

However, Kagan (2012) asserts that partnership based on equal contributions from ECE and compulsory school has not been the norm, with the latter more heavily shaping the former. Speaking of the Norwegian attempt to export kindergarten education to school and reflecting on this model of relationship, Haug (2012: 122) says:

> What I find of most interest in this situation is the ambition that it is possible to 'take' the best from different traditions and just mix them together. From a technical or instrumental perspective this could be done, just like baking a cake. You take a bit of this and that and stir it together, and a new type of 'education' grows out of it.

For him, the idea appears fundamentally naïve and overlooks the power of different educational traditions and of the institutions that have contoured early childhood and primary education. Values, ideas and practices are embedded and cultivated under different institutional conditions, such as those related to buildings, materials, rules, norms and expectations. The strong and equal partnership may be too idealized a vision (Kagan, 2012). But, as ECE has valuable contributions to make to primary school practices and in the interest of continuity of learning and well-being for children which is attentive to their individual strengths, characteristics and developmental levels, the vision of strong and equal partnership is important. How can we concretely work toward this vision? Three directions can be suggested:

- Develop meeting places, actionable strategies and policies: as stakeholders in the early childhood and primary education sectors often work in isolation, it is necessary to provide them with regular 'meeting places' where they can learn about and from each other and have opportunities to explore possible collaborations together. Such meeting places could be envisaged in transition efforts, teacher education and professional development, intellectual fora (e.g. research journals and seminars) and at the level of government administration (Bennett, 2012; Carr, 2012). Moreover, it is crucial to design and implement actionable strategies and policies that expressly address the unequal relationship (Kagan, 2012), such as policy, programmatic and pedagogical alignment (Kagan, 2012), alignment of curricula documents and outcomes (Carr, 2012), teamwork among ECE staff, schoolteachers and free time pedagogues (Moss, 2012), joint initial and continuous education (Britt and Sumsion, 2003) and equal pay and working conditions for ECE and school teachers (Bennett, 2012).
- Identify differences and common heritage, and develop shared visions and understanding: drawing on Dahlberg and Lenz Taguchi (1994), a strong relationship of equality can be facilitated by identifying differences as well as potentially common heritages of ideas embedded in ECE and primary education. These might be, for example, conceptions of child, childhood, learning, development and education – and may be discussed among stakeholders from both sectors, exploring their impacts on pedagogy and teaching practices. This process can be informed by the differences and common heritages derived from the past as well as from new orientations and practices, such as Loris Malaguzzi's conception of 'a rich child' (Children in Europe, 2008) and the child as a right holder (Committee on the

Rights of the Child, 2005). Once the differences and common heritages are clearly defined and their implications discussed, the development of shared visions and understanding among ECE and primary education stakeholders can be productively explored.

- Make parallel conscious efforts to build up the ECE sector: a strong and equal partnership seeks a strong and coherent ECE sector that can receive appropriately the increasing numbers of young children applying for services. Elements for building up the sector include a systemic and integrated approach to policy development and implementation; a universal approach to access with attention to children in need; sufficient public investment in services and infrastructure; quality regulation with a participatory approach to quality improvement; appropriate staff training and working conditions (OECD, 2001). In terms of quality, placing health, well-being, early development and learning at the core of ECE work while respecting the young child's agency and natural learning strategies (OECD, 2006) is important, and calls for establishing, within the ECE sector, the theory and practice of holistic pedagogy.

Final thoughts

There is no longer the choice of total dissociation or separation between early childhood and primary education. They are connected, and the connection will probably intensify further in the near future. ECE is encountering a kind of paradoxical situation whereby, on one hand, the level of interest, attention and support that it receives was never so great, and is being increasingly recognized as a legitimate and fully-fledged policy area; and on the other hand, it is more and more subject to the pressure to become like primary school and assimilate into the education system, losing its uniqueness and autonomy. In other words, ECE is coming closer to being an 'equal' partner of primary education, while it is expected to look up to primary school, to align to its goals and practices, and to be accountable, perform and produce outcomes as part of the greater picture of an education system and human capital development effort. Nevertheless, possibilities for real advancement towards a constructive relationship are present more than ever, and must be seized upon by placing children's well-being and development at the very centre of the endeavour.

☐ Summary

- The issue of the relationship between early childhood and primary education is important because it not only helps improve children's experience of transition between ECE services and school, but it also has the potential of

(Continued)

(Continued)

generating common understanding, aims and practices of education that cut across different educational stages, leading to the realization of a vision of lifelong learning.

- The relationship varies between countries and is shaped by the historical and structural contexts in which it is embedded. Relating the sectors is complex because they have distinct cultures and traditions and are in power relations.
- The school-readiness model of relationship defines the central aim of ECE as a preparation for primary schooling, and tends to support the 'schoolification' of ECE. The ready-school model of relationship suggests the transformation of primary school to provide conditions familiar to ECE services and to adjust expectations and practices to children's level of development and capacity. In the 'strong and equal partnership' model of relationship, the two sectors are closely connected and interact as equal partners, building on the strengths of each other. Certain conditions, such as an integrated ECE system with its specific identity, are considered to have helped build such a relationship in certain countries. Directions in which to take this model include: developing meeting places, actionable strategies and policies; identifying differences and common heritage and developing shared visions and understanding; and building up the ECE sector.

Questions for discussion

1. What relationship between early childhood and primary education exists in your country?
2. Is the schoolification of ECE an issue in your country? What signs of schoolification do you find, and what causes schoolification?
3. In your view, what efforts are needed to move towards a strong and equal partnership between early childhood and primary education (*Higher-level question*)?

Further reading

Levels 5 and 6

Ackerman, D.J. and Barnett, W.S. (2005) Prepared for kindergarten: what does 'readiness' mean? In: *Preschool Policy Brief*, March. New Brunswick, NJ: National Institute for Early Education Research at Rutgers University (NIEER). Available at: nieer.org/resources/policy reports/report5.pdf

This policy brief presents notions of school readiness and ready school, and provides policy recommendations on the issue.

Kaga, Y. (2008) What approaches to linking ECCE and primary education? In: *UNESCO Policy Brief on Early Childhood No. 44*. Available at: unesdoc.unesco.org/images/0017/001799/179934e.pdf
This policy brief summarizes the main approaches to linking early childhood and primary education, including the school-readiness and ready-school approaches, and highlights several strategies that support the continuity of learning and smooth transition for children.

Woodhead, M. and Moss, P. (eds) (2007) *Early Childhood and Primary Education. Early Childhood in Focus 2: Transitions in the Lives of Young Children*. Milton Keynes: Open University Press.
This volume includes a reappraisal of traditional concepts of school readiness and a strong and equal partnership between early childhood and primary education, and a review of strategies required to ensure continuity and successful transitions for children.

Levels 6 and 7

Moss, P. (ed.) (2012) *Early Childhood and Compulsory Education: Reconceptualising the Relationship*. London: Routledge.
This volume discusses the issue of the relationship between early childhood and compulsory education – what should be the relationship, and what can we learn from one another and by working together? It contains reflections on the issue by leading early childhood figures from Belgium, France, Italy, New Zealand, Norway, Sweden, the UK and the USA.

OECD (2006) *Starting Strong II: Early Childhood Education and Care*. Paris: OECD. Available at: http://www.oecd.org/edu/preschoolandschool/startingstrongiiearlychildhoodeducation andcare.htm
This publication offers examples of policy initiatives adopted in the early childhood field in 20 OECD countries, and identifies 10 policy areas for government attention. In the volume, the strong and equal partnership concept is treated extensively.

Websites

http://blogs.tc.columbia.edu/transitions/
This web page features the National and International Transition Analysis project implemented by the National Center for Children and Families, Columbia University. A compendium of US and international transition efforts, produced through the project, is available.
http://www.education.vic.gov.au/childhood/professionals/learning/Pages/transition.aspx
This web page of the Department of Education and Early Childhood Development of Victoria, Australia, suggests useful resources that help early childhood professionals support children's smooth transition from ECE services to primary school.

References

Ackerman, D.J. and Barnett, W.S. (2005) Prepared for kindergarten: what does 'readiness' mean? In: *Preschool Policy Brief*, March. New Brunswick, NJ: NIEER.
Barnett, W.S., Schulman, K. and Shore, R. (2004) *Class Size: What's the Best Fit?* New Brunswick, NJ: NIEER.

Bennett, J. (2006) 'Schoolifying' ECEC: accompanying pre-school into education. Lecture given at the Institute of Education, London, 10 May.

Bennett, J. (2007) A strong and equal partnership. In: M. Woodhead and P. Moss (eds) *Early Childhood and Primary Education: Transitions in the Lives of Young Children*. Milton Keynes: Open University Press, pp. 40–41

Bennett, J. (2012) A response from the co-author of 'a strong and equal partnership'. In: P. Moss (ed.) *Early Childhood and Compulsory Education: Reconceptualising the Relationship*. London: Routledge, pp. 52–71.

Blair, C. (2008) School readiness. In: L.J. Salkind (ed.) *Encyclopedia of Educational Psychology*. London: SAGE, pp. 877–879.

Blatchford, P., Goldstein, H., Martin, C. and Browne, W. (2002) A study of class size effects in English school reception year classes. *British Educational Research Journal*, 28(2): 171–187.

Bodrova, E. (2008) Make-believe play vs. academic skills: a Vygotskian approach to today's dilemma of early childhood education. *European Early Childhood Education Research Journal*, 16(3): 357–369.

Britt, C. and Sumsion, J. (2003) Within the borderlands: beginning early childhood teachers in primary schools. *Contemporary Issues in Early Childhood*, 4(2): 115–136.

Brown, C. (2010) Balancing the readiness equation in early childhood education reform. *Journal of Early Childhood Research*, 8(2): 133–160.

Carr, M. (2012) Making a borderland of contested spaces into a meeting place: the relationship from a New Zealand perspective. In: P. Moss (ed.) *Early Childhood and Compulsory Education: Reconceptualising the Relationship*. London: Routledge, pp. 92–111.

Children in Europe (2008) *Celebrating 40 years of Reggio Emilia: The Pedagogical Thought and Practice Underlying World-renowned Early Years Services in Italy*, Issue 6. Edinburgh: Children in Scotland.

Committee on the Rights of the Child (2005) *General Comment 7: Implementing Child Rights in Early Childhood*. Geneva: UNCRC.

Dahlberg, G. and Lenz Taguchi, H. (1994) *Förskol aoch skola – omt våskilda traditioner ochom visionen omen mötesplats [Pre-school and school – two different traditions and the vision of a meeting place]*. Stockholm: HLS Förlag.

Dowker, P. (2007) Ready or not, here we come: what it means to be a ready school. *Young Children*, 62(2): 68–70.

DREES (2010) Les modes d'organisations des crèches collectives et les métiers de la petite enfance [The modes of organization of daycare and the early childhood profession]. *Etudes et résultats*, no. 732, July.

Edwards, C., Gandini, L. and Forman, G. (1998) *The Hundred Languages of Children: The Reggio Emilia Approach – Advanced Reflections*. Westport, CT and London: Ablex Publishing.

Elkind, D. (2007) *The Power of Play: Learning What Comes Naturally*. Cambridge, MA: Da Capo Press.

European Commission (2011) *Communication from the Commission: ECEC – Providing all Our Children with the Best Start for the World of Tomorrow*. COM(2011)66 final. Brussels: European Commission.

Eurydice (2009) *ECEC in Europe: Tackling Social and Cultural Inequalities*. Brussels: European Commission.

Eurydice (2009/2010) *Organisation of the Education System in Sweden 2009/2010*. Brussels: European Commission.

Fabian, H. and Dunlop, A. (2006) Outcomes of good practice in transition processes for children entering primary school. Paper commissioned for the EFA Global Monitoring Report 2007: Strong Foundations: Early Childhood Care and Education. Paris: UNESCO.

Government of Sweden (2010) *Curriculum for the Preschool Lpfö 98: Revised 2010*. Stockholm: Skolverket.

Government of Sweden (2011) *Curriculum for the Compulsory School, Preschool Class and the Leisure-time Centre 2011*. Stockholm: Skolverket.

Haddad, L. (2008) For a specific dignity of ECE: policy and research issues relating the education of young children and sustainable society. In: I. Pramling Samuelsson and Y. Kaga (eds) *The Contribution of ECE to a Sustainable Society*. Paris: UNESCO, pp. 31–36.

Hart, B. and Risley, I. (1995) *Meaningful Differences in the Everyday Experience of Young American Children*. Baltimore, MD: Paul H. Brookes.

Haug, P. (2012) From indifference to invasion: the relationship from a Norwegian perspective. In: P. Moss (ed.) *Early Childhood and Compulsory Education: Reconceptualising the Relationship*. London: Routledge, pp. 112–129.

Heckman, J. and Masterov, D.V. (2004) The Productivity Argument for Investing in Young Children. Working Paper 5, Invest in Kids Working Group, Committee for Economic Development, 4 October. Economic Research at the University of Munich, 6(2): 3–8.

Kaga, Y. (2008) What approaches to linking ECCE and primary education? In UNESCO Policy Brief on Early Childhood No. 44.

Kagan, S.L. (2012) David, Goliath and the ephemeral parachute: the relationship from a United States perspective. In: P. Moss (ed.) *Early Childhood and Compulsory Education: Reconceptualising the Relationship*. London: Routledge, pp. 130–148.

Marcon, R.A. (2002) Moving up the grades: relationship between preschool model and later school success. *Early Childhood Research and Practice*, 4(1). Available at: http://ecrp.uiuc.edu/v4n1/marcon.html (accessed 28 February 2013).

Moss, P. (2008) What future for the relationship between early childhood education and care and compulsory schooling? *Research in Comparative and International Education*, 3(3): 224–234.

Moss, P. (ed.) (2012) *Early Childhood and Compulsory Education: Reconceptualising the Relationship*. London: Routledge.

Myers, R. and Landers, C. (1989) Preparing Children for School and School for Children. A discussion paper prepared for the 5th meeting of the Consultative Group on ECCD, UNESCO, Paris, 4–6 October.

Organisation for Economic Co-operation and Development (OECD) (2001) *Starting Strong I: Early Childhood Education and Care*. Paris: OECD.

Organisation for Economic Co-operation and Development (OECD) (2006) *Starting Strong II: Early Childhood Education and Care*. Paris: OECD.

Organisation for Economic Co-operation and Development (OECD) (2012) *Starting Strong III: A Quality Toolbox for Early Childhood Education and Care*. Paris: OECD.

Piketty, T. and Valdenaire, M. (2006) L'impact de la taille des classes sur la réussite scolaire dans les écoles, collèges et lycées français: estimations à partir du panel primaire 1997 et du panel secondaire 1995 [Impact of class size on student success in French schools, high schools and colleges: primary panel 1997 and secondary panel 1995 assessments], *Les dossiers*, 173, March. Paris: Ministère de l'Éducation nationale, de l'Enseignement Supérieur et de la Recherche, Direction de l'Evaluation et de la Prospective.

Rayna, S. (2010) Research and ECEC for children under three in France: a brief review. *International Journal for Early Childhood*, 42: 117–130.

Richards, C. (2008) Primary school/education. In: G. McCulloch and D. Crook (eds) *The Routledge International Encyclopedia of Education*. London: Routledge, pp. 452–454.

Shore, R. (1998) Ready Schools: A Report of the Goal 1 Ready Schools Resource Group. The National Education Goals Panel.

UNESCO (2006) *Education for All Global Monitoring Report. Strong Foundations: Early Childhood Care and Education*. Paris: UNESCO.

Vandenbroeck, M., De Stercke, N. and Gobeyn, H. (2012) What if the rich child has poor parents? The relationship from a Flemish perspective. In P. Moss (ed.) *Early Childhood and Compulsory Education: Reconceptualising the Relationship*. London: Routledge, pp. 174–192.

Woodhead, M. and Moss, P. (eds) (2007) *Early Childhood and Primary Education: Transitions in the Lives of Young Children*. Milton Keynes: Open University Press.

CHAPTER 4

HOW TO CONSTRUCT A CURRICULUM IN AN ITALIAN *NIDO*

Tullia Musatti, Donatella Giovannini, Susanna Mayer and Group Nido LagoMago

---

Overview

In this chapter, we propose a new perspective on the definition of curricula for early childhood education and care (ECEC) centres. Should children be provided with educational experiences directly geared to the acquisition of specific skills and knowledge? Or is it better to pursue broader educational goals and support the development of children's full potential? The debate is mostly focused on programmes immediately preceding children's enrolment in primary school at age 5 or 6. However, where infants and toddlers are concerned, it would be improper to consider the quality of curricula less crucial. We discuss the potential role of the content of experience provided to younger children while analysing educational practices in an Italian *nido* (an early childhood education centre for children under 3 years of age), practices which are based on the assumption that such centres are places of children's daily life and should provide them with significant social and cognitive experiences. Our analysis shows how it is possible to construct a powerful and detailed curriculum for children in their earliest years.

Introduction

Given that the youngest children's activities are quite basic, the content of the experience provided to them appears to be incidental. With regard to the youngest, the 'what' of children's learning looks much less important than the 'how' and 'why', and the boundary between 'curriculum' and 'pedagogy' (Hyson, 2007) is blurred. Underpinning much early childhood practice is a reductive interpretation of Piaget's theory, according to which children develop in stages characterized by increasingly complex cognitive and social competences, and the role of the educating adult is merely to provide children with developmentally appropriate opportunities to exercise their emerging skills (NAEYC, 1986). Even when it is suggested that, in proposing experiences to children, it is necessary to take account both of their age and their individual characteristics and their linguistic and cultural background (Bredekamp, 2007), the content of the experience proposed is viewed simply as a trigger for eliciting 'normal' child development.

A more comprehensive Piagetian interpretation considers that children have to learn 'how to learn', that is, they acquire their basic mental structures during their interaction with the physical and social elements of their environment. This view highlights the active role played by children in learning, as well as the essential role of an adequate environment in which they can express and consolidate their cognitive processes in a balanced dynamic interplay between assimilation and accommodation (Piaget, 1936/1952). In early childhood education, such a perspective fits with a holistic approach which 'assumes the inseparability of care and education, reasoning and emotion, body and mind' (Children in Europe, 2008: 6) and pursues broad educational goals rather than children's acquisition of specific skills and knowledge (see also Chapters 2 and 3). According to this perspective, the issue of balancing and integrating the 'what', 'how', and 'why' of pedagogical intervention remains highly significant, although taking on new nuances.

Early education and care centres, in which several young children live together with their adult caregivers, mostly every day and for long hours, represent a peculiar social situation. Their organization is governed by more or less explicit norms and rules of behaviour, moulded by habits and routines, and characterized by relational styles. Their participants have particular features and roles: adults, whose specific professional role orients their activities as well as their relational styles and attitudes; and children, who are the numerical majority, but who, although having a strong impulse to inter-subjectivity (Trevarthen, 1995), might not govern it. The activities of all participants intersect and convey meanings to each other, even unintentionally. These meanings can be further elaborated and shared by children and adults, and eventually memorized or represented. Half a century ago, Goffman (1964) argued that the social situation in which communication occurs should be considered attentively when analysing interaction and communication. In this chapter, we argue that both the social and cultural dimensions of the contexts where children and adults meet are not to be neglected (Goffman, 1964), and both have to be considered for pedagogical intervention. This consideration entails new pedagogical questions. How should we support, orient and integrate the activities of very young children in a group care context? How do we favour their elaboration and sharing of meanings with other children and adults? In this regard, what possible significance and function have specific play experiences proposed or supported by adults?

We investigated these topics by documenting, analysing and discussing the developments in the overall experience of a group of toddlers in the three years they spent in an Italian *nido*, and the educational practices that accompanied it. In the following, we present the conclusions we have reached, illustrating them with examples drawn from the documentation collected. First, we discuss the general arrangements for ECEC in Pistoia.

Pistoia's general pedagogical framework

The *nido* is one of the municipal ECEC centres of Pistoia that are all inspired by a common general pedagogical framework (Bennett, 2004), elaborated over the years through attentive policies and support for the continuous professional development of ECEC personnel (Musatti et al., 2011). The framework, that is realized in high-quality ECEC centres catering for children aged 0 to 3 years (*nido*), and aged 3 to 6 years (*scuola dell'infanzia*), is based on the assumption that ECEC centres represent places of everyday life for children in which their present and future well-being is cared for, their processes of socialization are favoured, and their curiosity and commitment in exploring the surrounding world are supported. Emphasis is laid on building positive interpersonal relations among all ECEC participants and stakeholders – children, practitioners, parents – and on sharing educational goals among service providers, children's families and the city community (Galardini and Giovannini, 2001). In common with other high-quality ECEC centres in Italy (Edwards et al., 1993), the Pistoia centres devote much attention to the aesthetic dimension of the physical environment: the choice of furnishings, and materials used to support autonomous exploration, play and interactions among children – the city's educational project has been defined as a 'pedagogy of good taste' (Becchi, 2010: 54). Special attention is paid to documentation (Galardini, 2009; Giovannini, 2001) and the standing of the service vis-à-vis the local and international community.

The study

Over the years, several action research projects have been carried out by the Italian National Research Council group on early childhood, in collaboration with the Department of Education of the Municipality of Pistoia. The study presented here was carried out by a group of researchers, a coordinator of Pistoia ECEC and *nido* practitioners.

Between December 2000 and June 2003, over three educational years, we collected systematic documentation regarding the everyday life of the same group of 14 children, aged 9–12 months, and three educators, starting from the first few months of their experience in a municipal *nido* and continuing until they left, at around the age of 33–36 months. Every week, the group's educators wrote narrative notes on the children's experience according to a plan (Picchio et al., 2012), and, once a week, a 45-minute video was recorded at the beginning of the morning to allow an in-depth analysis of the processes described in the written notes. Over the three-year period, this material was discussed during periodic meetings among the *nido* educators, the pedagogical coordinator and the researchers in order to high-light both the development of the children's experience and the educational choices made in everyday practice. In the following two years (2004 and 2005), the entire process was re-analysed and discussed, tackling three issues in particular: (1) the social processes underlying the children's and adult's shared everyday life; (2) the role of the organization of the context in directing these processes; and (3) the shar-ing of meanings by children and adults. We discuss some findings from each of these three areas below.

The *nido* is a place of everyday life shared by a group of children and adults

Focusing on the social situation (Goffman, 1964) in the *nido* implies analysis of the development of a group of children and adults not merely as being together in the same place, but also analysis of the way each child participates in the group, and a questioning of which experiences, rules, habits, routines or rituals orient how the group itself develops.

The starting point for this analysis was a comprehensive outlook on children's everyday life in the *nido* that has to be considered as a coherent whole rather than the juxtaposition and succession of freestanding experiences. Educators themselves are participants in that shared life and take a fresh view on how each child under-stands it as a common situation in which she eventually will participate with pleasure. With this participant role in mind, educators began to adapt their communicative and relational styles and assumed a more equal position vis-à-vis the children. They observed that it is important to communicate to the children that each situation develops as a result of the involvement and the contribution of everyone. For this reason it was important, as far as possible, for adults and children to share activities that are normally specific to the adult – for example, sorting out photographs, caring for books, preparing a space for an ordinary event such as lunch or an extraordinary event such as the arrival of a guest. Even though adults obviously have different capacities with respect to children and play a different role in the *nido*, the oppor-tunity to take part in what the adult was doing transmitted to the child a message of confidence in her capacities. Even more important, in this way a different equi-librium could be generated in child–adult relations, as the role of adults was not established by institutional rules, but was defined by acting together to achieve a shared objective. For example, it became customary to ask even very young children to prepare the bibs for the group snack, to fetch the scissors needed for an activity performed by a small group, or to take a message to the cook in the kitchen, verbally or in a written note. Furthermore, the educator often passed on a request received from one child to another child who, in that particular moment, was in a position to respond to it. In this way, the adult was no longer the only referent for the individual's needs and supported links of solidarity among children.

The educators re-interpreted their role as participant in the social situation during meals. Each adult sat down with a small group of toddlers and shared their meal, and stimulated the children's active participation in all the phases of the routine (such as setting or clearing the table or distributing food). During children's play and exploration activities, the educators gave priority to supporting the children's participation in a shared activity. Rather than attract children's interest to what the adults proposed, they chose to focus on what the children were interested in, in order to make the meaning of their activity or the links between the activities of the various children explicit to everyone. The adults' attention to the children's activities could be shown by commenting on their actions verbally, *echoing* what they said, or by mere physical proximity to the children.

The notion that life in the *nido* is an experience shared by a group of children and adults also formed the basis for defining the rules to be respected. Rules are needed to guarantee the social life of the group, individual well-being and mutual respect and must be defined in terms of these objectives. The educators considered that the message 'doing this makes it better for everyone' must be transmitted to the children clearly. The rules must be functional to each specific group of children but must also be adapted to suit the (developmental, emotional, family) needs of each individual child, ensuring that she can respect the rules of the group at her own pace or else offering an alternative.

Taking this perspective on the overall social situation does not mean neglecting the well-being and development of each child. We considered thoughtfully how to keep a balance between the individual and the collective needs of adults and children. Attention paid to the network of group interactions should not compete with attention paid to each child's needs, competences and moods. For some children, being in a group can be tiring and each child should be able to participate at her own pace and according to her style of behaviour. Indeed, the educators claimed that whenever a child felt uneasy in coping with the interactive and cognitive processes going on in the group, her discomfort could be relieved by making verbally explicit her emotions, feelings and moods both to herself and to the other children. At the same time, this practice made explicit the child's belonging to the group. The feeling of each individual's belonging to the group could also be boosted using simple strategies. For instance, whenever children were absent from the *nido* they would receive a telephone call at home from their *nido* companions to find out how they were and when they would be returning, and they were told what had happened during their absence.

In common with most Pistoia *nidi*, each educator had special responsibility for a group of 4–7 children, although both play and care activities could be performed all together or among different partners according to occasional preferences.

Although each small group composition is stable over the three years the children spend in the *nido*, there will be some changes in the staff or children in the group through departure and arrival. We discussed whether these changes could undermine the development of group life, but we concluded that a group with a strong identity is capable of accepting new elements and of growing, thanks to them. The identity of the group of children is the result not so much of its permanent composition but of the continuity of the experience shared by its members.

The organization of everyday life in the *nido* orients the children's experience

The organization of space and time in the *nido* was considered an important influence on social and cognitive processes. Pistoia ECEC centres typically have an abundance of materials organized into well-defined interest centres. The arrangement of furniture guarantees that children can play both in small groups and have moments of privacy and individual comfort. Over time, changes are introduced in the spatial organization as the children develop and their activities evolve.

Analysis of the documentation highlighted that the spatial organization of the context has important effects on the social processes developing in it. Earlier research had shown that interactions among children are influenced by the arrangement of furniture and materials in play areas (Campos-de-Carvalho and Rossetti-Ferreira, 1993; Legendre, 1989; Moore, 1986). We found that the stable position of the adult in the course of a play activity helps the children, especially the younger ones, to maintain their focus of interest, counteracting their fluctuating attention and typical impulse to move around (Musatti and Mayer, 2011). Children's overall understanding of their everyday life space and their continuous engagement in play was also enhanced by keeping containers for materials in the same place, as well by their active participation in rearranging them after play. Keeping visible traces of activities was also important in sustaining children's continuous involvement in the same activities over time – for example, by keeping constructions or other play productions or photographs of what they had done. The environment thus becomes a container for children's experiences in which individual or shared knowledge is stored.

Also, the temporal dimension of life in the *nido* was considered important: as with other Pistoia ECEC centres, the days in the *nido* go by at a leisurely unhurried pace to allow each child to act easily and become part of the social situation in their own time. Each morning, when a child arrives at the *nido*, she has to re-establish contact with her experience in the social situation (Rayna et al., 1991). A new day begins that has to be shared and linked significantly to what was done previously and what will be done later. To support this, the educators decided not to wait for all the children to arrive before proposing play activities. Instead, they invited each child to take part in the shared situation when they arrived. In this way, both the child and the accompanying parent received the message that they were entering an active community. Moreover, we considered that drawing conscious attention to the temporal rhythms of the day helps children grasp passing time and anticipate the succession of events and their participation in them. Most important, the day must be perceived by the children as a significant whole. As for all young children, everyday life in the *nido* is divided up into units of time that are regulated by the temporal scansion of children's physical needs and anchored to care activities, the significance of which is easy to identify and important in the eyes of the children. These particular phases thus represent for the children recognizable elements marking the course of their day. The stable organization of these phases helps the children to predict their succession: after lunch is diapering time, then nap time, and so on. These phases must also be rendered significant for the children and their expectations concerning them stimulated by educators.

In the practice that we documented, temporal phases were marked by stable routines related to the specific features of each care activity, as well as by habits that helped children's development and by the social processes going on within the group. In these phases, the individual satisfaction of children's physical and psychological needs mingles with the social dimension of group life. The context was organized to enable the children to relax and express emotions, to learn how to do things on their own, drawing pleasure and self-confidence from this experience, and to provide opportunities for meeting together where everybody can identify with what it is going on and with what is narrated. An important role was played by the elaboration of several play rituals that were set up within these contexts. As they were the outcome of an activity shared by the whole group and recognized by the children as such, they increased children's reciprocal familiarity and feeling of belonging to a community. All these elements evolved over time due to new proposals suggested by adults or children or to the development of children's competences. Thus, the children could take on a significance shared by the group and become part of that group's history.

The analysis of these phases focused on care activities allowed us to recognize an implicit strategy on which the *nido*'s educational practice was based: building everyday life contexts in which children's cognitive engagement and participation in group life is stimulated and supported and that become 'containers' in which children's shared experience and knowledge can be stored and potentially rehearsed and re-elaborated. In the case of these care phases, care activities represent an important frame of reference for children's engagement, as well as for the processes of interaction among children and between children and adults. We examined our documentation data to understand whether and how contexts focused on play and exploration activities could provide similar frameworks.

Sharing processes in the group of children

In their first three years of life, research has shown that children gradually master the fundamental relations among objects (proto-logical processes) and between their properties (proto-physical processes) by producing quite elementary actions such as putting in–taking out, moving up–down, grouping–separating, pushing, throwing, blowing to make an object fall, breaking up, and so on (Sinclair et al., 1982/1989; Verba et al., 1982). It has also been shown that during the same period children can coordinate these activities with their peers and share the underlying cognitive processes (Stambak et al., 1983). In ECEC centres that offer opportunities to a group of children to resume and elaborate their activities at successive moments and days, it was found that children go back to exploring the same objects and repeat and elaborate shared activities or play rituals even over long periods of time (Brenner and Mueller, 1982; Musatti and Mayer, 1993, 2001; Musatti and Panni, 1981; Verba and Musatti, 1989). These phenomena were interpreted as evidence that children memorized both the activities and the interactive format by means of which they were performed (Musatti, 2005). A principal goal of our investigation was to examine whether and how the evolution of children's play activities will intersect with the social processes taking place in the group.

At the beginning of the study period, once the children and educators were familiar with both each other and the environment, several activities were identified which repeatedly attracted the attention of one or more children. Rather than just repetition of the same activity, we found that the children showed a shared interest for a set of phenomena or relations arising out of a random event (a falling object makes a certain noise) or out of the incidental action of a child or adult. The educators chose to encourage these interests in the children by giving them the chance to develop their explorations and also proposing them to other children. In the discussion, the educators repeated on several occasions how only a few of the proposals they made were accepted – as one said, 'we baited the hook and [sometimes] the bait was taken' – and developed by the children and could become knowledge shared by several of them.

A deliberate and systematic re-proposing by the educators did not follow a pathway dictated by the development of the children's competences and was not aimed at stimulating their acquisition of specific skills or knowledge. The aim was to ensure the continuity of the children's experience and help them to overcome the fragmentary nature of their behaviours and knowledge – as one said, 'we provided the children with a map'. Eventually, some 'pathways to reflection' of various durations and complexities emerged.

In the course of the reflection pathway, the educators supported the development of children's exploration, by combining and varying the elements that the children were likely to reflect upon, introducing symbolic and notational elements, proposing new materials or new actions, and resuming the same activities in different situations and at different times. Re-proposing the same materials or play areas from one year to the next contributed to ensuring the continuity of the experiences. The educators' major commitment was to broaden the extent of their sharing among the children. The aim was to involve the whole group of children by communicating the 'discoveries' made by some to those not having participated, elaborating on narrations around them and constructing play rituals linked to the activities performed. Families were involved; they were informed about the activities, asked to supply materials and given occasions for participating in the activities directly.

As an example, we illustrate the evolution of one pathway to reflection that we named 'Blowing and Air'. This pathway was built up around an exploration of the movement of objects caused by air movements (achieved by blowing or other bodily movements), leading up to an exploration of the wind and followed over two educational years. At the beginning of the first year of the study, children's interest was captured by blowing on a mobile that hung over the nappy changing table. This play was repeated over a number of days, and, sometime later, the activity of moving objects by blowing was extended to other contexts and objects (feathers, pieces of paper, small balls, windmills). Over the following months, these objects were introduced into containers (boxes, tubes), into which adults blew. The children, individually or in a small group, spontaneously blew on other objects in order to move them (once, at lunch, a child tried to move a fork by puffing on it!). An interactive format between a child and an educator (throwing a piece of paper to each other on a table by puffing on it) was ritualized. During the snack break, the adults proposed a play activity: 'switch off the lights in the room (one child in turn moves her chair near the light switches, stands on it and switches off the lights) + light a candle that each child will puff out'. The activity was repeated almost every day for many months and all the children participated with great expectancy, engagement and pleasure. In the following years, the play ritual of blowing out a candle was rehearsed at the end of lunch and performed by producing an air movement by clapping the hands together or just pretending to puff. During the summer break, parents are solicited to help children collect objects that they will be able to blow and bring them back in a small bag to the *nido* in September. In the second year, among the younger children in the group several new versions of blowing are carried out and the play ritual of blowing pieces of paper to each other over a table is rehearsed spontaneously between children. At the same time, some older children together with new friends rehearse their explorations by blowing on old and new objects and their combinations, also outside the *nido* in the neighbouring park. The construction and use of artefacts that produce or exploit air movements, such as hairdryers, kites, windmills, led to exploring the wind, its characteristics and potential. The older children were encouraged to represent them by drawing. Some imaginary characters (the Ghost of the Wind, the Puffing Owl that lives in the park and communicates by blowing air) were created. Parents were involved in building kites and windmills and at the end of the year they all participated in a meeting at an airfield and flew kites.

Space precludes discussion of other pathways to reflection, an examination of which led to extensive discussion. We observed that, although they mostly consisted of very elementary activities (such as blowing on a sheet of paper, beating hands on a drum), during their elaboration the children were focused on the exploration of quite general questions, such as basic physical phenomena like air movement or sound. Over time, like a set of Chinese boxes, these explorations developed into more targeted actions performed along separate pathways by different subgroups of children or at different times. Most importantly, in addressing these issues, the children's active role in the cognitive interaction with the environment is strongly supported. Gauging the effect of their own actions, becoming familiar with the artefacts by means of which the culture to which they belong produces or dominates these effects (musical instruments, wind vanes, hair dryers, kites, as well as the narratives elaborated around them), and possibly creating other artefacts (fantastical instruments or imaginary characters), allow the child to acquire cultural competences that also valorise her identity and status in social networks outside the *nido* context. The involvement of families in the elaboration of the pathway also takes on this significance.

The second important issue concerns the function performed by these pathways in the formation and consolidation of the group of children and adults. In the course of the pathway, different activities were connected, the significance of which was made apparent to each child by participating in them or observing the activities performed by their peers and listening to comments and narratives about them. All this provided the group of children with a common ground (Clark, 1996). In our discussions we named it 'compost', like a matter which nourishes children's group life, as it represented an important reference framework for sharing play activities but also for communicating in other everyday contexts. The propagation of the pathway within the group and its development over time formed a *red thread* which transformed the meeting of children and adults at the *nido* into a group and narrated its history through the more repetitive aspects of the everyday routine. One educator asserted that 'it becomes a way of communicating among ourselves. Each family has its own way of expressing things. This is our way.' Once again it was found to be essential to involve parents and let them share the significance of children's activities and rituals so that the two worlds of the child could be mutually transparent (see the discussion in Chapter 5).

One further issue at the heart of heated debate in the action-research group was the participation of individual children in elaborating the pathway. Clearly, each child was involved to different degrees in the pathway (as active or passive participant, or bystander) more or less continuously and according to her competences and her own history within the group. Above and beyond these individual differences in the way the pathway was experienced by children, we all agreed that the development of a pathway did not marginalize the less active children but indeed encouraged their familiarization with the social situation and promoted their feeling of being part of an experience of shared life. The main message conveyed by the existence of a shared pathway did not concern its specific content but rather the experience of sharing attention and activities on a common ground.

Reflection pathways developed across everyday life in the *nido* and we found numerous instances of their migration from one activity context to another: some exploration activities turned into play rituals and crossed over into contexts of care activities in which the whole group of children were involved and where they underwent further elaboration.

Final thoughts

The analysis of the experience of a group of children during the three years they attended the *nido* shows how it is possible to construct a powerful and detailed curriculum for children in their earliest years. This curriculum is not a top-down instruction model along assumed universal developmental stages, but arises through detailed documentation and analysis of everyday practice and building activities and shared situations around a common philosophy.

The educational practice of the *nido* implemented the general pedagogical framework elaborated in ECEC centres of the city of Pistoia, according to which the *nidi* are children's places of life within the city community. This practice was based on the acknowledgment that, although each child's experience is unique and unrepeatable, it takes place in a social situation and in a continuous process within the framework of everyday life in the *nido*. This view considers as complementary the objectives of guaranteeing the well-being and promoting the involvement of each child (Laevers, 2004) and proposes an ecological perspective for children's well-being, asserting that being together with others in an atmosphere of sharing is a basic condition for well-being (see Chapter 10 for further discussion of this).

Within the educational approach we have described, educating children means acknowledging the global nature of their experience in the *nido* and accompanying their development by offering significant contexts of life. The expert organization of these contexts and their knowledgeable enrichment with material, social and symbolic elements make them an organizing framework both for children's social processes and their activities. From this perspective, even if broad educational goals are pursued, the content of children's activities is not incidental and is inextricably linked to the way they have the opportunity to perform, elaborate on and share them with their peers and adults.

In this process, in which many elements are in tune with the Reggio Emilia approach (Rinaldi, 2005), support of the children's reflection around specific themes, which emerge from their own interests, is interwoven with an attention to each child's well-being and overall development. The question of the trade-off between the time commitment required for the two educational actions (Bennett, 2004) loses importance.

The adults participate in the social situation by devoting considerable attention not only to the well-being and interests of each child but also to the network of interactions among children and between children and themselves. The adult's action is not meant to replace that of the child but to render explicit the significance of what the children are doing, even in the eyes of the actors themselves, to let communication circulate among children, activities be shared by children, and parents get involved.

The young age of the children and the big individual differences observed in the rate of development in the children's early years call for special flexibility in the adult's intervention and great creativity to provide coherent experiences across the various daily life contexts. The great care taken to ensure coherence and continuity in the children's experience, helps render these contexts harmonious and significant. In the observed educational practice, it was found that the element guaranteeing continuity of the children's experience is the formation of a group of children and adults, grounded in mutual familiarity, reciprocal affective participation and a sharing of everyday life routines, as well as a firm anchoring in a network of shared meanings; in other words, in a micro-culture of the small community of very young and adult persons. We have seen that constructing a suitable curriculum for children of this age means also building a bridge between this micro-culture and that of the broader society in which they are growing up.

Summary

- In this chapter, we have proposed a new perspective on education and care provision for children aged under 3, highlighting the social dimension of their experience in group care contexts.
- The analysis of the experience made over three years in an Italian early childhood education centre shows that educational practice can combine attention to children's development and well-being with support of children's socialization in their group of peers.
- The educational practice was aimed at providing significant contexts of daily life that could represent important reference frameworks for children's cognitive and social experience. It has been argued that the quality of the activities offered to children within such contexts influences both children's reflection and their interactions. Claims are made for a fresh outlook on the relationships between the 'what', 'how' and 'why' of young children's education.

Questions for discussion

1. Compare and contrast the approach to curricula described in this chapter with a pedagogical framework you are familiar with. What are the similarities and differences?
2. How are views of children and childhood reflected in the two curricula you have compared?
3. How can children's well-being be embedded in and enhanced through educational practice? (*Higher-level question*)

Further reading

Levels 5 and 6

Children in Europe (2008) Young children and their services: developing a European approach. A Children in Europe policy paper. Available at: www.childrenineurope.org

This is an important document issued by European experts which proposes 10 principles as the basis for a European approach to services for young children.

Musatti, T. and Mayer, S. (2011) EDUCARE in the *nido*: how to weave a tapestry from many threads. *Children in Europe*, 20: 6–7.
This article discusses how children's experiences in an educational setting can develop over time as a meaningful succession of related events.

Rinaldi, C. (2005) *In Dialogue with Reggio Emilia: Listening, Researching and Learning*. London: Routledge.
This book illustrates the different components of the Reggio Emilia educational approach by presenting a collection of writings by one of its major representatives.

Levels 6 and 7

Gandini, L. and Pope Edwards, C. (eds) (2001) *Bambini: The Italian Approach to Infant/ Toddler Care*. New York: Teachers College Press.
This book presents practices and reflections on early childhood education from the experience of four Italian cities.

Musatti, T. and Mayer, S. (2011) Sharing attention and activities among toddlers: the spatial dimension of the setting and educator's role. *European Early Childhood Education Research Journal*, 19(2): 207–221.
This article presents a detailed analysis of how the spatial organization of the educational context and the quality and arrangement of furniture and play materials affect infants and toddlers' social and cognitive performances.

Picchio, M., Giovannini, D., Mayer, S. and Musatti, T. (2012) Sharing reflection on children's experience among practitioners. *Early Years: An International Journal of Research and Development*, 32(2): 159–170.
This article illustrates the documentation procedures that *nido* professionals accomplish continuously and systematically, forming the basis of a collegial reflection on children's experience and practice improvement.

Websites

www.reggiochildren.it

This site provides current information on events and activities concerning Reggio Emilia ECEC services and educational experiences.

Acknowledgement

The action-research project, on which this chapter is based, was conducted with the financial support of the Region of Tuscany and was made possible by the collaboration of the *LagoMago nido* whole staff and the direction of the Department of Education of the City of Pistoia, whom we thank heartily.

References

Becchi, E. (2010) *Una pedagogia del buon gusto: Esperienze e progetti nei servizi educativi per l'infanzia del Comune di Pistoia*. [Pedagogy of 'good taste': Experiences and projects in Pistoia municipal ECE services]. Milano: Franco Angeli.

Bennett, J. (2004) Curriculum issues in national policy making. Paper presented at the 14th EECERA conference. Paris: OECD.

Bredekamp, S. (2007) Developmental appropriate practice(s). In: R.S. New and M. Cochran (eds) *Early Childhood Education: An International Encyclopedia*, Vol. 1. Westport, CT: Praeger, pp. 282–286.

Brenner, J. and Mueller, E. (1982) Shared meaning in boy toddlers' peer interactions. *Child Development*, 53(2): 380–391.

Campos-de-Carvalho, M.I. and Rossetti-Ferreira, M.C. (1993) Importance of spatial arrangements for young children in day care centers. *Children's Environments*, 10(1): 19–30.

Clark, H.H. (1996) *Using Language*. Cambridge, MA: Cambridge University Press.

Children in Europe (2008) Young children and their services: developing a European approach. A Children in Europe policy paper. Available at: www.childrenineurope.org

Edwards, C., Gandini, L. and Forman, G. (eds) (1993) *The Hundred Languages of Children: The Reggio Emilia Approach to Early Childhood Education*. Norwood, NJ: Ablex.

Galardini, A.L. (2009) Réseau et documentation: l'expérience italienne pour la qualité éducative. In: S. Rayna, C. Bouve and P. Moisset (eds) *Pour un accueil de qualité de la petite enfance: quel curriculum?* Toulouse: Édition Érès, pp. 79–86.

Galardini, A.L. and Giovannini, D. (2001) Pistoia: creating a dynamic, open system to serve children, families and community. In: L. Gandini and C. Pope Edwards (eds) *Bambini: The Italian Approach to Infant/Toddler Care*. New York: Teachers College Press, pp. 89–104.

Giovannini, D. (2001) Traces of childhood: a child's diary. In: L. Gandini and C. Pope Edwards (eds) *Bambini: The Italian Approach to Infant/Toddler Care*. New York: Teachers College Press, pp. 146–151.

Goffman, E. (1964) The neglected situation. *American Anthropologist*, 66(6): 133–136.

Hyson, M. (2007) Curriculum. In: R.S. New and M. Cochran (eds) *Early Childhood Education: An International Encyclopedia*, Vol. 1. Westport, CT: Praeger, pp. 176–181.

Laevers, F.V. (2004) *Experiential Education: Effective Learning through Well-being and Involvement*. Directorate for Education, Paris: OECD.

Legendre, A. (1989) Young children's social competences and their use of space in day care centers. In: B.H. Schneider, G. Attili, J. Nadel and R. Weissberg (eds) *Social Competence in Developmental Perspective*. Dordrecht: Kluwer, pp. 263–276.

Moore, G.T. (1986) Effects of the spatial definition of behavior settings on children's behavior: a quasi-experimental field study. *Journal of Environmental Psychology*, 6: 205–231.

Musatti, T. (2005) La qualité de l'expérience cognitive dans les milieux collectifs de la petite enfance. In: J.J. Ducret (ed.) *Scolariser la petite enfance? SRED, Cahier 12*. Genève: Service de la recherche en éducation, République et Canton de Genève, pp. 24–34.

Musatti, T. and Mayer, S. (1993) Pretend play in the schoolyard: propagation of play themes among a group of young children. In: M. Stambak and H. Sinclair (eds) *Pretend Play Among 3-Year-Olds*. Hillsdale, NJ: Lawrence Erlbaum, pp. 31–54.

Musatti, T. and Mayer, S. (2001) Knowing and learning in an educational context: a study in the infant-toddler centers of the city of Pistoia. In: L. Gandini and C. Pope Edwards (eds) *Bambini: The Italian Approach to Infant/Toddler Care*. New York: Teachers College Press, pp. 167–180.

Musatti, T. and Mayer, S. (2011) Sharing attention and activities among toddlers: the spatial dimension of the setting and educator's role. *European Early Childhood Education Research Journal*, 19(2): 207–221.

Musatti, T. and Panni, S. (1981) Social behavior and interaction among daycare center toddlers. *Early Child Development and Care*, 7: 5–25.

Musatti, T., Picchio, M. and Mayer, S. (2011) A continuous support to professionalism: the case of Pistoia ECE provision. In: *CoRe: Competence Requirements in Early Childhood Education and Care: A Study for the European Commission Directorate General for Education and Culture.* Available at: http://ec.europa.eu/education/more-information/doc/2011/core_en.pdf

NAEYC (1986) Position statement on developmentally appropriate practice in programs for 4- and 5-year-olds. *Young Children*, 41(6): 20–29.

Piaget, J. (1936/1952) *The Origins of Intelligence in Children*. New York: International University Press.

Picchio, M., Giovannini, D., Mayer, S. and Musatti, T. (2012) Sharing reflection on children's experience among practitioners. *Early Years: An International Journal of Research and Development*, 32(2): 159–170.

Rayna, S., Mazet, P. and Pérалès, D. (1991) L'entrée en crèche: une expèrience d'accueil. In: CRESAS. *Accueillir à la crèche, à l'école. Il ne suffit pas d'ouvrir la porte*. Paris: INRP – L'Harmattan.

Rinaldi, C. (2005) *In Dialogue with Reggio Emilia: Listening, Researching and Learning (Contesting Early Childhood)*. London: Routledge.

Sinclair, H., Stambak, M., Lézine, I., Rayna, S. and Verba, M. (1982/1989) *Infants and Objects*. San Diego, CA: Academic Press.

Stambak, M., Barriére, M., Bonica, L., Maisonnet, R., Musatti, T., Rayna, S. and Verba, M. (1983) *Les bébés entre eux: inventer, découvrir et jouer ensemble* [Among babies]. Paris: Presses Universitaires de France.

Trevarthen, C. (1995) The child's need to learn a culture. *Children & Society*, 9(1): 5–19.

Verba, M. and Musatti, T. (1989) Minor phenomena and major processes of interaction with objects and peers in day care centers. *European Journal of the Psychology of Education*, 4: 215–227.

Verba, M., Stambak, M. and Sinclair, H. (1982) Physical knowledge and social interaction in children from 18 to 24 months of age. In: G. Forman (ed.) *Action and Thought*. New York: Academic Press, pp. 267–296.

CHAPTER 5

THE FRENCH APPROACH TO FAMILY INTERVENTION WITH FAMILIES WITH YOUNG CHILDREN

Anne-Marie Doucet-Dahlgren

Overview

France has a highly developed system of early childhood education and care (ECEC) which is split between *Ecole Maternelle* for almost all children aged 3–6 and a mixture of group-based crèches and domestic-based care arrangements for children under 3. In this chapter, I provide an overview of some of the characteristics of the French approach to ECEC and then describe specific forms of early intervention organized within the framework of the Service de Protection Maternelle et Infantile (PMI). I consider the ways in which specific groups of parents respond to a Folk University parenting initiative and make suggestions about how to take some elements of the French experience as a model in an international perspective.

A European focus on parenting

Guiding families in their parenting role with their children has become a central issue in Europe in terms of family policy. Indeed, following the Final Statement and Declaration of the Ministers Responsible for Family Affairs in Lisbon, Portugal (16–17 May 2006), a recognition of Positive Parenting was taken into account, as it concerns the private sphere as well as public policy. Consequently, the Council of Europe (2006), in its Policy to Support Positive Parenting, made a number of recommendations to ensure that measures were taken towards families in terms of parenting support. One recommendation was that governments of European states should create the conditions for positive parenting that reflect the rights and best interests of the child. In this respect, measures should be taken to eliminate all forms of neglect and physical or psychological violence against children. In addition, the principles outlined in the UN Convention on the Rights of the Child (Resolution 44/25 of 20 November 1989) should be respected.

Parenting experienced in situations of social exclusion or at risk of exclusion is complex because the difficulties are often multiple and shared by all members of the same family. In this case, professionals have a specific role to play and qualitative guidelines are proposed for them. More precisely, this regards parents as both potential participants and requiring financial support. The guidelines in the report 'Aider les parents à être parents' (Centre d'analyse stratégique, 2012) highlight that professionals are able to assist parents in a non-stigmatizing and non-judgemental way. The guidelines recommend that methods for the identification of risk factors observed by social workers as well as health, youth, pre-school practitioners and school teachers are developed to help identify and support families. Families from a range of socio-economic backgrounds have various capacities to provide their child with a nutritious and healthy lifestyle. Following these principles, French policy (Décret – 1 August 2000 and Décret – 20 February 2007) made efforts to provide quality childcare and education for all families and, in particular, since 2012, to focus on families experiencing economic hardship which results in educational stress for many parents with young children. One issue for families in poverty is that childcare and medical care arrangements are often of low quality and sporadic. It is necessary to reinforce the ECEC services and parenting support to help them to cope with specific poverty-related matters. In this way, the initiatives taken by the Service de PMI with mothers and fathers with young children have characteristics described in the OECD report *Starting Strong*: 'Almost all OECD countries have some form of a framework – either in the form of a curriculum or standards. The age groups, which curricula are defined by, differ among countries' (OECD, 2012: 99).

The French ECEC system is a characteristically 'split' system, where 'child care and early education are governed and managed by different ministries' (OECD, 2012: 99). It is structured around care provision for children aged 0–3 years, based on a health and hygiene model and managed by the Ministry of Health (Ministère de la Santé). The system provides full- or part-time provision for children whose parents are in full- or part-time employment or who are not working. Inclusion of children with special needs is recommended and parental fees are required. At the age of 3, children move into education provision, until they are 6 years old, which is based on nationally prescribed curricula and organizational models. Nearly all children of the relevant age attend, as do one third of 2-year-olds, and this provision is managed by the Ministry of Education (Ministère de l'Education Nationale). There are no parental fees and children are not obliged to attend. This early education is a good example of what *Starting Strong* calls a 'learning framework for children in the older age bracket of ECEC: from around age two-and-a-half or three to compulsory schooling' (OECD, 2012: 97). Alongside this educational orientation, there is also, in France, an explicit parenting objective: *Action-Passerelle* programmes open to children from the age of 2 up to compulsory schooling. This is an approach with a strong health and social orientation to bridge home and school for working parents or children in need of special support.

The origins of the Service de Protection Maternelle et Infantile

At the end of the Second World War, many French families were faced with increasingly difficult living conditions. The death rate remained very high from the French state perspective. By the edict 'Ordonnance de 1945', the Service de PMI combined medical and social programmes which aimed at prevention, protection and assistance. From the beginning, the PMI was part of the 'Code de la Santé Publique' (public health code). It focused particularly on pregnant women, young children, families and children with disabilities, and monitored the quality of group- and home-based early childhood services.

Two milestones mark the progress of the Service de PMI at French and international level. The first is linked to the decentralization laws which organized the French state that is centrally run and is now also run by the regional governments or *Départements*. Second, at an international level, the Ottawa Charter for Health Promotion, launched on 21 November 1986, recognized the concept of global health, and specifically that creating supportive environments for health implies the existence of a relationship between environment and child development. This charter endorsed the work of the Service de PMI and in this way the ECEC systems were integrated with the health and prevention tasks entrusted to the PMI initiatives.

The French system is made up of divisions between national authorities (defining general goals) and local *Départements* which have the autonomy to implement policies that meet the needs of local constituents. Numerous stakeholders express the importance of developing a local-level decision-making procedure in order to better respond to family needs and circumstances. Stakeholders also pointed out the necessity of national guidelines to ensure equity goals. Since 2007, the PMI programmes have been conducted in two directions defined by the *Loi de Protection de l'Enfance* (Child Protection Act) and the *Code de la Famille et de l'Action Sociale* (Family Social Welfare Code). The aim is clearly to provide the means to support and reinforce the establishment of services at a universal level as well as at a targeted services level.

At a universal level, decentralization facilitates the collaboration across ECEC services and between services for children in the *Ecole Maternelle*. In addition to overseeing the Service de PMI which monitors the childcare sector, the *Départements* support coherent policies directed at specific geographical areas and targeting families in poverty and from minority ethnic groups. It is worth noting that there are universal guidelines for all families, whether from a public health or parenting support perspective.

At a targeted services level, focus is on the protection of children in danger or at risk. In this case, professionals carry out priority initiatives for vulnerable populations where new objectives are defined in order to prevent miscarriage, stillbirths and premature births, promote early screening of disability and re-enforce child–parent attachment.

The Service de PMI is a very complex system with specific objectives that are often part of the everyday life of families. The programmes of the Service are organized and delivered via the Centres de PMI established in districts of small or big cities.

What are the objectives of the Service de PMI?

The PMI service is universal and is composed of experts in child-rearing issues and family education in the broadest sense. They come from two sectors: the medical sector represented by doctors, psychiatrists, gynaecologists, midwives, nurses and care assistants and the child-rearing sector, represented by psychologists, therapists, family counsellors, educators and childminders. Two orientations can be distinguished which are detailed below. The first, orientation A, concerns the before and after birth programme with medical supervision, and the second, orientation B, concerns early childhood intervention; within both orientations there are possibilities for creating networks (for example, for parenting support).

Characteristics of the programmes

Orientation A: Ante- and post-natal programme

This programme consists of health services, both during pregnancy and after women have given birth, via the *Plan National Périnatal* of 2010 and initiatives for children under the age of 6. These initiatives include: free consultations; home visits by care workers; individual medical appointments (physical, psychological, sensorial, language or learning screenings) with the parents of children attending *Ecole Maternelle*; collective initiatives for specific groups such as parent–child conferences, disabled children, children at risk and disadvantaged families. Subsidies can be offered by the *Département* to create innovative services (i.e. for families in need). The aims are, on the one hand, to improve accessibility to all initiatives for high and low income families, and on the other, to facilitate the reconciliation of work and family life tasks. Among all the initiatives, the Network *Réseau d'Appui et d'Accompagnement des Parents* (discussed below) is a significant example. There are also community health projects and initiatives which look at child-rearing issues. The projects aim at fighting against isolation and promote child socialization.

Alongside these universal services and innovative projects are specific objectives for particular groups. These are: to prevent and detect disability; to include children with disabilities in the *Crèches* and *Ecole Maternelle*; to ensure access to the *Centre d'Action Médico – Sociale Précoce* for those families where a child has a disability; to address the needs of children who are at risk of abuse, or who have been abused, and offer them protection (*Protection de l'Enfance*); assessment of problems and reporting to the public prosecutor; and a more general objective around deprived populations and those who are vulnerable or in poverty.

Orientation B: Early childhood intervention programme

Programme B consists of group care in the form of full-day crèches, part-time *Halte-Garderie* and *Multi-Accueil* (playgroups), as well as flexible arrangement services such as *Action-Passerelle, Jardin d'éveil, Lieu d'Accueil Enfants* – parenting support carried out by educators, nurses and *Assistantes Maternelles* (childminders).

Coordinating early childhood systems

The above brief description of the universal and specialized responsibilities of the PMI, undertaken by professionals from a range of backgrounds, which sits alongside the education system, requires considerable coordination to ensure policies and practices are coherent. Since 2002, such efforts have taken place at two administrative levels: *Municipalités* (towns) and *Départements*. Many municipalities in each *Département* employ early childhood coordinators whose tasks include offering opportunities for exchange across professionals working in different ECEC services and the *Ecole Maternelle*. One of their tasks is to work with the Service de PMI, to organize collaborations between those two systems in the *Commission Départementale de l'Accueil des Jeunes Enfants*, which is a department-wide, early childhood commission. Each commission is organized in committees in order to facilitate links among the various ECEC policies and services. Specific responsibility is also carried by both systems to try to provide the most appropriate environment for children, along with appropriate parenting support.

Networking

One particular role of the Service de PMI is to develop and lead on networks that support dialogue and understanding about key social and cultural issues in order to support policy coherence. At a policy level, the Service de PMI sits at the apex of a large number of administrative organizations, including the regional government or

Département's health and social care responsibilities, the *Conseil Général* and civil society stakeholders, as well as the Ministry of Education and services for disabled people. The development of different ECEC services is based on local political priorities and resources, as well as parental choices and cultural attitudes towards ECEC. In the light of this combination of both central policy making and complex local and regional delivery of services, cohesion is needed for policies directed at young children at the local level with support and guidance from national policy makers and ministries.

It is possible to finance the running of experimental projects for pre-schools or innovative parenting support from Service de PMI funds (in collaboration with other partners). Below, I detail the operation of one network, which aimed to offer child-rearing and parenting support: *Réseau d'Ecoute, d'Appui et d'Accompagnement des Parents* (REAAP) (the Network for Parental Listening, Support and Guidance).

The network Réseau d'Ecoute, d'Appui et d'Accompagnement des Parents

The evolution of the family in French society and the changes affecting married life and parenting roles sometimes make child rearing difficult. In France and in Europe, the ability to parent consists of providing the child with cues and moral and practical guidance given with love, so that she can grow and flourish in the best way possible. The aim of the network is that professionals provide support for parents, including those who have difficulties at different stages of children's development.

The diversity of options in ECEC for children under 3 means that parents have to learn to use, on the one hand, group care such as the *Crèche* or *Crèche Parentale* as a day care system, and, on the other hand, individualized care such as *Assistantes Maternelles* (childminders). This is not easy for families who are struggling. Even if the trend is to recognize that needs and preferences for different arrangements vary according to local circumstances and the situation of each parent, choice seems to be an illusion for many. Family income, the number of children, whether a single parent or two-parent family and the mother's employment status, determine the type of arrangement and subsidy parents receive. Households with lower incomes have limited options regarding a *Crèche* or an *Assistante Maternelle* because both are expensive. This means that lower income families are more likely to take advantage of longer-term parental leave than to remain employed while their children are young. Another issue is that children from lower income families disproportionately benefit from quality childhood experiences when attending an ECEC service through increased opportunities for social and cognitive development, socialization and parent–child interaction. As explained above, a continuum between ECEC services, parents and other civil stakeholders should enhance cooperation and social intervention in the best interests of the child. In that case, both medical and psychological supervision may be needed.

The well-established network *Réseau d'Ecoute, d'Appui et d'Accompagnement des Parents* (REAPP) is an example of educationally oriented parenting support, one of many initiatives aimed at guiding parents to have appeared in recent decades.

Besides individual help for families, other forms of guidance were introduced in order to enable parents to better cope with the various difficulties they may meet in terms of child-rearing practices. These networks have developed in most countries in the European Union. They are often established in contexts of inter-institutional partnership and are inspired by innovative models such as day care centres, supporting services and parenting support programmes, family training and Folk Universities (see below). Since 2000, the French parenting support programme (REAPP) has supported the bringing together of groups of parents in France.

The starting point of the network is to offer the possibility for all parents involved in bringing up children from pre-birth to 18 years of age to receive help and advice when needed. The aim is to consolidate information and advice on parenting skills, through exchange and dialogue. For this purpose, parents are brought together with professionals such as teachers, educators and psychologists. There is no intention to directly control parents' lives and practices. Rather, the main objective is to create a group where questions can be raised – for example, discussing the place of the mother and father in relation to the child as well as their confidence in their educational role. Parental responsibility in protecting the child is underlined, such as upbringing and education without violence, family education including authority, conflict management, rules of life, sexuality and challenging teenage behaviour. Other issues, such as parental awareness of the importance of education, the use of the Internet, video games and family transculturality, are also emphasized.

The Network's main principles are to:

- avoid stigma by being open to all families
- promote parents as privileged actors of the networks
- enrol each group of parents in a partnership with other stakeholders in associations
- involve professionals in a support and/or facilitation role
- invite networks to participate in other groups formed at children's schools and at the information centre for early childhood
- participate in family policy workshops.

Parent groups

There are four types of group, as follows:

1. 'Generic groups', which correspond to those based on regular meetings of adults (men and women) performing parental roles with their children. Their goal is to establish a formalized method of communication between participants.
2. 'Informal groups' of parents meeting in places attended by their children (for example, pre-school, school, recreation centre) to discuss their responsibilities. There are multiple types of conversation such as debates and information on specific topics. They can be considered as a space for reflection on parenting. In this social and informal context, parents build a social network, thus preventing isolation and promoting the inclusion of members of the family in its environment.

3. Groups of parents with 'special profiles' are formed from associative or institutional initiatives (mostly from the network REAAP, as detailed above) around a topic. Parents gather for a specific purpose, such as to discuss child and teenager upbringing. These groups can offer a specific orientation and are organized in different ways to meet the needs or expectations of parents. The main objectives are to debate topics considered centrally by parent groups in child rearing. The parents lead the group dynamics, while at the same time they are participants and actors. Most of the groups are built from the *Université Populaire* (Popular Education) point of view (see below) and take shape in Folk University study circles (see example below).

4. Still other 'target groups' are concerned with parents eager to learn in order to prepare for or respond to a particular situation in family life (disability, adoption, illness, birth, a premature baby). They were developed in the 1980s and are aimed primarily at mothers but are now beginning to welcome fathers.

Folk University aimed at parenting: historical overview

In 1844, the first Folk High School was established by the Danish pastor and writer, Nicolai Frederik Grundtvig. He believed that University should educate young people for active participation in society and considered two types of schooling: School for Life (Folk High School) and School for Passion (Folk University). In 1868, the Swedish Worker Movement and Free Church Movement took over the Grundtvig project and built many Folk High Schools (*Folkhögskola*) and Folk Universities (*Folk Universitet*) with a social purpose to educate the working class. A popular movement was established following Popular Education principles and in opposition to the educational authority of the Swedish State. The movement to educate workers started with individual initiatives and state support was sometimes given to the groups established in study circles (Ambjörnsson, 1988).

What characterizes study circles today?

A key method of the Popular Education approach is study circles formed of 10–15 participants with a teacher or leader that meet around 10 times a year. Study circles offer a democratic means of sharing and extending knowledge held within the group participants. Regular participation makes it possible for participants' search for knowledge to progress. The learning methods offer flexibility and are connected to John Dewey's ideas of learning by doing (Dewey, 1916). One essential point is that the methods have to achieve immediate goals for the participant's actions in their everyday life. Different types of study circles include: reading circles, report circles, youth circles, parent circles, immigrant circles and university circles. An increasing number of such initiatives are now established in the Nordic countries, Germany, Italy and France (Doucet-Dahlgren et al., 2008).

Université Populaire in France: an illustration

There are many cultural themes and topics for the *Université Populaire* in France, and the ideas generated are disseminated and broadcast by the French philosopher Michel Onfray (2012). There are also specific *Groupe de Parents en Université Populaire* (parents' groups), which are a forum for groups of parents who meet monthly to discuss parenting issues. Each group is free to choose a relevant theme and is led by a host-organizer. Academic researchers regularly participate in meetings to help structure the group and support reflections on a specific theme, but do not directly supervise the group.

Outsiders, such as acting groups, give drama lessons in accordance with the principles called *Theatre of the Oppressed* (Boal, 2002), which shows how theatre can transform and liberate actors and non-actors (who are parents) to think in new ways. Parents may participate and act to enable the work of reflection and decision making concerning their child-rearing practices. Through the experience of acting together, parents gain new confidence and knowledge (Boal, 2002).

Each established group in a study circle works on an issue that has been accepted (in this case related to parenting), using specific methodologies (taking notes, reporting, recording, filming) collected by parents to account for progress and reflections on a regional or national level.[1]

Reflections from three groups of parents

The objective of Folk University parent groups is to discuss relevant issues from everyday life relating to 'what does it mean to be a parent today'? A researcher regularly attends meetings to help the group to organize and to support reflections, focusing on work in progress. Specifically, it is about establishing a dialogue and building a cooperative project between researcher and parents. The researcher is not only there to hear the group's issues but also to observe the group in a given space and time. Together with parents, the role of the researcher is to find a study theme that is of interest to the parents. From the researcher's point of view, roles are reversed. There is a shift in parents' role from the position of object, to subject, through participating in the group. Parents conduct their own literature research and inquiry, rather than receiving knowledge from specialists. The intention is to empower parents and for them to be recognized as citizens.

Between 2005 and 2009, I took part as a researcher (Doucet-Dahlgren et al., 2008) in three French study circles in Folk University aimed at parenting, with 45 participant parents. The groups were initiated by associations linked to the network *Réseau d'Ecoute, d'Appui et d'Accompagnement des Parents*. The groups took place in three towns in three *Départements*. The parents attended the Centre de PMI that disseminated information about the network organizing these circles.

All participants were parents of young children, but half were also responsible for adolescents and young adults studying or seeking employment. All the children of these families attended ECEC services. All the families took part in 'family leisure activities' organized by the REAAP network in each of the *Départements* that supported the Folk University aimed at parenting. Families came either from France or from West or North Africa. Education levels of the mothers and fathers varied; some were illiterate, most had elementary schooling (up to age 12) and, exceptionally, a few had high school or even higher education.

Group 1: Town 1 (North)

This group involved 15 parents (12 mothers and three fathers) aged 27 to 45 years from low socio-economic backgrounds (part-time working, long-term unemployment). These parents chose to focus on the issue of *intergenerational transmission* between two different worlds (disadvantaged families and ECEC services and school) with the question: 'What is it important to transmit from grandparents and parents regarding child-rearing rituals and routines?'

Group 2: Town 2 (East)

Twelve parents (10 mothers and 2 fathers) aged 30 to 45 years from working-class and minority ethnic groups or impoverished backgrounds comprised this group. Most of the parents experienced economic hardship and only part-time working or long-term unemployment. These parents chose to focus on the issue of *transmission from an intercultural perspective* (family and professionals) with the question: 'As values, rituals and practices are different in Europe from those in other continents (i.e. Africa), do the different ethnic groups find different ways to raise their children? What are the responses from the professionals?'

Group 3: Town 3 (South)

The group was made up of 18 working-class parents coping with poverty (16 mothers and 2 fathers) aged 23 to 40 years. The local association of *ATD Quart Monde* empowered the families to cope with their poverty-related problems. This group of parents chose to work on the issue of *parental responsibility* with the question: 'Do fathers and mothers share upbringing and responsibility for their children with the professionals?'

The three groups reflected on the concrete issues described above related to child rearing. Parents discussed the routines they created for their children and the reasons for these. They considered that routines and limit-setting were necessary in order to train children to become participants in civil society, but they also observed contrasts, such as different approaches to sleep routines and carrying infants, with the professional practices they saw in ECEC services, at school and on television. They faced dilemmas such as 'What is best for my child?' For example, the care of babies and toddlers may be thought about in a similar way by the parents (listening to the professionals' advice) due to the regular physical routines of eating, sleeping, nappy changing and play time, however such routines can disguise differences in parenting. It is therefore important for group facilitators to enable parents to elucidate their thinking and to articulate their goals for their children.

Discussion between parents

Relevant changes in child-rearing practices are enabled if parents and researcher are able to share reflections and translate this process into action. Argyris and Schön (1978) distinguish between 'reflection in action' and 'reflection on action'. Reflection in action is how parents act at the time (i.e. putting the child to bed and participating in bedtime routines) while 'reflection on action' is where parents reflect after the interaction (i.e. parents' feelings, ideas, sleep problems). Parents might pose questions such as 'how easy or difficult is it for young children to fall asleep in their own bed and bedroom?' Parents' questions about sleep practices may be associated with different themes such as the impact of the child's need for time on their own, or how to set limits and create rituals and routines. Parents know that creating time for the child and establishing routines are important in creating security for the child. Discussion in the circles enables parents to share what other parents do and hear what the views of the ECEC professionals might be.

In reflecting on the group experience, I found the main themes emerging from group discussions were: the importance of communication between parents and their child; and meetings between parents and professionals. Two positions became evident in group reflections:

1. Allowing parents to express themselves about their experiences, their relationship with carers and their role as parents;
2. Opportunities to participate in meetings where institutional stakeholders (such as ECEC services and the PMI centres) and parents can share mutual understanding about child upbringing.

The parents were convinced that their own involvement is necessary and in the best interests of the child, but that it is not a sufficient condition. Bringing up children today raises issues, doubts and uncertainties. The parents recognized that they do not completely control their children's socialization process, which is increasingly happening outside the family environment. All mothers and fathers in the three groups wanted to take part in the activities carried out by their children in the ECEC service and to have contact with the ECEC professionals. In other words, they concluded that they wanted to be involved in the life of their children within the ECEC service and solutions were found. Parental engagement took place for those families with experience of the Folk University groups.

Final thoughts

Starting Strong (OECD, 2012: 218–219) states:

> parental engagement refers to the formal and informal relations that parents have with ECEC services. The engagement can take a variety of forms and meanings, depending on the education stage of the child concerned (e.g. early childcare or pre-school) and the perspective taken on the issue (e.g. early years practitioner, teacher, parent, researcher).

The French investment in ECEC and family support is important. New French family policy aims at promoting equality of educational opportunity by expanding access to the Service de PMI and ECEC services for families in poverty by providing healthcare and an educational approach. The main missions of the Service de PMI are to supervise and monitor health for mothers and their children (0–6 years) and provide information about parenting support. Tensions exist between the interests of the children and those of the families (conflict, misunderstanding and neglect). The REAAPP initiative discussed in this chapter shows that the orientations of the Service de PMI and the ECEC services highlight the importance of taking into account parents' needs and children's well-being. Parental engagement is required in order to strengthen the relationships between these two aspects and the services provided (see also Chapters 6 and 7).

The experience of Folk University aimed at parenting shows that a strong community can be used as a social support network. Consequently, parental stress is reduced and positive engagements develop and empower parents in their upbringing role. At the start of the group initiatives described above, I observed that the quality of the social network was fragmented, with low involvement, poor cohesion and little community engagement. Participation in the Folk University appeared to raise the level of community engagement and lead to a higher level of social cohesion (i.e. mutual understanding and trust between participants and their neighbours and teachers). Parents moved from a position of social exclusion to acknowledged citizenship. The French initiatives described in this chapter appear to show that the Service de PMI, through the REAAP network, empowers families in need to cope with specific child-rearing issues. The model is an example of the 'centre-oriented' type of parental and community engagement described in the *Starting Strong* report (OECD, 2012), in particular the centre characteristics of providing volunteering opportunities and making facilities available to the community, and encouraging parental involvement in decision making and community collaboration to strengthen family practices and so enable children's learning and development.

☐ Summary

- This chapter reviewed the development and organization of ECEC services in France, where there is a complex and highly developed system of ECEC and family support services.

- In the chapter, I explored methods of family support and examined the use of parent networks as one form of early intervention, aimed at empowering parents living in poverty in their child rearing.
- Parent networks are based within the Folk University tradition and use study circles as one form of parenting support and education.
- The chapter reports on the process of change in parenting behaviour within these groups and identifies issues of concern to parents and their perspectives on parenting.
- Parent networks generated increased social cohesion among parents and a greater sense of active involvement in and control over parenting.
- Communication between parents and ECEC professionals was critical to the success of the groups.

Questions for discussion

1. Why do you think parental and professional engagement is important for children's well-being, learning and development?
2. What are the main factors in providing successful group support for children and families?
3. What do you consider to be the strengths and weaknesses of the notion of families 'in need' and related intervention strategies? (*Higher-level question*)

Further reading

Levels 5 and 6

Boddy, J., Statham, J., Smith, M., Ghate, D., Wigfall, V., Hauari, H. et al. (2009) *International Perspectives on Parenting Support: Non-English Language Sources*. Research Report No. DCSF-RR114. London: Institute of Education, University of London.
This report highlights different theoretical and empirical approaches to parenting support on an international level.

James, C. and Chard, G. (2010) A qualitative study of parental experiences of participation and partnership in an early intervention service. *Infants and Young Children*, 23(4): 275–285.
This article emphasizes coordinated experiences between parents and carers in early intervention services.

Levels 6 and 7

Belsky, J., Lowe Vandell, D., Burchinall, M., Clarke-Stewart, K.A., McCartney, K. and Tresch Owen, M. (2007) Are there long-term effects of early child care? *Child Development*, Mar–Apr, 78(2): 681–701.

This article outlines the effects of early childcare on children's functioning from age 4 1/2 years through to the end of 6th grade (M age = 12 years) examined in the National Institute of Child Health and Human Development Study of Early Child Care and Youth Development (n = 1364).

Organisation for Economic Co-operation and Development (OECD) (2012) *Starting Strong III: A Quality Toolbox for Early Childhood Education and Care*. Paris: OECD.
This publication is a quick guide to five policy levers based on earlier Starting Strong reports, designed to enable policy makers to improve quality in ECEC.

Sanders, M.R., Markie-Dadds, C. and Turner, K.M.T. (2003) Theoretical, Scientific and Clinical Foundations of the Triple P-Positive Parenting Programme: A Population Approach to the Promotion of Parenting Competence. Parenting Research and Practice Monograph, 1: 1–21. Parenting and Family Support Centre, University of Queensland.
This paper deals with the theoretical and empirical foundations of multi-level parenting and family support interventions in order to reduce behavioural and emotional problems. These interventions include universal population-level media information targeting all parents, with two levels of brief primary care consultations.

Note

1. The Folk University is considered an arena in which participants develop knowledge and citizenship. The methods described were first used in 1972 by the French and international non-governmental organization Aide à Toutes Détresses: ATD *Quart Monde* in several regions of France, targeting groups living in poverty.

References

Ambjörnsson, R. (1988) Den skötsamme arbetaren: Idéer och idealer i ett norrländskt sågverk 1880–1930 [The conscientious worker: ideas and ideals in a northern sawmill community 1880–1930]. Stockholm: Carlssons.

Argyris, C. and Schön, D.A. (1978) *Theory in Practice: Increasing Professional Effectiveness*. San Francisco, CA: Jossey-Bass.

Boal, A. (2002) *Games for Actors and Non-actors*, 2nd edition. London: Routledge.

Centre d'analyse stratégique (2012) *Aider les parents à être parents*. Rapports et Documents 2012 – N°50. Paris: La Documentation Française.

Council of Europe (2006) Committee of Ministers: Policy to Support Positive Parenting. Available at: https://wcd.coe.int/ViewDoc.jsp?id=1073507 (accessed 13 March 2013).

Dewey, J. (1916) *Democracy and Education: An Introduction to the Philosophy of Education*. London: Macmillan.

Doucet-Dahlgren, A.M., Francis, V., Sita, C. and Cadei, L. (2008) A way of conducting groups of parents: which work? An overview of practices in France and Italy. In: C. Canali, T. Vecchiato and J.K. Whittaker (eds) *Assessing the 'Evidence-base' of Intervention for Vulnerable Children and their Families*. Padua: Fondazione Emanuela Zancan Onlus, pp. 325–327.

Onfray, M. (2012) Université Populaire de Caen (France). Available at: http://upc.michelonfray.fr

Organisation for Economic Co-operation and Development (OECD) (2012) *Starting Strong III: A Quality Toolbox for Early Childhood Education and Care*. Paris: OECD.

CHAPTER 6

THE ROMA EARLY CHILDHOOD INCLUSION (RECI) RESEARCH PROJECT

John Bennett

Overview

This chapter describes an initiative to gather data and information in four Central and South-Eastern European (CSEE) countries – the Czech Republic, Macedonia, Romania and Serbia – on the inclusion of young Roma children and their access to public services. An introduction is followed by a description of the research methodology and a discussion of its strengths and weaknesses. The chapter then gives a description of the Roma people with some surprising information about the size of the Roma population and the persecution they have had to suffer over the centuries. The fourth section outlines the main findings, drawn from the national reports of the selected countries. In summary, the national reports found that:

- there is a large gap between EU and country aspirations for the Roma and the actual implementation of policy
- extreme poverty undermines the health and development of Roma children
- majority prejudice against the Roma is a major challenge in all countries

(Continued)

(Continued)

- early development from pre-natal to 3 years is not given sufficient attention
- kindergarten and primary education systems are failing Roma children
- countries are not collecting sufficient data on Roma children, not least about their access to early childhood services. This is a remarkable ostrich-like situation: no data, no problem, no progress.

The final section charts some tentative conclusions arising from the research.

Introduction

The Roma Early Childhood Inclusion (RECI) Project is sponsored by three leading European organizations – the Open Society Foundation, the Roma Education Fund and UNICEF. Its purpose is to gather data and information about the inclusion of young Roma children in the early childhood services of four Central and Eastern European (CEE) countries: the Czech Republic, the former Yugoslav Republic of Macedonia (hereafter 'Macedonia'), Romania and Serbia. For each country, national researchers and specialists have researched and written a RECI national report, based on a common format. The *RECI Overview Report* (OSF-UNICEF-Roma Education Fund, 2012), on which this chapter is based, summarizes the main findings of these national reports.

Research focus, methodology and issues

A major focus of the RECI Project was to gather reliable data and information on the inclusion/exclusion of young Roma children in the early childhood services of the selected countries. Not only do many Roma individuals not declare themselves as Roma, but governments also fail to collect reliable data on the ethnic background of impoverished populations and service users. Even for as simple an indicator as population size, census data significantly undercount Roma because of the common practice of relying on self-identification (Table 6.1).

The focus of the research was therefore to gather accurate data and information about the inclusion of young Roma children in the early childhood services of four Central and Eastern European (CEE) countries. To achieve this purpose, a national team of researchers was established in each country, supported by the national office of one of the sponsoring organizations. Each team was composed of two or three researchers, one of whom was an expert of Roma origin. The exercise was a first attempt in the Central and Eastern European region to capture and present systematically the situation of young Roma children. Four national RECI (Roma early childhood inclusion) reports were prepared, one each for the Czech

Table 6.1   Size of the Roma population in selected countries: official figures (in thousands) and alternative estimates

Countries	Official Roma population in 000s	Official Roma as percentage of national population	Official Roma under 18 years in 000s	Alternative Roma population in 000s	Alternative percentage of national population	Alternative Roma children at 18 years of age in 000s
Bulgaria	371	4.8	152.8	700–800	9.7	309
Czech Republic	11.7	0.1	5.6	160–300	2.3	110
Hungary	190	1.9	81.1	550–600	5.7	246
Macedonia	53.9	2.7	22.4	80–130	5.2	44
Romania	535.1	2.5	230.9	1,800–2,500	9.9	926
Serbia	108.2	1.4	44.4	350	4.7	144
Slovakia	89.9	1.7	39.1	350–370	6.7	157

Source: McDonald and Negrin (2010)

Republic, Macedonia, Serbia and Romania. The purpose of the reports was to provide a detailed picture of early childhood policy and provision frameworks in these countries, highlighting the barriers and opportunities for improving the access of Roma children to appropriate, high-quality early childhood services. Once reliable data was collected, a national meeting of key policy makers (including governments) and stakeholders was convened to verify the findings and to establish priorities for action, which were then included in the final version of the national RECI reports.

Research methodology

For each country, data collection was carried out over a six-month period by the national research team. Available data from European sources, international organizations, national statistics and research, and the leading Roma organizations were sifted in an attempt to provide accurate figures of the numbers of Roma children and to identify the priority early childhood issues and concerns of Roma populations. The views of Roma communities, families and parents were gathered through focus group discussions and interviews. Technical experts, representatives of ministries of health, education and social welfare, academics, as well as members of civil society organizations, were invited to read the draft versions of the national reports. More than a hundred contributions were received concerning the articulation of policy reforms and the practical steps required to improve the situation of disadvantaged Roma children.

A final step was to synthesize the findings from the research in the four countries. The *RECI Overview Report* was published in February 2012 (OSF-UNICEF-Roma Education Fund, 2012; see http://www.unicef.org/ceecis) based on the country reports. It presents the findings of the national reports, compares and contrasts the different policy contexts and proposes a series of recommendations for the expansion of early childhood development provision for Roma children. It also includes a brief summary of each of the national reports, allowing researchers to have a rapid overview of the state of Roma children in each country. Its findings and recommendations are particularly relevant at this time when the European Commission requires member states and countries seeking accession to the European Union to develop reporting processes and national strategies for Roma inclusion.

Research issues

A number of research issues arise in regard to the various reports. For example, although the reports provide valuable new information and insights into the condition of Roma children, the national authors in each country faced a serious difficulty. Data on young Roma children are often scant and unreliable as many governments fail to collect disaggregated data on young children and their participation in services. In sum, Roma communities and their children have been ignored or neglected for decades. Research teams, no matter how talented, cannot invent complex social data if such does not exist. In addition, many Roma families in all countries do not identify themselves as such, fearing in many cases that a Roma ascription will bring them unwelcome attention.

The methodology used by the researchers to collect information was primarily qualitative. Data on the situation of the Roma in each country was collected through literature reviews and semi-structured interviews with key informants, such as central and local government policy makers and officials, Roma experts and NGOs, early childhood centres and educators, and various focus groups. While the authors were unable to use a strictly representative sampling approach in the organization of focus groups and interviews, a broad range of actors was consulted and a wide variety of perspectives obtained. While the reports often offer insights rather than a rigorous analysis of interviews, it is reassuring from a methodological perspective to know that a strong concordance of views emerges across the different countries concerning the general situation of Roma populations.

The Roma people

Origin and languages

According to the European Union website, the term 'Roma' refers to a variety of groups of people who describe themselves as Roma, Gypsies, Travellers, Manouches, Ashkali, Sinti, as well as other self-ascriptions. Strong linguistic and genetic evidence exists to suggest that ancestors of the original group or groups emigrated from the north-western Indian lands (possibly from Rajasthan and what is now modern-day Pakistan), in the late 10th and early 11th centuries, via Persia, Anatolia and the

Balkans to Central and Eastern Europe by the 14th century, and on into western and northern Europe by the early 15th and 16th centuries. They speak a number of related dialects of the Romani language, which are Indic in origin and contain admixtures of Persian, Greek and the Balkan languages, frequently mixed with words from the majority national language of the country in which modern Roma populations live. In some cases, these dialects are heavily influenced by the dominant language to form contact languages such as Anglo-Romani or Scandinavian Romani. Some groups have maintained their language competence while others have lost theirs, due to assimilative processes or attempts at forced eradication of Romani language and culture, in a national context.

Today, with an estimated population of around 12 million people, they constitute the largest ethnic minority in Europe, present in all 27 EU member states. Because of their heterogeneous background and the range of countries and environments in which they live, there cannot be a single strategy suitable for all Roma groups. A Hungarian survey has shown, for example, that the share of Roma with less than basic education was 23% for the Romungro Roma (whose native language is Hungarian), 42% for the Bayash (native Romanian speakers) and 48% for the Wallach or Vlach Roma (whose mother tongue is Vlach Romani). There is a need, therefore, for differentiated approaches that take account of the diverse backgrounds of Roma groups and individuals and of the different geographical, economic, social, cultural and legal contexts of the countries in which they live. However, a unifying feature of the situation of Roma across Europe is the widespread rejection and social exclusion practised toward them by majority populations. As a result, too many Roma children live in dire poverty and are denied the educational opportunities that could break the inter-generational transmission of deprivation and exclusion.

Discrimination

Historically, Roma populations have been a target for discrimination and xenophobia. During the Second World War and the Nazi occupation of central Europe, between 200,000 and 800,000 Roma people lost their lives because of their ethnicity. Under communist regimes, Roma communities, though restricted in the expression of their cultural traditions and language, fared better; children were integrated into education systems and many Roma adults were employed in state-controlled economies. However, the period of transition from 1989 led to a heavy loss of employment among Roma, forcing many families into long-term unemployment and the need to seek social assistance.

In sum, although they have been an integral part of European society for about 700 years, Romani cultures are rarely spoken about or included in school programmes, beyond stereotyped references. In their daily lives, Romani people face discrimination and social exclusion, based on racial prejudice and stereotyping, and, as a consequence, are confronted by profoundly negative attitudes, frequently articulated by populist politicians, ultra-nationalist political parties and the mass media.

Demographic patterns

Roma populations have been traditionally concentrated in south-eastern, Central and Eastern European (CEE) countries, with the largest populations in Turkey and the Balkans, although, today, they are migrating northwards and westwards throughout Europe in search of work. Reliable data are hard to come by, but they form a significant (estimated) proportion of the population in Bulgaria (around 10%), Slovakia (9%), Romania (8%), and Hungary (7%). They are also present in the western Balkans, including Serbia and the former Yugoslav Republic of Macedonia. Many Roma do not possess identity documents, or are included in the general category of minority groups, or, for a variety of reasons, prefer not to identify as Roma.

Today, Roma groups have significantly higher fertility (and mortality) rates than mainstream populations in the CEE countries. According to the *EU Framework for National Roma Integration Strategies up to 2020* (European Commission, 2011):

> The Roma population is young: 35.7 per cent are under 15 compared to 15.7 per cent of the EU population overall. The average age is 25 among Roma, compared with 40 across the EU. The vast majority of working-age Roma lack the education needed to find good jobs. It is therefore of crucial importance to invest in the education of Roma children to allow them later on to successfully enter the labour market. In Member States with significant Roma populations, this already has an economic impact. According to estimates, in Bulgaria, about 23 per cent of new labour entrants are Roma, in Romania, about 21 per cent. (*Source*: http://ec.europa.eu/justice/policies/ discrimination/docs/com_2011_173_en.pdf)

The *RECI Overview Report* draws a more child-centred conclusion. If given the opportunity, Roma children – through education – can have a better life and contribute to their own culture and to the economies and societies of their respective countries. Countries with a sizeable Roma minority must address issues of social justice and education concerning these children (see also Chapter 7).

Main findings of the *RECI Overview Report*

The following are some of the key issues identified in the national reports:

1. A large gap between aspirations and implementation. Progress is being made but a large gap exists between aspirations for Roma populations at EU level and actual implementation of policies at national level. This can be seen in Table 6.2 comparing the situation of Roma populations with that of the majority population in Serbia.

    Among the reasons advanced for the slow progress are the following:

    - Though national legislation in each of the four countries has developed remarkably, under the influence of membership of or preparation for accession to the

Table 6.2   Size of the Roma population in selected countries: official figures (in thousands) and alternative estimates

Serbia	Majority	Roma
Functionally illiterate (15+)	Less than 4%	c. 80%
Not in formal employment	19%	70–80%
Households in severe poverty – less than 100 Euros per month	6.1%	55.5% (WB 60.1%)
Children in extreme poverty	5.6%	57.8%
Infant mortality rate	7 infants per 1,000	14 infants per 1,000
Life expectancy	74 years	c. 45 years (women 48 yrs)
Education enrolments Nursery (0–3 years) Kindergarten (36–59 months) PPP year Special school or class	c. 15% 44% 88% (OSI) c. 60%	m* 8% 45% (OSI) 31% of all pupils (2008/9)

Source: UNICEF (2012)

Note: m* = missing data

European Union, it rarely requires public authorities to take specific actions or to achieve measurable results.

- In the Roma policy field, a lack of indicators, institutional audits and evaluations severely hamper knowledge of which policies work.

2. Extreme poverty undermines the health and development of Roma children. Extreme poverty, intolerable living conditions, low educational levels and lack of employment undermine Roma family life and the health of infants and young children. The great majority of Roma families suffer from severe poverty, which the Marmot Review (2010) identified as one of the greatest barriers to the holistic development of young children. The impact of poverty is reinforced by family stress (due to lack of employment and income), malnutrition (sometimes severe) and intolerable living conditions, such as severe overcrowding and lack of running water and other basic community infrastructure.
3. Majority prejudice is a major challenge. The social exclusion of the Roma is greatly reinforced by the discrimination and prejudice of the majority population. The national reports and various European surveys (notably the Gallup Poll organized by the EU Fundamental Rights Agency in 2009 and the EU Minorities and Discrimination Survey [EU-MIDIS, 2009]) testify to the widespread prejudice against Roma groups in the four countries. Prejudice ranges from negative stereotyping to political extremism, with threatening marches on neighbourhoods, used to injure, intimidate or evict Roma residents.

The EU Minorities and Discrimination Survey (EU-MIDIS) 2009

EU-MIDIS asked a sample of Roma respondents about discrimination they had experienced, in the past 12 months or in the past 5 years, in nine areas: 1) When looking for work; 2) At work; 3) When looking for a house or an apartment to rent or buy; 4) By healthcare personnel; 5) By social service personnel; 6) By school personnel; 7) At a café, restaurant or bar; 8) When entering or in a shop; 9) When trying to open a bank account or get a loan.

47 per cent of all respondents indicated they were victims of discrimination based on their ethnicity, in one or more of these areas, during the previous 12 months. In the Czech Republic, Roma respondents reported the highest levels of overall discrimination (64 per cent), closely followed by Hungary (62 per cent). In the context of being victims of crime, and racially motivated crime, the EU-MIDIS survey was even more explicit:

On average – 1 in 4 Roma respondents were victims of personal crime – including assaults, threats and serious harassment – at least once in the previous 12 months.

On average – 1 in 5 Roma respondents were victims of racially motivated personal crime – including assaults, threats and serious harassment – at least once in the previous 12 months. Roma who were victims of assault, threat or serious harassment experienced on average 4 incidents over a 12 month period.

81 per cent of Roma who indicated they were victims of assault, threat or serious harassment in the previous 12 months considered that their victimisation was racially motivated.

(*Source*: http://fra.europa.eu/fraWebsite/eu-midis/index_en.htm)

4. Early development from pre-natal to 3 years is not given sufficient attention. The early development of Roma children, during infancy and the pre-kindergarten period, is often neglected at governance level for two reasons: first, because of a general under-estimation of the importance of the period 0–3 years, with CSEE governments spending little on specific developmental programmes for children in the age group. Second, national spending on the public services that critically affect young children – that is, public health, social protection and family policies – is, in most instances, well below the EU average.

5. Kindergarten and primary education systems are failing Roma children. The basic findings of the national reports can be summarized as follows:

- A high percentage of Roma children never enrol in the education system.
- The participation rate of Roma children in pre-school education is extremely low.
- The drop-out rates of Roma children, especially in lower secondary education, are extremely high. Drop-out rates are even higher in segregated educational settings.
- Roma adolescents, in particular girls, have a very low transition rate into upper secondary education.
- The total number of years spent by Roma children in the education system is, in general, about half the national average.
- Thousands of Roma children are tested each year for entry into primary school and a significant proportion are then channelled into special classes or schools.

The segregation of Roma children in school education

Although a promising start has been made in Serbia to end the practice, the segregation of Roma children within education systems remains a significant challenge. To justify the practice of segregation, children are tested at the age of 5, 6 or 7 for entry into primary school. True to the defectology tradition still influential in the former Soviet bloc countries, these tests look for weaknesses and not strengths. In addition, they are generally culturally biased in the sense that they are designed with the majority child in mind and are administered through the majority language (few psychologists speak Romani languages). According to the national reports, the time spent with each child may be as short as 15 minutes. Not only is the methodology suspect but the fact that disability and cognitive delays in Roma children are routinely attributed to cultural and racial factors, rather than to the serious malnutrition of expectant and nursing mothers, is a matter of real concern. As a result of these tests, a disproportionate number of Roma children are allocated to special classes or placed in special schools where simplified curricula are used. 'Graduation' from these schools has little value in the eyes of potential employers or of society at large. Table 6.3 provides a brief summary of the information on segregated education found in the national reports:

Table 6.3   Percentage of total children in special classrooms, centres or segregated schools who are Roma

Percentage	Czech Republic	Macedonia	Romania	Serbia
Percentage of Roma children in special schools, classes or segregated schools	26.7% is the MoE figure[1] but according to research by Romani NGOs, around 70% of children placed in special schools and classes are Roma	Roma children make up around 36% of children of primary school age who are placed in special schools and classes	c. 60% of children of primary school age, who are placed in special schools and classes, are Roma[2]	32% of children in special schools and 38% of children in special classes are Roma[3]

Source: RECI National Reports, 2011

Notes:

[1]Romani organizations in the Czech Republic place the figure at around 70% (see text below). *Source*: ERRC (2009).

[2]The Romania National Report provides a figure of 70%, based on research from 2001 (ERRC, 2001). Research conducted in 2008 for the Romani CRISS Organization found that of the 90 schools studied, 67% had some segregation of Roma pupils (Surdu, 2008).

[3]*Source*: OSI (2010) – 30% in special schools (almost wholly for intellectual difficulties) and 38% in special classes.

As can be seen, large numbers of Roma children also escape being placed in segregated classrooms or schools. Their inclusion in mainstream classrooms can be due to a number of factors:

- The children may have passed the school entry test without difficulty.
- They may have attended a kindergarten for a number of years and have a good knowledge of both school routines and the national language.

- Their parents may not declare themselves Roma.
- They may live in a district and/or apply for a school where discrimination against them is low or does not exist.
- They may live in a country where testing for placement in special schools is now forbidden, e.g. Serbia.

The reasons are multiple but one thing is certain: in most countries with large Roma populations, Roma children find themselves being disproportionately segregated and placed in special schools and classes. And even when they are included in mainstream classrooms, their progress is not ensured. National school and kindergarten systems tend to be highly mono-cultural. Few Roma staff are employed, and, frequently, according to the focus groups that were organized by the authors of the national reports, open prejudice is shown toward Roma children by teachers, majority parents and children:

> I never saw the teacher showing him something in the books, not a letter in his books by his teacher, not in notebooks, nor did he help him in anything. (Focus group mother, Barajevo, Serbia)

> If she had good grades, the teacher used to say: 'You see, she gets good grades even if she is a gypsy'. (Focus group parent, Craiova, Romania)

> We love them (the Roma children), we help them but at school their colour starts to matter; the children start to separate, to marginalize Roma, to be unwilling to sit on the same bench with them. (Focus group, teacher, Bucharest, Romania)

> Children start going to (regular) school, attend it for a while, then become less and less successful and they start to feel neglected, unwanted. They don't have trainers, or the things that other kids have. Everyone avoids them. So the child doesn't want to go anymore, simply refuses to go, so his parents transfer him to a special school, where they also get benefits. (Health mediator, Novi Sad, Serbia)

By contrast, a recent study by Fremlova and Ureche (2011) followed the educational progress of Roma children whose families had emigrated to England from the Czech Republic and Slovakia. In their former countries, many of these children had been assigned to special classes and schools for children with disabilities, whereas in England they were fully integrated with mainstream British children. The research shows that after a few years in English schools, the average attainment of Roma pupils (aged 9–15 years) in literacy, numeracy and science was just below the national average. In terms of the children's spoken English, 89% spoke fluent or almost fluent English. The younger the respondents were when they first came to the UK, the more quickly they were able to speak English fluently. According to one of their educators: 'I do not see any difference between the Roma pupils and the non-Roma ones in terms of their ability or their potential, it is just a question of catching up. After a year or so they are at the same level as their peer group' (2011: 48).

When the Roma parents were interviewed, they agreed that they:

> valued the overall atmosphere at school, their children's feeling of being welcome there and their experience of equal treatment, equal opportunities, and the absence

of anti-Roma sentiments and racism expressed by their children's non-Roma peers and educators, which they all said their children had experienced in various forms in the Czech Republic and Slovakia. They all said the prospect of their children's education and employment was one of the most powerful driving forces behind their decision to move to the UK. (2011: 41)

6. No data, no problem, no progress. The lack of disaggregated data on Roma children and their progress in education prevents evidence-based planning, monitoring and evaluation. Ministries and organizations working for social inclusion do not know the exact number of Roma children, what measures are successful or whether they were implemented effectively. Without data and research, policy units remain in the realm of opinion: *no data, no problem, no progress.*

Conclusions

From the data and qualitative information gathered, not least from Roma people themselves, the *RECI Overview Report* formulated the following recommendations:

1. Roma children are valuable: Europe and its member states cannot afford to neglect their future

Because of the demographic profile of the Roma population and given the ageing of Europe and its chronic lack of labour, Roma children are an extremely valuable asset, if they can be educated and brought into the skilled workforce. Action needs to be taken urgently: to invest more in the developmental readiness of Roma children for both kindergarten and school and to eliminate the many barriers experienced by Roma families in accessing public services.

The costs of not taking action are clearly indicated by the European Parliament in its *Explanatory Note on the EU Strategy on Roma Inclusion* (2010/2276/INI). By not prioritizing Roma inclusion, member states incur significant losses that include:

- the indirect cost of lost GDP: as a result of social exclusion, unemployed Roma fail to produce domestic product
- social assistance and welfare costs which will continue to grow; in addition, the administrative costs of supervising the flow of welfare expenditure will increase
- higher health costs incurred due to substandard living conditions
- wasted education expenditure: the funds put into segregated and/or low-standard schools that fail to provide quality education is wasted money
- extra safety costs, due to higher crime rates caused by socio-economic deprivation.

2. In addition to legislation, governments need to invest in communication and education to renew majority notions of citizenship and democracy

Discrimination against young Roma children takes the form of: the non-provision of services; enrolment procedures that favour dual-income parents; a hostile or neglectful kindergarten climate; lack of outreach to parents; the practice of streaming or 'ability-grouping'; and even the segregation of Roma children into 'special' schools and classes.

An urgent task is to change negative majority attitudes toward the Roma and particularly – within early childhood services – negative attitudes toward Roma children among majority children and their parents. Already, much is being done at EU levels, for example through the PROGRESS programme, including the *For Diversity: Against Discrimination* information campaign (European Commission, 2008b). These activities need to be supported at national level by similar information programmes. Given the long history of prejudice and discrimination against Roma in Europe, it will also be necessary to establish anti-discrimination bodies and procedures that can be invoked whenever rights and obligations are disregarded.

3. The major responsibility for early childhood policies remains with national government. Their efforts will be more effective if linked closely with EU Roma initiatives

Member states are primarily responsible for Roma integration, including access to the key areas of employment, healthcare, housing and education which hold back Roma inclusion the most. The inclusion of Roma children will not happen unless countries take on their responsibilities, begin to set measurable goals and priorities and coordinate the policies and activities of different ministries.

Moreover, Roma early childhood programming should be part of national social inclusion and education policies. The mainstreaming of Roma inclusion issues into national policy areas – rather than treating them as a separate issue (which may isolate Roma children even more) – is in line with Principles No. 2 and No. 4 of the *Common Basic Principles on Roma Inclusion* (Council of Europe, 2011). These principles promote 'explicit but not exclusive targeting', as well as 'aiming for the mainstream'.

In certain circumstances, for example in the case of very young children, services need to be brought to where people are, with the support of the local community. In a situation characterized by lack of services, community-based programming for very young children becomes necessary. In addition, community programming supports the role of the family in the upbringing of children and assists minority groups to preserve their language and culture.

The EU framework offers member states and pre-accession countries powerful policy and financial tools to develop and implement Roma inclusion policies effectively. Among the key initiatives in which the EU is actively involved is the 2005–2015 *Decade of Roma Inclusion* and the *Integrated Platform for Roma Inclusion* (European Commission, 2008a). In addition, through its *Social Protection and Social Inclusion Process*, the EU coordinates and supports member states' actions to combat poverty and social exclusion.

4. In contexts of extreme poverty and exclusion, developmental readiness for school requires a multi-dimensional concept of early childhood programming that places a strong emphasis on early intervention and women's education

In contexts of extreme poverty and exclusion, a multi-dimensional concept of early childhood services is needed. Before getting Roma children into centre-based kindergartens and school, community intervention programmes are urgently needed to ensure the developmental readiness of young Roma children within the family and community. These interventions should include pre- and postnatal health, parenting and adult education, and play and stimulation programmes for toddlers, conducted in the relevant Romani dialect. Such interventions can be implemented in an economical and sensitive way by the local health and paediatric services, in consultation with Roma communities and NGOs, and with the help of Roma health and education assistants. Only Roma participation can ensure the legitimacy, accountability and success of such services.

Interventions will also pay special attention to the education of girls. In all countries, the educational level of mothers is a significant indicator of a child's success (or lack of it) in school. The improved education of Roma girls will make possible the early stimulation, language inputs and educational support that future Roma children will receive.

5. For successful policy implementation, effective governance of the sector is critical

All the RECI national reports refer to weaknesses in the current governance of early childhood programming for national and Roma children. A common critique is the failure to develop and coordinate national policy. Ministries continue to pursue their traditional aims without reference to each other or to Romani (and other) NGOs working in the field.

The *RECI Overview Report* recommends for consideration the establishment of an Early Childhood Council in every local government to coordinate policy, with responsibility for social inclusion, child health and education, from infancy to school age. This Council could involve a wide range of stakeholders, including Roma representation in those municipalities where Roma communities exist.

6. Effective kindergartens and schools for excluded children need clear goals, high quality, expanded services, outreach to parents and appropriate pedagogies. A free place in kindergarten should be provided for at least two years to every child coming from an 'absolute poverty' background

In summary form, government policy makers might wish to consider the following goals for young Roma children at different ages:

Table 6.4   An early childhood development agenda for Roma children

Developmental stage	Issues to address
A. Pre-natal to birth	Ensuring quality pre- and post-natal healthcare for mothers and infants within communities, through visiting health services and the use of Romani bridging personnel; reasonable family living standards; parent education; counselling for self-care; preparing for delivery, parenting and family planning.
B. Birth to age 3	Birth registration; communication and counselling for healthcare, nutrition and feeding, with an emphasis on infant–caregiver interaction; attention to the play, social development and language development of toddlers through providing a responsive, rich and stimulating learning environment.
C. 3–6 years	Access to quality early learning opportunities in public kindergartens: a safe, hygienic and stimulating environment; qualified providers; a quality curriculum; developmentally appropriate and interactive; culturally and linguistically sensitive; gender sensitive; active parental participation; continuous assessment of programme quality and child development outcomes.
D. 6–8 years	Focus on developmental school readiness; getting schools ready for children, eliminating all forms of segregation, special schools and classrooms, etc.; getting families ready for children's schooling.

Source: UNICEF (2008)

Research suggests that steps 1 and 2 above are critical, that is, to secure reasonable living standards for Roma families from which to ensure health, social care and stimulation for young children in the first three years. The need for special schools and classrooms would quickly disappear if Roma families had better living conditions in which to rear their children and if the early services and kindergartens were empowered to do comprehensive work.

In all countries, every disadvantaged child (including Roma children) should be given an entitlement to a free place in kindergarten for at least two years before compulsory schooling, and disadvantaged Roma parents provided with the necessary support to enable their children to take up such an entitlement. Recent analyses of the funding of pre-school provision suggest that the CSEE countries could achieve such an aim within their present budgets, if afternoon kindergarten services (which cater for dual-working parents) were financed more equitably by users and abolished where they are not needed. In communities where, at present, no kindergartens exist, community services for families and young children under 3 years of age should be extended upwards to include children of kindergarten age and should employ trained Roma teachers and assistants to initiate and supervise these services.

7. Evidence-based policy in favour of Roma children will not be achieved without research, consultation and data collection

The Open Society Institute has contributed to the debate on the lack of data on Roma children through its publication: *No Data, No Progress* (McDonald and Negrin, 2010), which makes a case for the collection of disaggregated data, noting that the lack of reliable data about Roma communities remains a major obstacle to reducing inequality and eliminating discrimination. However, reasons for greater optimism about data collection now exist: there is new focus at European level on the need for rigorous data collection, benchmarking, monitoring and evaluation (see the *EU Framework for National Roma Integration Strategies up to 2020* [European Commission, 2011] – which gives attention to the need for better data in individual national plans for Roma inclusion).

Final thoughts

Young Roma children share many of the disadvantages that all children in poverty confront, but they experience either more intense or additional challenges to holistic development than even the poorest of majority children. For example:

- *The level of material poverty and deprivation experienced by Roma children is generally far greater than that experienced by children from unemployed families.* A saving grace may be that, despite their enormous difficulties, Roma families are often very united around children. This is a strength that policy makers can build on.
- *Many Roma children have additional language and developmental needs.* According to the RECI national reports, there was often little understanding in the countries reviewed of the importance of prenatal to 3 years for the development of language (concepts, cognitive development) or of the need to support the home learning environment and mother tongue acquisition.
- *Roma children have supplementary access difficulties because of prejudice, local neglect of their enrolment or flagrant lack of provision.* As researched by Havas and Liskó (2004), 29% of municipalities in Hungary are without a kindergarten, about half being Roma settlements. Because of centuries of oppression, many Roma communities are settled in isolated rural areas, far from the services provided in larger municipalities.
- *Many Roma families are reluctant – sometimes with good reason – to entrust their children to national early childhood services.* Their reluctance means, however, that children are not enrolled early enough in kindergarten services or, if enrolled,

do not participate sufficiently due to chronic absenteeism, segregation into special classes and teacher neglect.

- *When Roma children do access services, teachers (many of whom teach in appalling conditions) entertain very low expectations in their regard.* These teachers often lack appropriate anti-bias training and/or training to support diverse families and children who speak a different home language.
- *Within kindergartens and school, it is often recorded that Roma children are excluded or even bullied by majority children.* In addition, when Roma children become a significant minority or majority within a school, 'white flight' can take place, with majority parents withdrawing their children and sending them to majority-only schools.

 **Summary**

- Roma children are valuable: Europe and its member states cannot afford to neglect their present and future.
- Governments need to invest in legislation, communication and education to renew majority notions of citizenship and democracy.
- The major responsibility for early childhood policies remains with national governments. Their efforts will be more effective if linked closely with EU Roma initiatives.
- For successful policy implementation, effective governance of the sector is critical.
- In contexts of extreme poverty and exclusion, developmental readiness for school requires a multi-dimensional concept of early childhood programming that places a strong emphasis on early intervention, family support and women's education.
- Effective kindergartens and schools for excluded children need clear goals, high quality, expanded services, outreach to parents and appropriate pedagogies.
- A free place in kindergarten, with attendance support, should be provided for at least two years to every child coming from an 'absolute poverty' background.
- Evidence-based policy in favour of Roma children will not be achieved without research, consultation and data collection.

 Questions for discussion

1. 'Developmental readiness for school' includes not only verbal and intellectual skills and knowledge, but also social abilities, health and nutritional status that predict preparedness for life and not just for school (Bowman et al.,

2001). Do you agree? How important for young children is knowledge of group routines or 3R skills, before they enter school?

2. 'The improved education of Roma girls will make possible the early stimulation, language inputs and educational support that future Roma children will receive.' Why does the author of the chapter believe that the education of Roma girls is particularly important? Can formal education compensate for the practical experience young Roma girls now have in looking after younger siblings, one of the main reasons why they are withdrawn early from school?

3. The author of the study points to governance failures to explain the lack of attendance by Roma children at kindergarten and primary school. Do you agree? Could their poor attendance record be attributed to family negligence? To the low educational levels of Roma mothers? To too many children to look after? To the alleged lack of interest of Roma families in education? (*Higher-level question*)

Further reading

Levels 5 and 6

Common Basic Principles on Roma Inclusion – these 10 principles are a framework for the successful design and implementation of actions to support Roma inclusion. They can be accessed from the Council of Europe website: http://www.coe.int/t/dg4/youth/Source/Resources/Documents/2011_10_Common_Basic_Principles_Roma_Inclusion.pdf
The site provides a comment on each principle. The 10th principle (Active participation of the Roma in all polices and activities directly concerning them) is often expressed by the phrase: Nothing about us without us!

Levels 6 and 7

Foster, B. and Norton, P. (2012) Educational equality for Gypsy, Roma and Traveller children and young people in the UK. *Equal Rights Review*, 8. Available at: http://www.equalrightstrust.org/ertdocumentbank/ERR8_Brian_Foster_and_Peter_Norton.pdf
This study provides a critical account of policy and attitudes toward Roma children in the UK.

OSF-UNICEF-Roma Education Fund (2012) *The Roma Early Childhood Inclusion (RECI) Overview Report*. Available at: http://www.romachildren.com/?page_id=504
The RECI Project is sponsored by three leading European organizations – the Open Society Foundation, the Roma Education Fund and UNICEF. Its purpose is to gather data and information about the inclusion of young Roma children in the early childhood services of countries where there are significant Roma minorities. The first overview report, referenced above, provides data and information about Roma in four Central and Eastern European (CEE) countries: the Czech Republic, Macedonia, Romania and Serbia.

Websites

http://ec.europa.eu/justice/ – European Commission
http://www.romadecade.org – Decade of Roma Inclusion, 2005–2015
http://www.unicef.org/romania/children_1599.html – this site offers concise information about the situation of young children in Romania, including their education, health, care and protection.

References

Bowman, B., Donovan, S. and Burns, S. (eds) (2001) *Educating Our Preschoolers*. Washington, DC: National Academy Press.

Council of Europe (2011) *Common Basic Principles on Roma Inclusion*. Available at: http://www.coe.int/t/dg4/youth/Source/Resources/Documents/2011_10_Common_Basic_Principles_Roma_Inclusion.pdf

European Commission (2008a) *Integrated Platform for Roma Inclusion*. Available at: http://ec.europa.eu/justice/discrimination/roma/roma-platform/index_en.htm

European Commission (2008b) *For Diversity: Against Discrimination*. Available at: http://ec.europa.eu/justice/fdad/cms/stopdiscrimination/

European Commission (2011) *EU Framework for National Roma Integration Strategies up to 2020*. Communication from the Commission to the European Parliament, the Council, the European Economic and Social Committee and the Committee of the Regions, Brussels, 5.4.2011, COM(2011) 173 final.

European Roma Rights Centre (ERRC) (2001) *State of Impunity: Human Rights Abuse of Roma in Romania*. Budapest: ERRC.

European Roma Rights Centre (ERRC) (2009) *Persistent Segregation of Roma in the Czech Education System*. Budapest: ERRC.

EU-MIDIS (2009) *EU Minorities and Discrimination Survey*. Available at: http://fra.europa.eu/fraWebsite/eu-midis/index_en.htm

Fremlova, L. and Ureche, H. (2011) From Segregation to Inclusion: Roma Pupils in the United Kingdom – A Pilot Research Project. Budapest: Roma Education Fund. Available at: http://equality.uk.com/Education_files/From%20segregation%20to%20integration_1.pdf

Foster, B. and Norton, P. (2012) Educational equality for Gypsy, Roma and Traveller children and young people in the UK. *Equal Rights Review*, 8. Available at: http://www.equalrightstrust.org/ertdocumentbank/ERR8_Brian_Foster_and_Peter_Norton.pdf

Havas, G. and Liskó, I. (2004) *Szegregáció a roma tanulók általános iskolai oktatásában* [Segregation of Roma in primary education]. Kutatási zárótanulmány, Felsőoktatási Kutatóintézet, Kézirat.

Marmot Review (2010) *Fair Society, Healthy Lives*. London: Department of Health.

McDonald, C. and Negrin, K. (2010) *No Data, No Progress*. Budapest: Open Society Foundation.

Open Society Institute (OSI) (2010) *Roma Children in Special Education in Serbia: Overrepresentation, Underachievement, and Impact on Life*. Budapest: OSI.

OSF-UNICEF-Roma Education Fund (2012) The Roma Early Childhood Inclusion (RECI) Overview Report. Available at: http://www.romachildren.com/?page_id=504

Surdu, L. (2008) Monitorizarea aplic`rii m`surilor împotriva segreg`rii colare în România. Romani Criss/UNICEF. Bucharest: Editura MarLink.

UNICEF (2007) An Overview of Child Well-being in Rich Countries: A Comprehensive Assessment of the Lives and Well-being of Children and Adolescents in the Economically Advanced Nations. Innocenti Report Card 7. Available at http://www.unicef-irc.org/publications/pdf/rc7_eng.pdf

UNICEF (2008) *Toward Roma Inclusion: A Mapping of Roma Education Initiatives in Central and South-Eastern Europe*. Geneva: UNICEF.

UNICEF (2012) Roma Early Childhood Inclusion (RECI): Serbian Report. Available at: http://www.romachildren.com/wp-content/uploads/2013/02/RECI-Serbia-Report.ENG_.pdf

PART 2

CHILDREN'S SPACES

CHAPTER 7

SPACE AND PLACE AS A SOURCE OF BELONGING AND PARTICIPATION IN EARLY YEARS SERVICES IN CHIAPAS, MEXICO

Margaret Kernan and Kathia Loyzaga

Overview

In this chapter, we make a case for including spatial and place perspectives when exploring the notions of belonging, participation and citizenship in relation to services for young children in urban societies. We pay particular attention to the position of marginalized children, especially migrant children, who often experience barriers to accessing services and challenges to their rights of citizenship and positive identity. Three topics are addressed: (1) what belonging and interdependence can mean in the context of early childhood education and care (ECEC); (2) the interrelationship between children's physical, social and cultural environments; (3) belonging and participation in interconnecting zones of experience in the community. These are illustrated with reference to two of the projects of Melel Xojobal, a non-governmental organization (NGO) working to improve the quality of life of indigenous migrant children and their families in the city of San Cristóbal de Las Casas, Chiapas, Mexico.

Introduction

By 2030, it is estimated that 60% of the world's population will live in cities. This is due, in large part, to increased transnational and internal migration as families search for a better quality of life. It means that young children's lives, more than ever before, are being shaped by urban environments and the kinds of experiences that are open or closed for them there. Studies of urban childhood draw attention to the changing spatial conditions of childhood and children's lives. Those located in Western industrialized societies point to the linked phenomena of traffic danger, children's reduced independent mobility outdoors in the city (Atkinson and Flint, 2004; Hillman et al., 1990) and their 'insularization' into child-specific institutions or 'islands', i.e. houses, day care settings, after-school centres and leisure centres (Karsten, 2002). The impact of migration on children's well-being in both industrialized and non-industrialized countries is also beginning to receive attention (Dobson, 2009). Many children who migrate with their parents to cities flourish and contribute positively to their communities. However, a significant majority of migrant young children, especially those who are members of minority groups, those who are refugees or without documents and those living in informal urban settlements on the margins of cities, experience barriers to accessing services and challenges to the rights of citizenship and identity. These groups of children are often negatively affected by their parents' economic insecurity (Bryant, 2005) and stress-related mental health issues (Bartlett, 2010). All of these phenomena point to children's invisibility and marginalization in urban space, as well as their separation from the social capital of communities. They also raise questions regarding the possibilities for children's sense of belonging and opportunities to participate and be active citizens.

By and large, studies of urban childhood have focused on children in middle childhood and in the teenage years. Much less attention has been paid to researching younger children's spatial and place experience as it applies to understandings of citizenship and participation in society. This chapter considers the possibilities available to young children to construct a secure self-identity, a sense of belonging and active participation within urban areas in the context of their life at home, in ECEC settings and in public space in the city.

ECEC spaces as refuge and opportunity

Since the 19th century, ECEC settings have been viewed both as a 'bridge' between the private and public worlds, between the child and the family and wider society (Liebschner, 1992) and as a separate, protected and 'containing' space for children (Vandenbroeck, 2006). Both perspectives persist today. In contexts of inequity, oppression, violence or abuse, it is recognized that early years settings can provide a 'safe haven' for children to play, to learn, to engage in peer culture and to nurture their resilience (Nimmo, 2008). Early years settings can function both as a refuge and opportunity for young children and their carers, especially those growing up in difficult circumstances, when they are accompanied by measures which reduce stress in families' lives. In the case of poor urban settlements, such measures include adequate housing, reliable water supplies and sanitation (Bartlett, 2010). The notion of the ECEC setting as a 'safe haven' is also apparent in less harsh urban environments, where parents look to ECEC institutions to provide children with socialization and outdoor play opportunities in secure environments, since they are perceived as not being available in the public space of the neighbourhood.

Typically, however, debates on the role of ECEC in relation to migration, urbanization and the resultant diversity of societies have focused on the 'problem' of language and the need for young children to learn the dominant language in any society if they are to succeed (Adair, 2011; Karoly and Gonzalez, 2011). However, there are alternative views of ECEC pedagogy and alternative images of the ECEC service. These place to the fore the notion of the active participating child citizen supported by interdependent and inclusive relationships with peers and with significant adults and the significance of space, play and belonging for young children (Brooker and Woodhead, 2008; Nimmo, 2008). (See also Chapters 4, 6, 8 and 10 for a discussion of these issues.)

Conceptually, the 'new' geography of childhood has much to offer these understandings of ECEC in contemporary urban societies. This field of study has emerged from a blurring of the edges around other disciplines such as anthropology, environmental psychology, urban studies, architecture and the sociology of childhood. Geographical dimensions of children's lives include the intersection of human and physical worlds, and of time and space, spatial variation, the importance of scale, place knowledge, the distinctiveness of place and the meanings and feelings attached to significant sites of everyday life (McKendrick, 2000).

One of the outcomes of such cross-disciplinary work has been a theoretical and practical interest in the notions of space, 'placeness', belonging and connection to others as they apply to children's experiences in their early years (Fog Olwig and Gullov, 2003; Moss and Petrie, 2002) (see Chapter 8). Below, we examine these ideas in more detail.

Why belonging is important

The experience of belonging has been conceptualized as a fundamental human need, right and motivation (Melton, 2006). Belonging and interdependence have also been articulated in terms of a sense of togetherness and the expression of an experience of a common ground for young children (de Haan and Singer, 2001). Furthermore, within psychology and education, it is increasingly acknowledged that acting together is the basis for all learning (Bruner, 1996) (see Chapter 4). During the childhood years, the need to belong is also clearly visible in the importance afforded by children to peer relations, friendships and play (Kernan and Singer, 2011). Belonging may also be evident in the appropriation of spaces with their own meanings and reference points and from which new meanings can be invested and shared.

Experiencing a sense of belonging or a sense of connection to community, whether through togetherness in peer relations, the experience of a common ground or acting, learning and playing together, may be more challenging for children who are 'different', whether due to culture, language, economic status, gender or ability, and whose experience is one of exclusion rather than inclusion. Furthermore, as Kjørholt (2008: 29) argues, being excluded from the social relationships and belonging that ECEC offers can also mean 'being deprived of the possibilities to practise citizenship'. In these respects, ECEC has a critical role given that attendance at such a setting may be the child's first exposure to 'the other' or first experience of being different, and that is often the place where children are confronted with diversity for the first time (Vandenbroeck, 1999). ECEC settings have also been conceptualized as sites for social justice or for democratic political practice (Dahlberg and Moss, 2005). This assumes a particular relevance in urban environments given that cities offer physical and social opportunities for their citizens, including child citizens, to meet and mobilize to claim their rights and promote solutions to shared problems (Child Friendly Cities, 2008).

Space and place matter: the interrelationship between the physical, social and cultural environments

Within the ECEC literature, belonging and interdependence have primarily focused on social relations and interactions within and between generations – in relation to secure attachments between children and caregivers and participation in cultures. Our intention in this chapter is to extend understandings of belonging to highlight the interrelationship between the physical, social and cultural conditions of young children's lives.

In a seminal text published in 1977, human geographer Yi-Fu Tuan conceptualized the relationship between space and place as follows: space, meaning room and permitting movement, is often associated with freedom and is 'longed for'. Place, on the other hand, is security and often the notion of being 'attached to' place is expressed. According to Tuan, space and place require each other and humans require both. From the security and stability of place, there is an awareness of openness, freedom and, sometimes, threat of space. Human lives, Tuan suggests, can be described as a 'dialectic movement between shelter and venture, attachment and freedom' (Tuan, 1977: 54). Tuan conceptualizes a young child as being 'adrift or placeless' (Tuan, 1977: 29), without the security of a supportive parent close by. Yet, at the same time, young children are open to the world. Thus, in the early years of life there is a tension between what is old and new or between the secure, familiar and safe, and adventuring outwards to what is novel, facilitating growth and development and a sense of connectedness and belonging to the world.

Children thrive when they can get both meaning and value from their encounters with their surroundings (Reed, 1996), particularly when they are rich in sensorial quality, facilitate the freedom to express and create, and offer new and interesting experiences and activities that encourage children's natural curiosity (Blinkert, 2004; Jans,

2004). In these respects, play, and often play outdoors, is viewed as offering the quintessentially 'natural' means of learning and development in the early years, as well as a means of connectedness to the surrounding physical and natural world (Nabhan and Trimble, 1994). It is also recognized that it is important for children to have access to adults and other expert and experienced people who will provide a secure base, listen to them, answer and raise questions and jointly interpret everyday events and phenomena whereby there is a shared construction of knowledge. Reflecting these emphases, Lenz Taguchi (2010) has proposed an intra-active pedagogy, which is inclusive both of children's thinking and different strategies and ways of doing, and the materials, spaces and places children occupy and use in their daily lives.

Viewing early childhood settings through such a geographical, ecological and inclusionary lens helps focus our attention on the extent to which environments are rich in meaning and value for all children and families. One approach adopted has been to incorporate familiar characteristics into the early years setting, paying particular attention to making entrance areas welcoming and reflecting all children's backgrounds and life histories in the design, resourcing, artefacts and images displayed in ECEC environments (Houndoumadi et al., 2007). Here, importance is given to the notion of ECEC settings as common spaces or meeting places and communities of mutual respect and respectful communication (Children in Europe, 2008; VBJK and DECET, 2003) (for further discussion, see Chapter 4). A complementary approach has been to engage in a listening dialogue (Clark et al., 2005) and participatory research with children regarding their interests and priorities in space and place in ECEC (Clark, 2007), as well as a listening dialogue with parents of diverse backgrounds (Brougère et al., 2008). One important aspect of such an approach may be to attend to the life histories and stories of parents, practitioners and children (older and younger). This could focus on the changing spatial conditions of children and childhood over the life course (Sandberg and Pramling Samuelsson, 2003), and for migrant families and those working with them, attending to the competing values between dominant culture and home culture (see Chapters 5 and 6). This also supports critical reflection on what is 'permitted' for children or prohibited in terms of their engagement with their surrounding social and physical worlds in their everyday lives, wherever they are being lived.

Belonging and participation in interconnecting zones of experience and action in the community

In his discussion on 'child-sized' citizenship, Jans (2004) notes that children can identify themselves with larger social groups and communities which are '*in reach*' [emphasis added] of children in their environments. Viewing young children's engagement with their environment in terms of progressive or linked zones or fields of action offers a further space and place perspective when analysing children's sense of belonging and opportunity to participate. Studies in neighbourhoods in the Netherlands and Belgium have used the notion of 'play space networks' or 'webs' as design strategies for providing child-oriented public space where children can play and meet in formal and informal play spaces and where there are routes connecting these places and the surrounding social network (Vanderstede, 2008). The schools and pre-schools of Reggio Emilia, in the highly urbanized regions of northern Italy, are also envisioned as part of a web, being located at the centre of a neighbourhood, physically and metaphorically where the daily life of children and teachers are 'a visible point of reference for the community' (Gandini, 1998: 164), and the spaces surrounding the schools are considered as extended classroom space (Gandini, 1998). In 2010, a special issue of the *Children in Europe* magazine highlighted the benefits to children of ECEC services being open to the surrounding physical space and communities. This is made explicit in the following excerpt from a logbook of an early educator in Catalonia:

> We find nature in the squares, the hidden corners of the nearby routes that we walk day in, day out; privileged places where, near a small fountain, or a park, or a particular square, things happen ... such spaces can provide symbols and memories and create a sense of belonging and an urge to express to others what this means. (Cols, 2010: 8)

One further zone of learning experience for young children, which is also key in identity formation and connectedness, particularly in developing countries, is participation in work. As proposed by Dawes (2010: 28), 'Self-esteem and self-efficacy supported as new skills are recognized by family and community members. Cognitive abilities, technical skills and local cultural competencies develop in parallel'. The ways in which children work and play are often highly integrated. A study of children's experiences as street traders in Peru described street trading as a hybrid activity of work and play. In Cusco, the site of this research, child traders (aged 6–16 years) were frequently observed playing between attempts at selling goods (Bromley and Mackie, 2009). From the children's point of view, their work on the street was both enjoyable and economically empowering (as they could then pay for food and schooling). However, there were also dangers evident, such as substance misuse, physical abuse, accidents, theft (particularly from young children), and frequently heavy-handed confiscation of goods by police.

These themes – place–space relations, belonging, identity, play and work – provided a framework for analysing the daily lives and activities of indigenous migrant girls and boys living in the city of San Cristóbal de Las Casas and the work of Melel Xojobal, a local NGO in Mexico.

Case study

Background and introduction

Mexico is characterized by immense cultural and ethnic diversity and has one of the highest proportions of indigenous populations in the world (UNICEF, 2010). Vast disparities exist between indigenous and non-indigenous populations, children included, leading the UN Committee on the Rights of the Child to voice its concern about 'persistent discrimination against indigenous children' (UN Committee on the Rights of the Child, 2006: 6). San Cristóbal de Las Casas is the third largest city in Chiapas, one of the poorest states in Mexico. Its population has tripled since 1980 due almost entirely to the migration of indigenous groups of Maya origin from rural farming communities in the highland areas of the State to the city. Those leaving their community of origin do so in search of a better quality of life due to religious, political and, primarily, economic reasons. This migratory shift has changed the demography of San Cristóbal de Las Casas. According to estimates of local NGOs, more than 50% of the population is now indigenous, a dramatic change from 20 years ago, when it was just 20%. However, despite their majority status in the city in terms of population, adults and children from indigenous communities feel that 'they do not belong there', that it is not 'their place' – nor do they feel they have a role as citizens in the city.

Indigenous families tend to live in the northern margins of the city in informal settlements in very basic housing. Alternatively, they rent a room in a house that is shared with many other families. Women often become the sole providers for the household. When they manage to find work, it is generally as domestic workers or else in informal commerce in the large tourist outdoor markets in the city (Figueroa Fuentes, 2008). In their rural communities of origin, children are socialized into their responsibility to work on the land from an early age to support the economic activity of their household. Growing up in the city, young children are often required to go to work with their mothers. Alternatively, they stay at home alone or they are looked after by other children or adults who take little responsibility for them (Gutiérrez and Figueroa Fuentes, 2008). At the same time, most parents want their children to learn to read and write in Spanish, while maintaining their own indigenous language as the spoken language at home. This, they believe, is important for their children's future well-being.

Melel Xojobal is a Mexican NGO founded in 1997 and working on social issues. It began as a small diocesan project for young indigenous children who worked with their families in the Santo Domingo crafts market in San Cristóbal de Las Casas. In 1999, Melel Xojobal became an independent organization separate from the diocese. A key aim of Melel Xojobal (meaning *The True Light*) is to work with indigenous children and young people to promote, defend and exercise their rights through participative processes that improve their quality of life. It also draws the general public's attention to violations of human and children's rights, and informs the public about the risks and consequences of migration, particularly the rights of children and young indigenous people to education, health, good working conditions, protection from violence and freedom of speech. Melel works at the interface of poverty, ethnicity, migration and discrimination, the cumulative effect of which places children at risk of violence, poor health and exclusion from basic social and educational services. Although Melel is not the only NGO working with indigenous children in San Cristóbal de Las Casas, it is the only one explicitly giving attention to issues of identity, belonging and diversity.

Two of its intervention programmes involve young children. These are *Arrumacos* (meaning 'nurturing hugs'), a centre-based programme that strives to stimulate the all-round development of children from birth to 4 years through participation and play, and *Infancia Trabajadora* (meaning 'child workers'), which involves engaging with 6–12-year-old children in the squares and markets where they spend most of their day, working in the open air markets as vendors or accompanying adults working as vendors.

Data for this case study has been collected through an analysis of the documentary material, including publications and reports relating to Melel Xojobal, as well as informal interviews with project staff.

Supporting belonging and participation in a ECEC group context

Arrumacos is housed in three interconnected rooms in the Melel Xojobal premises in San Cristóbal de Las Casas: one room for babies from one month to 2 years, a second room for children aged 2–3 years and a third room for 3- and 4-year-olds. An inner open-air patio functions as an outdoor play space. The centre is attended by children of diverse backgrounds, those from the various indigenous groups and 'mestizo' (of mixed cultural heritage). Most of the children are being raised by lone mothers. Essentially, *Arrumacos* provides a safe, secure and nurturing space for young children while their mothers work. The activities are intended to work across generations. Close attention is paid to children's physical health and nutritional needs and social and emotional well-being, as well as that of their mothers thus reducing their stress.

Great importance is paid to fostering a positive identity and sense of belonging, taking cognizance of both the children's and their parents' life histories and the realities of their present living environments. In monthly creative workshops involving drawing, photography and story, mothers are supported in developing self-knowledge and confidence in their skills and abilities, and building affection and emotional bonds with family members. They are also supported in valuing their own culture, exchanging knowledge and respecting diversity (Gutiérrez and Figueroa Fuentes, 2008). Interrelated with this are daily activities and discussions with the children in the centre, which typically involve dressing up, drawing, use of masks and simple map making, as children express their views of themselves and experiences of their family, their home and the street where they live. Local fabrics, traditional 'rebozo' or 'chal' (shawls or baby-carrying cloths), hand-made artefacts, '*masa de tortilla*' (dough) and documented stories and drawings of communities of origin are everyday resources in *Arrumacos*. These are used along with more commercial materials and toys.

The physical landscape, rural and urban, is invoked in the way mothers and children describe daily life and 'who they are'. For example, in a book of stories written by mothers for their children, in which they explain their origins and identity, there is reference to hills, rivers, earth and cornfields, coffee and fruit trees as representing the rural landscape of both work and play (Melel Xojobal, 2008). Children's accounts include references to significant family members as well as other key physical markers in the city, such as to cars on the street, particular shops and bus stops. Walks in the immediate area are not considered advisable due to the very narrow footpaths and the dangers posed by traffic. Exploration beyond the boundaried area of the centre takes the form of organized visits to the zoo, botanical gardens, a children's park and other children's day care centres. The staff also organize group visits to children's individual homes in order to strengthen the link between the ECEC service and the family. Through all of these group activities, the staff support children to develop a sense of belonging and of 'common ground' in relation to their family, their place of origin, their group in *Arrumacos* and the spaces and places in the city which are significant for them.

Supporting children's belonging and participation in public space

One of the aims of the *Infancia Trabajadora* initiative has been to raise awareness, both with the children and at broader public level, including city governance, regarding the notion of children as citizens of the city with rights. Between three and four times a week, Melel Xojobal staff leave the centre in order to take materials and resources to the key outdoor sites in the city where children work as vendors. A sheet is spread out on the ground marking an identifiable space which 'belongs' to the children, and the beginning of a familiar ritual in which children, aged approximately 6–12 years, gather as a group. It begins with informal chat, followed by a game, chosen by the children; and then a creative activity led by the adult facilitators. The session ends with the children reflecting and sharing with the group. The whole activity takes less than one hour. The group size is typically 10–12 children. Younger children, most of them accompanying their older siblings, often form part of the group. In common with the *Arrumacos* project, the experience of play and creative activities in a group are viewed as contributing to the development of a secure self-identity, a sense of belonging and respect for 'the other'. In *Infancia Trabajadora*, these activities also take on the role of supporting children to become aware of their rights and responsibilities.

In practice, this activity is beset by a number of challenges. First, many of the children find it difficult to 'be in' and share experiences in a large group of peers, and conflicts often develop. If a tourist bus rolls in, with potential new customers, the children typically rush away from the group. Maintaining focus and interest in the group activity can be difficult. Second, despite the fact that the municipality has given Melel Xojobal a written permit for the *Infancia Trabajadora* project, the police often try to disband the group and threaten to confiscate the children's merchandise, citing the fact that the *Infancia Trabajadora* group is making the city look 'ugly' and negatively affecting the perception the city wants to create for tourists. In supporting the children to exercise their rights to reclaim their gathering, play and work space in the markets, the Melel staff discuss questions such as

'To whom does the city belong?' and 'Who is part of the city?' with the children. One of the outcomes of such a discussion has been for the children to make a banner with the message: 'I have a right to be here because I am hard-working and am not causing trouble.'

Through meeting with the children in the public space, the project team is able to identify other issues requiring attention. Recently, the *Infancia Trabajadora* project team has been focusing their energies on a programme called Riesgos en Calle, which helps children deal with risks and dangers they face in public spaces, which can include sexual exploitation, human trafficking and child abuse, as well as theft, accidents and police abuse. A further role is assisting indigenous children to secure a birth certificate, a basic requirement to register for kindergarten and school, and to access health services. As in the case of the child street traders in Cusco, Peru (Bromley and Mackie, 2009), many of the children involved in the *Infancia Trabajadora* project succeed in combining some hours attending kindergarten or school with time spent working in the markets on a daily basis.

Final thoughts

By examining the work of Melel Xojobal through a space, place and belonging 'lens', a number of competing tensions which impact on indigenous migrant children's ongoing construction of a positive identity and sense of belonging are revealed. These include:

- the position of children as contributors to the household economy working in the public space in street markets, versus the need and right to access education and care in ECEC settings and schools
- children's needs and rights to engage in cultural and play activities in city spaces, indoor and outdoor, organized and less organized, versus the need to preserve the public space for tourist and associated adult-oriented economic activities
- the needs and rights of young children to navigate and explore city spaces safely, with and without adults, versus the dominance of traffic networks in the city and the risks of abuse and exploitation.

These tensions underline the fact that ECEC programmes alone cannot address issues of poverty, discrimination and exclusion (Council of Europe, 2007; OECD, 2006). Rather, as emphasized throughout this chapter, multi-dimensional responses are required that connect ECEC 'spaces' with other community 'spaces' and initiatives, and unequal power relations need to be named and challenged.

Melel Xojobal endeavours to meet these challenges by being sufficiently flexible to respond to real localized needs, by attending to children's creative and playful expression, and engaging inter-generationally. Importantly, this engagement occurs in a range of significant sites of children's everyday lives – at home, in ECEC group settings and in the public space of a market square. In this innovative work, Melel helps create urban spaces where all citizens, including young migrant children, participate and belong. This is important at a time when urban living, and all its constraints and opportunities, is becoming the reality for the majority of the world's children.

Summary

- Young children benefit when ECEC services forge physical and social connections with the range of physical, social and cultural spaces which are significant for young children in urban areas.
- This requires attentiveness to the importance of everyday spatialities of children, encompassing personal histories and priorities, materials, artefacts and playable spaces.
- It also entails critically reflecting, in collaboration with parents, neighbourhood communities, schools, other services and municipal authorities, on what is permitted or prohibited in terms of children's engagement with their surrounding social and physical worlds in the city.
- Particular attention needs to be paid to ensuring that young migrant children can also be active participants in social and cultural life and have the opportunity to practise citizenship.

Questions for discussion

1. Think about an urban community you are familiar with. What might belonging to and participation in social and community worlds mean in practice for the young children in that community?
2. What are the particular challenges and opportunities for young migrant children in urban settings in developing a sense of belonging and actively participating in ECEC settings?
3. How can a focus on space and place support our understanding and implementation of children's rights to a positive identity, the experience of belonging and connectedness, and inclusive relations with others and with the surrounding physical environment? (*Higher-level question*)

Further reading

Levels 5 and 6

Young children in cities: challenges and opportunities, *Early Childhood Matters*, 115, November. The Hague: Bernard van Leer Foundation. Available at: http://www.bernardvanleer.org/English/Home/Our-publications/Browse_by_series.html?ps_page=1&getSeries=4
This downloadable illustrated publication consists of a series of 11 articles describing young children's experiences of growing up in urban settings around the world. Topics addressed include: the urban experience of young Roma children; child friendly cities: perspectives from the Rotterdam, the Netherlands and the Asia Pacific region; community care and education programmes in Caracas, Venezuela, Ciudad Juarez, Mexico, Delhi, India and Peru; post-emergency work with young children in urban areas.

Levels 6 and 7

Horton, J., Kraftl, P. and Tucker, F. (2008) The challenges of 'children's geographies': a reaffirmation. *Children's Geographies*, 6(4): 335–348.
This editorial from the journal *Children's Geographies* is recommended for readers who would like to further explore the subdiscipline of the same name. The editorial discusses nine challenges for children's geographers. The first of these is described as 'Missing children and young people' and readers are urged to 'constantly problematize the absence of children and young people from broader contemporary ways of knowing, writing and researching the world' (p. 338). The journal *Children, Youth and Environments* is also recommended for those interested in children's relationships with their physical environments. While neither journal focuses exclusively on children in the early years, there are sufficient articles addressing early childhood to merit a closer look.

Websites

http://www.childfriendlycities.org
The Child Friendly Cities Initiative was launched in 1996 to act on the resolution passed during the second UN Conference on Human Settlements (Habitat II), which declared that the well-being of children is the ultimate indicator of a healthy habitat, a democratic society and good governance. The International Secretariat for Child Friendly Cities is in UNICEF Innocenti Research Centre (IRC) in Florence, Italy. The CFC website provides useful information on how to build a Child Friendly City/Community. It includes data on good practices and initiatives, gathering relevant publications and updates on current research. Pay attention to the illustrated Child Friendly Community Assessment Tools, one of which is specifically designed for parents of pre-school children aged 0 to 7 years.

http://www.melelxojobal.org.mx/
This is the attractive website of Melel Xojobal, the Mexican child-focused organization featured in the case study in this chapter. It describes the organization's history, mission and vision, programmes and activities and publications. Most of the sections are available in both English and Spanish.

Note

1. The chapter is an adaptation of an article written by Margaret Kernan and Kathia Loyzaga in 2010, published by Taylor and Francis in *European Early Childhood Education Research Journal*, 18(2): 199–213, titled 'Space and place as a source of belonging and participation in urban environments: considering the role of early childhood education and care settings'. Copyright EECERA, reprinted by permission of Taylor and Francis, www.tandfonline.com on behalf of EECERA.

References

Adair, J.K. (2011) Confirming Chanclas: what early childhood teacher educators can learn from immigrant preschool teachers. *Journal of Early Childhood Teacher Education*, 32(1): 55–71.

Atkinson, R. and Flint, J. (2004) Fortress UK? Gated communities, the spatial revolt of the elites and time–space trajectories of segregation. *Housing Studies*, 19(6): 875–892.

Bartlett, S. (2010) Children living in urban poverty: a global emergency, a low priority. Young children in cities: challenges and opportunities. *Early Childhood Matters*, 115: 4–9.

Blinkert, B. (2004) Quality of the city for children: chaos and order. *Children, Youth and Environments*, 14(2): 100–112.

Brooker, L. and Woodhead, M. (eds) (2008) *Developing Positive Identities: Diversity and Young Children*. Milton Keynes: The Open University/The Hague: Bernard van Leer Foundation.

Bromley, R.D.F. and Mackie, P.K. (2009) Child experiences as street traders in Peru: contributing to a reappraisal for working children. *Children's Geographies*, 7(2): 141–158.

Brougère, G., Guénif-Souilamas, N. and Rayna, S. (2008) Ecole maternelle (preschool) in France: a cross-cultural perspective. *European Early Childhood Education Research Journal*, 16(3): 371–384.

Bruner, J. (1996) *The Culture of Education*. Cambridge, MA: Harvard University Press.

Bryant, J. (2005) Children of international migrants in Indonesia, Thailand and the Philippines: a review of evidence and politics. Innocenti Working Paper No. 2005–05. Florence: UNICEF Innocenti Research Centre.

Child Friendly Cities (2008) A Child Friendly Community Self-Assessment Tool for Pre-School Parents. IRC/CERG. Available at: http://childfriendlycities.org/research/final-toolkit-2011/

Children in Europe (2008) *Young Children and their Services: Developing a European Approach*. A Children in Europe policy paper. Edinburgh: Children in Scotland.

Clark, A. (2007) Views from inside the shed: young children's perspectives of the outdoor environment. *Education 3–13*, 35(4): 349–363.

Clark, A., Kjørholt, A.T. and Moss, P. (eds) (2005) *Beyond Listening: Children's Perspectives on Early Childhood Services*. Bristol: Policy Press, pp. 175–187.

Cols, C. (2010) Outside the school: a world full of possibilities. *Children in Europe*, 19: 8–10.

Council of Europe (2007) Towards quality education for Roma children in Europe: transition from early childhood to primary education. Report of UNESCO and Council of Europe Expert Meeting on the Education of Roma Children in Europe. Available at: http://unesdoc.unesco.org/images/0016/001611/161164e.pdf

Dahlberg, G. and Moss, P. (2005) *Ethics and Politics in Early Childhood Education*. London: RoutledgeFalmer.

Dawes, A. (2010) Learning through work, and learning how to work. In: L. Brooker and M. Woodhead (eds) *Early Childhood in Focus 6: Culture and Learning*. Milton Keynes: Open University Press, pp. 28–30.

Dobson, M. (2009) Unpacking children in migration research. *Children's Geographies*, 7(3): 355–360.

Fog Olwig, K. and Gullov, E. (2003) Towards an anthropology of children and place. In: K. Fog Olwig and E. Gullov (eds) *Children's Places, Cross-cultural Perspectives*. London: Routledge, pp. 1–19.

Figueroa Fuentes, P. (2008) Introduction to the bilingual edition. In: Melel Xojobal (ed.) *So that You Know, Aspirations and Stories by Women of Chiapas/Para que sepas, Anhelos e historias de mujeros de Chiapas*. San Cristóbal de Las Casas: Melel Xojobal, pp. 13–15.

Gandini, L. (1998) Educational and caring spaces. In: C. Edwards, L. Gandini and G. Forman (eds) *The Hundred Languages of Children: The Reggio Emilia Approach – Advanced Reflections*. Greenwich, CT: Ablex, pp. 161–178.

Gutiérrez, J. Haza and Figueroa Fuentes, P. (2008) Who are we? The Arrumacos children: identity and the sense of belonging. *Early Childhood Matters*, 111: 24–28.

de Haan, D. and Singer, E. (2001) Young children's language of togetherness. *International Journal of Early Years Education*, 9(2): 7–24.

Hillman, M., Adams, J. and Whitelegg, J. (1990) *One False Move … A Study of Children's Independent Mobility*. London: Policy Studies Institute.

Horton, J., Kraftl, P. and Tucker, F. (2008) The challenges of 'children's geographies': a reaffirmation. *Children's Geographies*, 6(4): 335–348.

Houndoumadi, A., Gill, G., Moussy, F., Lee, P., Vervaet, V. and Schallenberg-Diekmann, R. (2007) *Diversity and Equity: Making Sense of Good Practice*. Brussels: Diversity in Early Childhood Education and Training (DECET).

Jans, M. (2004) Children as citizens: towards a contemporary notion of child participation. *Childhood*, 11(1): 27–44.

Karsten, L. (2002) Mapping childhood in Amsterdam: the spatial and social construction of children's domains in the city. *Tijdschrift voor Economische en Sociale Geografie*, 93: 231–241.

Karoly, L.A. and Gonzalez, G.C. (2011) Early care and education for children in immigrant families. *The Future of Children*, 21(1): 71–101.

Kernan, M. and Singer, E. (eds) (2011) *Peer Relationships in Early Childhood Education and Care*. Abingdon, Oxon: Routledge.

Kjørholt, A-T. (2008) Children as new citizens: in the best interests of the child? In: A. James and A.L. James (eds) *European Childhoods: Cultures, Politics and Childhoods in Europe*. New York: Palgrave Macmillan, pp. 14–37.

Lenz Taguchi, H. (2010) *Going Beyond the Theory/Practice Divide in Early Childhood Education: Introducing an Intra-active Pedagogy*. Abingdon: Routledge.

Liebschner, J. (1992) *A Child's Work: Freedom and Play in Froebel's Educational Theory and Practice*. Cambridge: Lutterworth Press.

McKendrick, J.H. (2000) The geography of children: an annotated bibliography. *Childhood*, 7(3): 359–387.

Melel Xojobal (2008) *So that You Know: Aspirations and Stories by Women of Chiapas – A Compilation of Stories Created by Women for their Children/Para que sepas: anhelos e historias de mujeres de Chiapas, una compilacion de cuentos creada por mujeres para sus hijos e hijas*. San Cristóbal de Las Casas: Melel Xojobal.

Melton, G.B. (2006) Foreword. In: J. Barnes, I. Katz, J.E. Korbin and M. O'Brien (eds) *Children and Families in Communities: Theory, Research, Policy and Practice*. Chichester: Wiley, pp. xi–xx.

Moss, P. and Petrie, P. (2002) *From Children's Services to Children's Spaces*. London: RoutledgeFalmer.

Nabhan, G.P. and Trimble, S. (1994) *The Geography of Childhood: Why Children Need Wild Places*. Boston, MA: Beacon Press.

Nimmo, J. (2008) Young children's access to real life: an examination of the growing boundaries between children in child care and adults in the community. *Contemporary Issues in Early Childhood*, 9(1): 3–13.

Organisation for Economic Co-operation and Development (OECD) (2006) *Starting Strong II: Early Childhood Education and Care*. Paris: OECD.

Reed, E.S. (1996) *Encountering the World: Toward an Ecological Psychology*. Oxford: Oxford University Press.

Sandberg, A. and Pramling Samuelsson, I. (2003) Preschool teachers' play experiences then and now. *Early Childhood Research and Practice*, 5(1). Available at: http://ecrp.uiuc.edu/v5n1/sandberg.html

Tuan, Y-F. (1977) *Space and Place: The Perspective of Experience*. Minneapolis, MN: University of Minnesota Press.

UN Committee on the Rights of the Child (CRC) (2006) UN Committee on the Rights of the Child: Concluding Observations, Mexico, 8 June, CRC/C/MEX/CO/3. Available at: http://www.unhcr.org/refworld/docid/45377ee60.html (accessed 30 May 2012).

UNICEF (2010) UNICEF Annual Report for Mexico. Available at: http://www.unicef.org/about/annualreport/files/Mexico_COAR_2010.pdf

Vandenbroeck, M. (1999) *The View of the Yeti: Bringing up Children in the Spirit of Self-awareness and Kindredship*. The Hague: Bernard van Leer Foundation.

Vandenbroeck, M. (2006) The persistent gap between education and care: a 'history of the present' research on Belgian child care provision and policy. *Paedagogica Historica*, 42(3): 363–383.

Vanderstede, W. (2008) Childhood and Society Research Centre, Flanders-Belgium. Paper presented at the Child in the City conference, Rotterdam, the Netherlands, 3–5 November.

VBJK and DECET (2003) *Lullaby for Hamza: Childcare as a Meeting Place*. Ghent and Brussels: Expertisecentrum Opvoeding en Kinderopvang (VBJK) and Diversity in Early Childhood Education and Training (DECET).

CHAPTER 8

PLACE-BASED LEARNING IN EARLY YEARS SERVICES: APPROACHES AND EXAMPLES FROM NORWAY AND SCOTLAND

Bronwen Cohen and Wenche Rønning

Overview

What can we learn from services which help children to understand and engage with 'place' and community' and use this as a tool for active learning? Place-based learning is an approach to early childhood education and care (ECEC) that makes use of local economic activities and the unique history, culture, tradition and other community reference points to engage more effectively with children and young people within the context of their lives. Like 'forest schools' and 'wood' or 'nature' kindergartens, it may make extensive use of nature, which, in Norway, for example, is seen as part of the national identity. However, place-based learning encompasses other aspects of place and community, recognizing the role of place, culture and community in informing children's sense of their own identity and their social relationships in a variety of different ways. In this chapter, we look at its origins as a pedagogical approach and how it is developing in Norway and Scotland, associated in particular with protecting rural communities and their way of life. We consider its relevance to more urban settings and what it could bring to services in a globalized world in which 'place', 'space' and 'belonging' can have multiple meanings for children, and the role they can and should play as cultural meeting places, based on mutual respect.

The pedagogy of place-based learning

The American educator, John Dewey (1859–1952) was among the first to articulate the value of connecting a child's educational experience with their life outside the classroom. In his seminal work *Democracy and Education* (Dewey, 1916/1997), he criticized the isolation of schools and their failure to make use of children's experiences from their daily lives at home and in their communities in helping them to learn. Dewey's work, alongside that of educationalists such as Jean Piaget and Lev Vygotsky, contributed to experiential and constructivist learning in which a child uses experience to construct her own view of reality. Dewey, Piaget and Vygotsky share an emphasis on active and collaborative learning which are important elements in place-based learning. A common theme they would all have shared, if expressed differently, is that children's learning must recognize, value and engage with the child's life outside the kindergarten or school.

At the same time that educational reformers were pointing to the value of 'place' as a learning tool, anthropologists were exploring the mutual implications of place (and, more recently, community) and culture. In recent decades, psychologists and neuroscientists have investigated the biological basis underpinning relational interpersonal life and cultural learning. For example, according to psychologists Frank and Trevarthen (2012: 262–263):

> We live, work, learn and talk in a sphere of meaning made by persons sharing actions and experiences, passing on knowledge, techniques and beliefs about the world in ritual and symbolic ways. Our fates as individuals, our unique 'personal narrative histories', depend upon the health and pride of this sharing, on the affections and poetry or 'making' of life – how our families and communities appreciate and support us through all stages of development, and what we give to them in return.

Improved understanding of how children learn has undoubtedly contributed to interest not only in constructivist learning but also, more specifically, in place-based learning. But its development is not just about the enhancement of learning. It also lies in the linking of educational aims with wider societal goals, from stemming rural depopulation to developing awareness of local and national identities (see also Chapters 6 and 7).

The most systematic approach to place-based learning can be found in Norway where rural policy has been accorded high priority and where decision making has become progressively devolved downwards, giving local authorities great freedom in how they deliver their services. Place-based learning began in school but, as we see later, is now an important element in Norway's extensive system of full-day kindergartens which children are entitled to attend from the age of 1.

By contrast, developments in Scotland have generally been less systematic, but have also benefited from raised awareness of issues around local and national identity, accompanying discussion prior to, and following, the establishment of the Scottish Parliament, as well as a new and wide-ranging curriculum and local authority cultural strategies.

Place-based learning in ECEC services in Norway

Norwegian government encouragement for place-based learning dates back to the 1939 national curriculum, N39, based on what was called the 'work–school' principle. It promoted a cross-curricular approach aimed at connecting school with 'real-life' issues affecting communities and using nature as a learning arena (Rønning, 2010). As a result of the outbreak of the Second World War, N39 was never fully implemented but the principles of place-based learning, which it contained, fed into later national curricula. The current curriculum, LK06, maintains the emphasis on cooperation with the local community (Norwegian Directorate for Education and Training, 2012a: 2). Place-based learning developed in Norwegian schools. Pre-school services were few in number until the 1970s. As they developed into the extensive system that exists today, they began to adopt the principles of place-based learning introduced into schools. Since 2009, all Norwegian children between 1 and 6 years old (the latter being the age at which they start school) have had the right to a full-time kindergarten place. Currently, nearly 90% of Norwegian children in this age group attend highly subsidized kindergartens, either owned by the municipality or privately (Statistics Norway, 2012).

Outdoor education and activity is the most extensive strand of place-based learning in Norwegian kindergartens and is required within the national curriculum. The current 'Framework Plan for the Content and Tasks of Kindergartens' contains a chapter on 'Body, movement and health', which goes beyond physical activity to make a connection with sensory experience, developing a love of nature and links with the local environment.

The Framework stipulates that kindergartens must ensure that children:

- have positive experiences of outdoor activities and being outdoors in different seasons
- develop a love of using nature for exploration and physical challenge, and gain an understanding of how one can use the environment and countryside while also looking after it.

And to achieve this, kindergartens should:

- ensure good planning, flexible preparation and flexible use of the physical environment, and assess how the local neighbourhood can supplement the kindergarten's premises at different times of year. (Norwegian Ministry of Education and Research, 2003a: 35)

The main staff in Norwegian kindergartens are known as pre-school teachers but receive an initial education which is essentially that of a social pedagogue, with a wide range of skills focused on the 'whole child' and including health and sports (Norwegian Ministry of Education and Research, 2003b). Outdoor education is delivered as part of the education of pre-school teachers at both under-graduate and post-graduate levels, encouraging pre-school teachers to make use of outdoor environments. For example, one post-graduate course details in its prospectus how outdoor education students will learn how to stimulate children to play and wonder about, enjoy and experience mastery in nature based on the children's capabilities (University of Nordland, 2012).

Clear requirements for outdoor education in the national Framework Plan, as well as its inclusion within initial and ongoing teacher education, have led Norwegian kindergartens to make extensive use of outdoor environments. Drawing their inspiration from A.A. Milne's stories (1926) about Winnie the Pooh, the fictional anthropomorphic bear who lives his life and plays with his friends in the 'one-hundred acre' wood, many Norwegian kindergartens have an area close by which they name in this way. This is a piece of nature which they visit regularly, where they study the changes in the seasons and where children can climb, play and construct. In rural areas, this may be a real forest; in urban areas, a park or playground.

The Framework Plan's emphasis on active place-based learning has encouraged the development of more specifically themed kindergartens, including nature kindergartens predominantly based outdoors and farm kindergartens – see case study below. Since the first nature kindergarten was established in 1985, the number of themed kindergartens has increased considerably (Lie et al., 2011). However, all kindergartens are required to offer children challenging activities outdoors in their local environment, and, in general, kindergarten children spend a minimum of two to three hours a day outside.

Nature is a central element in Norwegian place-based education. But place-based learning in Norway encompasses other aspects of life and activities. Depending on the location of the kindergarten, they make use of art galleries, museums, fish farms or other kinds of local industry. A national programme has been set up to promote links and partnerships with local institutions as part of a focus on entrepreneurship in education – see the example in the Norway case study (Norwegian Ministry of Education and Research et al., 2008).

Another strand within Norwegian place-based learning is that of nurturing and passing on history, culture and traditions from the local environment. Children in schools and kindergartens undertake activities such as spinning and dying wool, making and using traditional tools and cooking traditional dishes. In some cases, this involves working with grandparents or other older people living in the area.

Although there is a strong focus on Norwegian traditions, Norway's diversity is also recognized in place-based learning. Norway's indigenous people, the Sami, with three official languages, have their own national curriculum, LK06-S (Norwegian Directorate for Education and Training, 2012b), with a focus on Sami culture, traditions and history and opportunities for local adaptation. School children take part in typical Sami activities such as reindeer herding, slaughtering and preserving meat and traditional arts, crafts and handicrafts linked to Sami mythology and history.

Norwegian schools and kindergartens make extensive use of the arts, which are not only used to pass on indigenous local traditions but also to bring Norway's children and young people into contact with other cultures – within and outside Norway. For school-aged children, Norway's Cultural Rucksack scheme (Norwegian Ministry of Culture and Norwegian Ministry of Education and Research, 2012) offers extensive access to the full range of arts and culture, and to work in the arts across the world. At pre-school level, the arts is also used as a window into the world outside, as well as for the immediate neighbourhood.

Norway case study: Medås farm kindergarten

One of a rapidly increasing number of farm kindergartens, Medås in Nordland was established in 1999 by two farmers who had over a number of years lost the sheep on their farm to predators such as lynx during the summer grazing season. In order that they could remain and make a living, they turned their farm into a farm kindergarten. The kindergarten is popular and now has full day places for nearly 100 children aged 1–6. It is no longer run as a farm but keeps a variety of animals and poultry, including cows, horses, sheep and hens, which feature in the daily activities of the kindergarten.

Every day, the children feed the sheep, the horses and the cows, collect eggs from the hens and help clean the barn. In spring, they plant vegetables and they follow the animals to their summer pastures. In the autumn, they harvest the crops they have planted, pick berries in the nearby wood and take part in preserving the food, including meat from the slaughtered sheep.

The farm kindergarten takes part in farm fairs where the children sell their produce such as home-made jam, potatoes and eggs – an example of the initiative 'Entrepreneurship in Education' promoted in Norway. In this way, the farm kindergarten not only aims at providing a good and healthy learning environment for the children, but also encourages them to value their local community, this way of life and the lifelong opportunities it offers.

Medås farm kindergarten tries to strengthen the children's links to their local environment through activities which introduce them to local traditions and history. They invite older, more experienced people in the area to work with them in cooking traditional food, telling stories and teaching local crafts. Links are built to the community in ways which are important not only for the children, but which also enable the older people to get to know the new generations.

Medås is a dedicated kindergarten. Some farm kindergartens form part of working farms which may also be used for visits or as a learning environment for young people requiring an alternative to school. Some of these are run by a voluntary organization known as 4H, which has traditionally focused on agricultural projects for young people but now also includes other activities such as open kindergartens, where parents and their children can spend time with other families with the support of a pre-school teacher (see http://www.4h.no).

Place-based learning in ECEC services in Scotland

Scotland, like Norway, has relatively easy access to its extensive countryside and nature has often been a popular learning tool with many urban local authorities which in the past have had their own outdoor centres. Similarly, there has been a long-standing interest in the relationship between schools and communities, contributing in the late 1990s to a pioneering programme known as New Community Schools, which drew on the vision of schools as institutions for delivering lifelong and community learning, and has fed into subsequent education strategies (Cohen, 2005: 6). Most recently, this led to the adoption of the Curriculum for Excellence in 2004 as a framework for active learning for children aged 3–18, including increased use of the outdoors and the natural environment, and more extensive community involvement (Scottish Government Curriculum Review Group, 2004).

The potential this has offered for more radical approaches to the use of place-based learning has been strengthened by the establishment of the Scottish Parliament in 1999 (subsequently the Scottish government) and by the increased freedom offered to local authorities through the 2007 Concordat agreed by the new Scottish Nationalist government and Scotland's local government association, the Convention of Scottish Local Authorities (Scottish Government, 2007).

Scotland's indigenous languages, in particular Gaelic, were early beneficiaries of the Concordat. Legislation enacted in 2000 required local authorities to include an account of their Gaelic medium provision in their reporting and allowed ministers to set national priorities which included Gaelic (Scottish Parliament, 2000). While still limited, Gaelic medium education at primary and nursery school level is increasing and has extended into urban areas as well as upwards in age. One Gaelic school in Glasgow is now offering Gaelic medium education for children aged 3–18 (Bòrdna Gàidhlig, 2012; Glasgow City Council, 2012).

Place-based learning has also benefited from a focus on culture which uses as its basis the broad definition adopted by UNESCO in its Declaration on Cultural Policies in Mexico City in 1982. This encompasses 'not only the arts and letters but also modes of life, the fundamental rights of the human being, value systems, traditions and beliefs' (UNESCO, 1982: 1). With the establishment of a Culture Commission in Scotland in 2000, local authorities began to develop their own local cultural strategies, using this broad definition (Scottish Government/Culture Commission, 2005: 276).

The Outer Hebrides strategy emphasizes culture as playing an 'essential part in creating and sustaining socially and economically healthy communities' (Comhairle nan EileanSiar, 2006: 6–7). The retention and development of Gaelic are seen as central to this strategy and one example of what this means can be seen in a traditional song and rhymes pack developed for pre-school services and in a pack for Gaelic learner parents of children under 3 based on the principle of family learning:

> A mum described how her 2 and 3 year olds, having learned a song at Rionnagan Beaga, a Gaelic child and family group, in the morning, sang it to their older sister after school and their dad at tea time. She estimates that they had spent at least half an hour as a family singing the song with each other at home and they all have new vocabulary. (Grey, 2011: n.p.)

In the far north of Scotland, the Shetland Islands' cultural strategy makes strong links between the islands' environment, history and cultural traditions and economic and social regeneration. They identify a clear role for education in this, including promoting interest in local dialects, place names, literature and traditional crafts (Shetland Islands Council, 2004, 2009).

In Scotland's crofting areas in the north and west of Scotland, a partnership formed in 2009 between the Scottish Crofting Federation and the Soil Association Scotland has been helping schools to develop awareness of their crofting heritage – a traditional form of land use (Rodway, 2012; see also the case study).

Notwithstanding these developments, the most visible strand within place-based learning to be found in Scotland's school and pre-school services lies in the increasing interest in and use of natural and outdoor environments. The Curriculum for Excellence is now being taken forward by the Scottish Nationalist government which took office in 2007. Its development has seen a growing emphasis on outdoor environments. Guidance published in 2010 by Learning and Teaching Scotland, the then non-departmental body responsible for promoting the curriculum, further details how the outdoors can be used in different subject areas in implementing the principles of the curriculum.

This includes:

- encouraging and capitalizing on the potential to experience learning and new challenges in the outdoor environment (health and well-being)
- teachers taking advantage of opportunities for study in the local, natural and built environments (science)
- learning outdoors through field trip visits and input by external contributors (social science).

The guidance contains an impassioned call for all educators and their partners to create, develop and deliver outdoor learning opportunities which can be embedded in the new curriculum:

> From school grounds to streets of cities, forests to farms, ponds to paths, coastlines to castles, moors to mountains, Scotland has a rich wealth of outdoor learning opportunities which will help children and young people make connections within and across the curriculum areas. (Learning and Teaching Scotland, 2010: 26)

The guidance has been supported by the appointment of a national development officer now based in Education Scotland – a new national body supporting quality and improvement in Scottish education. Education Scotland reports significantly raised awareness of outdoor learning and a developing spectrum of provision ranging from what are described as 'place-ambivalent' activities – which just happen to take place outside – to those taking place in very specific outdoor locations.

Some local authorities now have considerable experience in supporting their nurseries and schools in developing outdoor activities. Fife Council has been one of the pioneers in forest kindergartens, initiating a programme in 2005 with the help of Norwegian guidance and a visit to Norway. A 2012 survey found that over 70% of their own nurseries and partner nurseries are now involved in some way with their forest kindergarten and 'foreshore' (beach environment) programmes, alongside a range of outdoor play experiences including holiday and out-of-school play provision (Fife Council, 2012).

Local authorities are working with a variety of national agencies with an interest in this area. These include Forestry Commission Scotland and the Forest Education Initiative, Scottish National Heritage, Historic Scotland and the John Muir Trust, which, together with Education Scotland and Grounds for Learning, have come together in an ambitious 'Places' project. The aim is for a school or nursery or other institution to choose a place within walking distance to develop as an environment for outdoor learning. The project is likely to include a significant number of pre-school services – around half of the Forest education initiatives currently relate to this age group – but also reflects the different perspectives of the partners. For example, Scottish National Heritage has more of a focus on family learning and the environment. Some 50 Places projects for children aged 3–18 were confirmed in 2012, with the target 370 (Wilson, 2012, 2013).

There have been many developments in place-based learning in Scotland over the last decade but there are also still significant constraints. The main focus within education has been on outdoor learning and activities and there is no clear framework promoting a full understanding of place-based learning, although a number of local authority culture strategies reflect a wider understanding than the use of natural environments. The Scottish Government framework, published in 2008 as a means of taking forward the Curriculum for Excellence, refers to the need for an 'emphasis on Scottish contexts, Scottish cultures and Scotland's history and place in the world' (Scottish Government, 2008: 5). But the principles of place-based learning as a cross-departmental strategy at a *local level*, which have been the aim of local authority culture strategies, are not sufficiently understood and do not always work out in practice. For example, in the Shetland Islands, where knitting is not only valued as part of the islands' traditional culture but also contributes to its economy, education department support for knitting classes was stopped in 2010 (although some schools still continue with these).

Too many of the activities are short-term projects and are not being absorbed into services on a permanent basis. For example, Scotland has seen considerable investment over the past decade in the arts but the use of the arts in ECEC is still insufficiently understood and supported long term.

The greatest constraint on place-based learning in Scotland's ECEC services is structural. Scotland lacks the level of formal provision of ECEC services which Norway has developed over the last few decades. The most extensive area of provision is that of local authority school nurseries, to which children only gain access at age 3 and then only on a part-time basis. This significantly limits the activities which can be undertaken. While the Scottish government is committed to expanding the hours and access to services, it remains to be seen whether this will be sufficient to enable place-based learning to fulfil its potential within Scotland's ECEC services.

Scotland case study: Dunrossness Nursery and Primary School, Shetland

Dunrossness Primary, located in the south mainland of the Shetland Islands, has 140 children aged 3–12 years. It stands on around an acre of land and is one of some 60 schools and school nurseries supported by Crofting Connections in the crofting areas in the north and west of Scotland from Argyll to Shetland.

Crofts are small agricultural units held subject to the provisions of crofting legislation brought in to protect families from eviction, which historically led to thousands of crofters losing their land and homes in what is known as the Highland Clearances. Crofting Connections aims to help schools develop awareness in children of their crofting heritage and its future, helping to keep it alive for the benefit of rural communities as well as increasing children's understanding of environmental issues.

The head teacher of Dunrossness Primary School is an ecologist and has approached the use of its land from this perspective. There is a nature garden with a pond – with an occasional stickleback – and native Shetland plant species which the nursery uses to look at seasonal changes.

Poly-tunnels are used for growing vegetables and fruit – the nursery children grow peas and flowers or other plants for projects. The vegetables are used in the school canteen. Families, including a few grandparents, help with a rota for taking care of the poly-tunnel during the summer – the holiday out-of-school club also helps with this. They have *eco* days and invite other schools.

A third area is a meadow with wild orchids and other flowers and plants.

The school builds awareness of the local community and their local heritage from the nursery upwards, culminating in a heritage project in the last year of primary school. The nursery children visit and research where they are living and where all the children come from – the school has children from quite a few countries.

The school became a Crofting Connections school in 2009 through the local Crofting Association. Crofting Connections provides a little money – £2000 – which helps in growing and studying the yield from heritage vegetables and crops – for example, Shetland potatoes and grain. The project also helps the school to network with other schools.

(*Source*: Interview with Lesley Simpson, head teacher, Dunrossness Primary School, Shetland, 29 May 2012; Rodway, 2012)

Final thoughts

Place-based learning is an important means through which services for young children can make learning real and authentic, promoting active learning approaches and helping children to understand and relate to local culture, history, traditions and the natural environment.

Making use of natural environments is the most straightforward and easily understood element within place-based learning. Outdoor learning has obvious advantages for children's physical health and is a good learning environment, socially as well as educationally. Space and natural challenges reduce conflict and bullying and help in developing cooperative skills while conducting real-life tasks (Forestry Commission Scotland, 2011; Mårtensson et al., 2009).

Neuroscientists point to nature as an ideal environment for the free 'chaotic' play required for the developing brain. In the words of the renowned Finnish neurophysiologist, Matti Bergstrom: 'In nature they find a reflection of their own "possibility" world' (Bergstrom and Ikonen, 2005: 13).

But, as we noted earlier, place-based learning is more than outdoor education and making use of natural environments. It is about children's understanding of and engagement with the communities they grow up in: their people, their history, society and economy and their contribution to children's sense of place and identity wherever they live – in urban as well as rural areas (see also Chapter 10). This can be more complex than is sometimes thought. Our understanding of 'place' and 'identity' has to a significant extent been shaped by historical anthropological perceptions of culture as 'separate, bounded and unique wholes' (Hastrup and Olwig, 1996: 3). Today, anthropologists no longer take this view and our understanding of culture acknowledges the concept of place and identity as more complex and porous than simplistic images associated with local or national identity.

In recent decades, researchers have been examining the experience of children who have crossed borders, within or across countries, or whose families do not share the cultural values and practices of others in the community (for further discussion, see Chapter 6). Studies point to the importance of a better understanding of the diverse cultural contexts and multiple identities of the children and families for whom our services exist (Bertram and Pascal, 2008; Vandenbroeck, 2009).

Place based-learning is now seen as a more dynamic process – with the key provided by children and families themselves. By engendering an understanding of place and identity in its rich diversity, our services can not only engage with children more effectively but can also become cultural meeting places in which the voices of all children are heard, and where mutual respect is the norm.

Table 8.1   Key factors in supporting and promoting place-based learning at different levels

Level	Key factors
National	• Resource and legislative requirements for development of high-quality ECEC services. • Framework for cross-departmental and professional working. • Curriculum supporting local cross-curriculum and, where necessary, non-measurable outcomes. • Support for use of arts in services. • Inclusion in workforce initial education and professional development. • Support in developing models and guidance for place-based learning in different settings.
Local authority/ community	• Political support for resourcing and prioritizing place-based learning. • Effective community planning and cross-departmental cooperation. • Providing professional development for schools and ECEC services.
ECEC/school	• Gaining parental support through information and inclusive discussions. • Effective planning and cooperation with partners for use of local geographical areas and traditional, cultural and community resources, including families from minority languages or cultures. • Effective support, training and development of staff and volunteers.

 Summary

- This chapter has described experiences in developing place-based learning in ECEC services in Norway and Scotland, examining the varied purposes which it serves – from economic regeneration to active learning and the physical, social and emotional development of young children.
- It has explored multi-disciplinary perspectives on place, culture and identity and the broad approach across departments, and work with partners, required in its effective implementation.
- Use of the natural environment and outdoor learning and play has been particularly important in Norway and is the feature of place-based learning that is most easily understood and evident in Scotland, but it can be as relevant to urban as rural areas in helping children to understand and connect with their local community, culture and traditions.
- In Norway, where the development of place-based learning has been the most systematic, it has been associated with strategies to protect rural communities from depopulation and promote economic development and has benefited from the development of a substantial network of ECEC services attended by nearly 90% of Norwegian children aged 1–6 years.

- In Scotland, an increasing focus on national identity contributed to the development of local cultural strategies but the principles of place-based learning are less well developed than in Norway and in respect of ECEC it has far fewer community services.
- 'Place' and 'culture' have traditionally been seen as corresponding to particular localities. But place-based learning is a dynamic process with the key provided by children and families themselves. As such, it offers a tool for a better understanding of the multiple meanings which place, culture and identity can have for children in an increasingly diverse society and globalized world, and, potentially, it gives us a powerful means of enabling our services to become cultural meeting places.
- The key factors in supporting and promoting place-based learning are summarized in Table 8.1 above, requiring action at the level of national and local government and services themselves.

Questions for discussion

1. What are the reasons for promoting place-based learning from a pedagogical perspective?
2. What other reasons are there for developing it as part of the curriculum?
3. What kind of support is required at different levels (national, local and pre-school/school) for the successful implementation of place-based learning?
4. How can children help us make our ECEC services cultural meeting places and what is required for this to happen? (*Higher-level question*)

Further reading

Levels 5 and 6

Bergstrom, M. and Ikonen, P. (2005) 'Space to play, room to grow', *Children in Europe*, 8 (April): 12–13.
This paper provides an easily accessible summary of the implications of research on brain development and why nature's empty space is the best environment for young children's uninhibited learning.

Cohen, B. and Milne, R. (2007) *Northern Lights: Building Better Childhoods in Norway*. Edinburgh: Children in Scotland.
This is a short publication providing a snapshot of the Norwegian approach to children's services in comparison with Scotland and an introduction to place-based learning in the county of Nordland in northern Norway.

Levels 6 and 7

Bertram, T. and Pascal, C. (2008) *Opening Windows: A Handbook for Enhancing Equity and Diversity in Early Childhood Settings*. Birmingham: Amber Publications.
This text offers a critical examination of how the ECEC systems of five European countries are serving the children of recent immigrants and of what their parents want for them in these settings.

Solstad, K.J., Nygaard, V. and Solstad, M. (eds) (2012) Kunnskapsløftet 2006 Samisk – mot en likeverdig skole? [The Knowledge Promotion Reform 2006 Sami – Towards an Equitable Education?] NF-report no. 1/2012. Bodø: Nordland Research Institute.
This report provides a critical analysis of Sami educational reform.

Websites

Children in Europe – www.childrenineurope.org
Published in 15 languages, this website offers an insight into ECEC research, policies and practice across Europe and includes issues on place-based and outdoor learning.

Crofting Connections – www.croftingconnections.com
This is a project begun in 2009, working with schools to develop children's awareness of their crofting heritage. Useful reports on how schools are approaching this are included.

Norwegian Directorate for Education and Training – www.udir.no/stottemeny/English
This site includes the Norwegian national curriculum (LK06) and the Framework Plan for the Content of Kindergartens.

Norwegian Ministry of Education and Research – www.regjeringen.no/en/dep/kd.html?id=586
This website is in English with links to relevant resources such as the Education Act, information about ongoing development work, etc.

References

Bergstrom, M. and Ikonen, P. (2005) 'Space to play, room to grow', *Children in Europe*, 8: 12–13. Edinburgh: Children in Scotland.
Bertram, T. and Pascal, C. (2008) *Opening Windows: A Handbook for Enhancing Equity and Diversity in Early Childhood Settings*. Birmingham: Amber Publications.
Bòrdna Gàidhlig (2012) http://www.gaidhlig.org.uk/bord/en/our-work/education
Cohen, B.J. (2005) Interagency collaboration in context: the joining up agenda. In: A. Glaister and B. Glaister (eds) *Inter-Agency Collaboration*. Edinburgh: Dunedin Academic Press, pp. 1–13.
Comhairle nan EileanSiar (2006) Outer Hebrides Cultural Strategy 2006–10. Available at: http://www.cne-siar.gov.uk/artsandculture/documents/OHCS%202006.pdf
Dewey, J. (1916/1997) *Democracy and Education*. New York: Simon & Schuster.
Fife Council (2012) *Survey of Forest and Foreshore Kindergartens*. Kirkcaldy: Fife Council.
Forestry Commission Scotland (2011) *Natural Play: Making a Difference to Children's Learning and Wellbeing*. A longitudinal study of the Forestry Commission Scotland/Glasgow City Council/Merrylee Primary School Partnership, 2008–2011. Glasgow: Forestry Commission.
Frank, B. and Trevarthen, C. (2012) Intuitive meaning: supporting impulses for interpersonal life in the sociosphere of human knowledge, practice and language. In: A. Foolen, U.M. Lüdtke,

T.P. Racine and J. Zlatev (eds) *Moving Ourselves, Moving Others: The Role of (E)Motion for Inter-subjectivity, Consciousness and Language*. Amsterdam: John Benjamins, pp. 262–305.

Glasgow City Council (2012) Glasgow Gaelic School home page. Available at: http://www.glasgowgaelic.glasgow.sch.uk/

Grey, J. (2011) Young Musicians' Hebrides. Personal communication to authors, 24 June.

Hastrup, K. and Fog Olwig, K. (eds) (1996) *Siting Culture: The Shifting Anthropological Object*. London: Routledge.

Learning and Teaching Scotland (LTS) (2010) *Curriculum for Excellence through Outdoor Learning*. Edinburgh: LTS.

Lie, S., Vedum, T.V. and Dullerud, O. (2011*) Natur-, frilufts. og gårdsbarnehager. Hva kjennetegner dem? Hvabetyr de for barnasutvikling? [Nature, outdoor and farm kindergartens. What characterizes them? How do they influence children's development?]* Report no. 8/2011. Elverum: Hedmark University College.

Milne, A.A. (1926) *Winnie the Pooh*. London: Methuen and Co.

Mårtensson, F., Boldemann, C., Blennow, M., Söderström, M. and Grahn, P. (2009) Outdoor environmental assessment of attention promoting outdoor settings for preschool children. *Health and Place*, 15(4): 1149–1157.

Norwegian Directorate for Education and Training (2012a) The Core Curriculum. Available at: http://www.udir.no/Stottemeny/English/Curriculum-in-English/Core-Curriculum-in-five-languages

Norwegian Directorate for Education and Training (2012b) Sami Curriculum. Available at: http://www.udir.no/Stottemeny/English/Curriculum-in-English/_english/Sami-Curriculum

Norwegian Ministry of Culture and Norwegian Ministry of Education and Research (2012) The Cultural Rucksack. Available at: http://kulturradet.no/the-cultural-rucksack

Norwegian Ministry of Education and Research (2003a) The Framework Plan for the Content and Tasks of Kindergartens. Available at: http://www.regjeringen.no/upload/KD/Vedlegg/Barnehager/engelsk/FrameworkPlanfortheContentandTasksofKindergartens.pdf

Norwegian Ministry of Education and Research (2003b) Rammeplan for førskolelærerutdanningen. Abbreviated version in English at: http://www.regjeringen.no/en/dep/kd/documents/reports-and-actionplans/Actionplans/2006/Curriculum-regulations-.html?id=587302

Norwegian Ministry of Education and Research, Ministry of Trade and Industry and Ministry of Local Government and Regional Development (2008) Action Plan: Entrepreneurship in Education and Training. Available at: http://www.regjeringen.no/en/dep/kd/documents/reports-and-actionplans/Actionplans/2009/entrepreneurship-in-education-and-traini.html?id=575005

Rodway, P. (2012) Crofting Connections. Personal communication to authors, 27 April. See http://www.croftingconnections.com

Rønning, W. (2010) Norwegian Teachers' Conceptions of and Stances towards Active Learning. PhD thesis. Leeds: School of Education, University of Leeds.

Scottish Government Curriculum Review Group (2004) *A Curriculum for Excellence*. Edinburgh: Scottish Government Curriculum Review Group.

Scottish Government/Culture Commission (2005) *Our Next Major Enterprise: Final Report of the Cultural Commission*. Edinburgh: Scottish Government.

Scottish Government (2007) *Concordat between the Scottish Government and Local Government*. Edinburgh: Scottish Government.

Scottish Government (2008) *Building the Curriculum 3: A Framework for Learning and Teaching*. Edinburgh: Scottish Government.

Scottish Parliament (2000) *Standards in Scotland's Schools Act*. Edinburgh: HMSO.

Shetland Islands Council (2004*) A Vision for Cultural Life in Shetland 2004–8*. Shetland Islands Council.

Shetland Islands Council (2009) *On the Cusp: Shetland's Cultural Strategy 2009–13*. Shetland Islands Council.

Statistics Norway (2012) Barnehagar, barn og tilsette. Fylke. Available at: http://www.ssb.no/emner/02/barn_og_unge/2012/tabeller/barnehage/bhage0200.html

UNESCO (1982) Mexican City Declaration on Cultural Policies. Available at: http://portal.unesco.org/culture/en/files/35197/11919410061mexico_en.pdf/mexico_en.pdf

University of Nordland (2012) http://www.uin.no/omuin/ansatte/administrativstotte/studieplaner/Pages/default.aspx (the Norwegian text has been translated into English by the authors).

Vandenbroeck, M. (2009) Let us disagree. *European Early Childhood Education Research Journal*, 17(2): 165–170.

Wilson, J. (2012) National Development Officer for Outdoor Learning, interviewed 30 May.

Wilson, J. (2013) National Development Officer for Outdoor Learning, interview updated 9 January.

CHAPTER 9

PERCEPTIONS OF USING THE OUTDOORS IN EARLY CHILDHOOD EDUCATION AND CARE CENTRES IN ENGLAND, HUNGARY AND DENMARK: SOME QUESTIONS ABOUT THE RECRUITMENT OF MALE WORKERS

Claire Cameron

Overview

Very few men work in early childhood care and education (ECEC) centres. Searching for explanations for this, some researchers have argued that ECEC centres need to promote working outdoors in order to recruit more men. In this chapter, I consider the relationship between being a male worker and being outdoors, using data from a study of the views of practitioners and experts in three countries: England, Denmark and Hungary, as expressed when they observed films of everyday practice in the three countries. I argue that there are two main orientations to practice: a care orientation and a pedagogic orientation, and that these broadly map onto two perspectives about being outdoors: 'safety and care' and 'freedom to roam'. There were few comments about gender and male workers and no indication that being male was linked to being outdoors. However, I conclude that gendered practice is more likely to be visible in a care orientation to practice.

Introduction

In 2012, the first male undergraduate at Norland College for Childcare Training made national news in England, confirming that few men work with young children in early childhood education and care services. As Roberts-Holmes and Brownhill (2011: 128) point out, the workforce is 'virtually gender segregated'. Explanations for this usually centre on the generally poor conditions of work in ECEC and the normative association of 'care' work with women, whether as mothers, teachers or childcare workers (Cameron et al., 1999). Indeed, the proportion of male workers in ECEC services remains below 10% even in countries, such as Denmark and Norway, where there has been considerable policy and practice effort to realize gender equality opportunities in general, as well as in professional education programmes (Cameron, 2012; Cameron and Moss, 2007). One of the possible explanations for this is that what we define as ECEC practice is itself gendered. In other words, not only is the work carried out by women but the practice that is defined as 'care' is more likely to be evaluated as 'female', while practice that is defined as 'education' or 'pedagogy' is not so closely bound up with a gendered identity (Cameron, 2012). Timmerman and Schreuder (2008: 13) argue that an important element in promoting both the professionalism of ECEC staff and their role in stimulating a wide range of developmental opportunities for children is to avoid 'continuing to reduce the characteristics and qualities needed in the childcare sector to "female nature"'.

In this view, early childhood practice is 'pedagogic' rather than being primarily about 'care', and pedagogic practice is less associated with one gender or the other. By 'pedagogic', I am referring to the holistic, child-centred and learning-oriented tradition which embraces children's risk taking and values self-expression, common in Nordic countries (Jensen, 2011), and by 'care' I am referring to being mostly concerned with adults 'looking after' children, especially their bodily health and well-being, in early childhood settings (Bennett, 2006; Jensen, 2011). Although the divisions are less marked than in previous decades, the 'care' orientation is more associated with provision for children under 3 and with 'split' systems (such as in France; see Chapter 5), and, arguably, with settings in countries such as England, where the main occupation is known as 'nursery' or 'childcare worker' rather than having an educational training as preparation for practice (for further discussion, see Chapter 2). Such general orientations to practice may have an impact on male workers; it may be that few men work in ECEC because the organization and conception of the work keeps them out.

There is a growing body of literature about ECEC practice and use of the outdoors (e.g. Aasen et al., 2009; Austin, 2007; Waller, 2010). International comparisons show that Norway, as part of a Scandinavian tradition, values outdoor space highly, having a minimum outdoor space requirement for ECEC settings that is six times that of indoor space requirements and more than three times the OECD average (OECD, 2012). Norwegian ECEC settings reflect a cultural belief that experiential familiarity with the natural world outdoors, including the climate, 'contributes to the emotional health of children, to their sense of independence and autonomy' (OECD, 2006: 198). (For further discussion of Norway, see Chapter 8.)

Such comparisons also show that there are culturally informed distinctions in the valuing of outdoor space. For example, Taguma et al. (2012) found that the New Zealand curricula for ECEC does not prescribe or discuss outdoor activities as being important, while Sweden's ECEC curricula does. Little and Wyver (2007: n.p.) argued that, in Australia, 'legislation and regulations in the early childhood sector are becoming increasingly restrictive and prescriptive with an overemphasis on risk management'. In Ireland, 11% of childcare provision has no access to a dedicated outdoor space (Kernan and Devine, 2010). England's most recent statutory framework regulating ECEC services notes only that outdoor space should be 'fit for purpose' and that children should have access to outdoor space on a daily basis with no minimum space requirements (DfE, 2012: para 3.53).

Examining ECEC services from an international perspective has led both Mooney et al. (2003) and Bennett (2006) to conclude that while there are a number of similarities across countries, there are also marked differences (see the discussion in Chapter 2). These differences are sufficient to warrant a distinction between, on the one hand, English language countries, where services are characterized by the least paid parental leave; mostly age-segregated services; the favouring of private market provider participation; and relatively high levels of low trained, poorly paid childcare workers, and on the other, countries in the Nordic tradition, where there are generous parental leave entitlements; extensive non-school and age-integrated services; an entitlement for children to access services; generally high levels of public sector provision; and a well-trained workforce. Bennett (2006) termed the first group 'pre-primary' (being mostly concerned with preparation for school) and the second 'Nordics' (having more holistic and child-centred developmental concerns).

In this chapter, I explore this distinction further. I argue that the pre-primary group mostly conceptualizes the purpose of ECEC as catering for 'care' needs and preparation for school, while the Nordic or 'pedagogic' group is more in line with seeing children as active and in charge of their own learning, and ECEC as a place for citizenship. I will employ the distinction between 'care' and 'pedagogy' as characterizing two approaches to using the outdoors. I will also examine the premise put forward by Emilsen and Koch (2010: 551), who argue that 'the outdoors corresponds better to many men's interest' and should be promoted in order to recruit more male workers into ECEC, and conclude that the prospects are not promising.

Carrying out the research

This chapter draws on data collected for a European Commission funded study called *Care Work in Europe* (2001–2005) (see Cameron and Moss, 2007 for full details). The focus of the multi-method project was the quality of employment in 'care work' in six countries.

As part of the study, three films were made in 'ordinary' early childhood services offering full-day childcare and education, and in each case focused on the practice of two workers over the course of a day.[1] The films, made in England, Denmark and

Hungary, once edited, were shown to groups of 'stakeholders' in ECEC who had detailed knowledge of practice: practitioners and 'experts' from the fields of leadership, training and research.[2] These stakeholders were the primary data source. They were asked to observe and comment on the practice they saw. The films pose an open interview question: What do you think when you see this? The reflections and discussions that emerged from the stimulus of the film were analysed as reflecting contemporary perspectives on aspects of early childhood practice, perspectives which differed across the three cultural and professional contexts.

Posing an open question is a potentially useful approach to studying cross-national understandings of professional roles in ECEC. This is because the visual prompt of the film can bring to the surface perspectives that are embedded and unarticulated, while asking more specific questions can run the risk of assuming common knowledge. Using an open question reduces researcher influence on the discourse.

The three films

All the films followed a similar structure, and were made by the same cameraman and edited in conjunction with the principal researcher in each country. All show two workers who had agreed to be 'in profile' for the day, and who had typical professional qualifications for that country. Preparatory visits familiarized both children and staff with the cameraman and the camera, and permission from parents was sought. The films included children and parents being greeted, departures, group activities, one-to-one activities and conversations, meal times, being outdoors, toileting and sleep or quiet times.

The film made in England was of a small privately run day nursery for children aged 2–5 years located in the rear of a community centre in a highly urbanized area. The nursery offered flexibility to parents, who could book sessions by the hour; few children were full-time attendees.[3] There was one male and one female worker in profile. In Denmark, the film was of practice in a centre for children aged 1–6 years, with one part of the centre for younger children and one for older. It was run by the city municipality, with access to green open spaces. The two workers in focus were female, but one of the other staff seen in the film was male. Most children attended full-time. Finally, the Hungarian film was made in a 'methodological' centre (one known for its excellence) for children aged 0–3 years. Run by the city municipality, 80% of the children attended full-time. As is typical for Hungarian nurseries, the children were organized into groups of 12, each with two qualified workers, and one support staff for two children's groups. All the workers were female.

The stakeholder sessions

In each country, the films were shown and perspectives recorded, in sequence. First, the film was shown to the practitioners whose practice was the primary focus, the children and their parents. As well as collating their perspectives, this step was part of the ethical procedures adopted in the project. Second, the practitioners (termed 'care workers' here for ease of reference) met on two occasions with colleagues from another childcare centre and viewed the (subtitled) films from the other two countries. Third, all three films were shown to specially invited groups of 'experts', known for their contribution to the early childhood field. All the stakeholders brought to bear their wide experience when formulating views about the practice they saw. The filmed practice made the familiar become strange and opened a discursive space around practice knowledge. In total, in each country there were 27 transcripts of discussions among stakeholders, from nine showings of the films. Transcripts were summarized and used to write country reports (Cameron and Clark, 2004; Jensen, 2004; Korintus et al., 2004). This chapter focuses on data illustrating practitioner and expert perspectives in the summaries and country reports,[4] and not those of children and parents.

Being outdoors

Going outside was a dominant feature of the Danish film. Almost the first comment made by English care workers about the Danish film was that a baby was left outside to sleep, with little apparent means of observation or ensuring security for that baby. One said:

> I mean, you can't see whether there's, like, a fence around, or whatever. I know that sounds a bit dramatic, but just leaving the baby outside in the pushchair ... I mean, I was left outside in a pushchair as a child and my mum was fine about that, but...

Jensen (2011: 151) refers to this as a 'classic example of amazement (expressed by visitors to Danish early childhood centres) that very young children have their naps outdoors, even in the coldest weather'. For the English care workers, this was not just amazement but a concern for the safety of the child, which might be at risk if left outside. The phenomenon of babies sleeping outside was not remarked upon by Danish and Hungarian study informants, suggesting that it is a more usual practice and less worthy of comment than for the English practitioners.

Hungarian and English study informants commented on the amount of outdoor space there was in the Danish centre. Hungarian care workers 'expressed envy when they saw the conditions and the equipment in the courtyard' which was of a 'great size' and with 'various opportunities for play' in comparison to their own. One of the workers said:

> At our institution, we have an about 2–2.5 metre concrete-covered surface, which is a very bad solution. It is covered with paving-blocks, a few of which have sunken, which you cannot change. And there is a lawn surface, too. I mean, it is not optimal. Here (in the courtyard seen in the film) you can always let them go about safely, while there (at the childcare centre of the care worker), you always have to ban them from doing various things, otherwise it would be dangerous. That is all very bad.

This comment about safety and avoiding danger through controlling children's movements when outdoors is another example of risk-based thinking about being outside. The English male care worker also commented on the amount of space in the Danish film: 'It's great, all the space they've got. They must love all that. All the little bushes. They must really enjoy all that.'

His concern was more about the facilitation of enjoyment through the outdoor environment; bushes could be considered a supervisory risk, but this worker's line of thinking was more about what the children would 'love'. One of the English 'experts' said: 'I was struck by the space and freedom that they had', and another by the amount of time the Danish children spent outside. English care workers also thought the Hungarian film showed a 'lovely outdoor space (with) a nice garden' but also that use of the space must be 'very controlled' because the children seemed to stay in quite a limited area.

The discourse about being outside from the English and Hungarian perspectives was characterized by concerns about safety from danger versus enjoyment of space and freedom to roam. Arguably, a predominant concern about safety is aligned with a 'care' oriented perspective, while a concern with promoting freedom is more associated with a 'learning' or 'pedagogic' perspective.

All the study informants in all the countries valued children being outside. This was expressed in various ways. For example, there were frequent critical comments about the small size of the outdoor space in the English film. One of the Danish practitioners said she had a physical reaction to the English outdoor space: 'that makes me feel claustrophobic'. Other Danish study participants commented adversely on the 'many plastic tools and the artificial grass, the flower painting on the walls and they were puzzled about the lack of real flowers' (Jensen, 2004: 26). These comments can be seen in the context of a cultural and professional tradition. As Jensen (2011: 151–152) puts it, 'the outdoor life is central in Danish practice', where children can express themselves freely, 'play without interruption', 'children can get the feeling of being lost' and be physically challenged, with the 'obligatory sandbox' and where planned learning also takes place. The Danish perspective puts a high priority on 'nature' and 'freedom to roam', and situates this as learning, not risk.

Movement between indoors and outdoors

Practitioners in England commented on the movement between outdoor and indoor spaces. The children in the Danish film could be seen going outside and inside on their own, whereas in the English and Hungarian films children had clear 'outside' and 'inside' times. Hungarian study informants referred to this as part of the philosophy the Danish workers had of valuing children's 'freedom ... Their approach to child upbringing (education) is more permissive and they support the acts of children to a greater extent than the English practice, where in many cases it was the adult who told the children what to do'. Another informant thought this was not only about freedom but that Danish workers 'provide them with the opportunity to learn according to their own space and character, not only educate them' (Korintus et al., 2004: 16). In these comments, Hungarian study informants characterized the Danish practice as freedom to move around and self-directed learning, in contrast to the English practice, which they considered more adult-led.

English workers contrasted what they saw with their own practice. They saw the Danish children being able to wander between indoor and outdoor spaces as freedom that was difficult for them to provide. They saw it as not possible to provide staff supervision both for children who wanted to be outside and those that did not, while practice in the Danish film seemed to indicate that 'they don't seem bothered about' staff being with the children constantly or not. Within the context of thinking from a perspective of 'care', notions of freedom are fraught with dilemma. Participants in the expert group in England thought that what they saw in the Danish approach was a 'live and let live' ethos. One expressed this as deciding:

> that live and let live is valuing the strengths of children, that they can manage on their own, they don't have to be protected, and not having that very vulnerable view … that view of children as very vulnerable. Or whether it's don't care too much, really, just get on with it.

Here, English study informants raised their ambivalence about the idea of freedom to roam. They saw a tension between valuing children's strengths and ensuring that children felt cared about. Too much freedom might feel like a lack of care.

By contrast, the Danish workers were puzzled about why the children in the English film could not apparently move freely around the outdoor space. One said: 'Although it is a small playground, it is fenced off, so maybe they do not need the gate to separate the outdoor and indoor areas that the children cannot open themselves.' Furthermore, children of that age (2–4 years) know very well how to go outside on their own, and 'they stressed that practitioners know each child well enough to determine who can go alone' (Jensen, 2004: 27). Jensen (2004) argued that from a Danish perspective, decisions about going outside and inside should be made on the basis of detailed knowledge of each individual child's abilities by practitioners and not on the basis of whole-institution rules and routines.

This discussion about self-directed movement between inside and outside spaces illustrates two different perspectives: freedom to roam is central to the Danish approach; the English and Hungarian approaches appreciated this but raised more safety and care-oriented concerns.

Leaving the premises

Most discussion was provoked by scenes depicting Danish children leaving the premises. In one scene, children and staff visited a stream to watch for wildlife, poking sticks in the water.

The Hungarian workers thought they would not have such an opportunity to leave the nursery and that 'some older care workers in Hungary would have had a heart-attack worrying that the kid would fall into it headfirst'. The practitioners remarked that the Danish worker 'doesn't keep saying, unnecessarily, that they shouldn't go near the (water's) edge' but that they were also surprised it should take place. One said 'as we were watching it, (I was) thinking, my God what would happen next'. Another replied:

> in Austria, they never warn kids of anything and, interestingly, the child mortality rate has not soared. We are the only ones that are so over apprehensive, I'm afraid. Here, she will tell the child once that he shouldn't go further in, and that's all. I mean there are no unnecessary prohibitions, yet the kids will do whatever they are told.

These comments convey a concern with safety and control of children when outside the setting, and also a sense of surprise that the Danish children do what they are told given the freedom they enjoy. English practitioners thought leaving the nursery posed practical problems. As one worker said, parents don't expect the children to go outside:

> Some of our parents don't even bring their children in a coat, we find, because they just bring them in, like, in summer dresses in this sort of weather. Whether they think we're not going to take them outside because it might be drizzly. Or something like that, but we've got spare coats and things which they borrow, and tights and things, but I think some parents just presume that because it's raining a bit … But they have to experience rain as well as the sun.

Next, there were supervisory constraints. Another worker commented that there didn't appear to be any counting of the children as they left the Danish nursery:

> If we went outside we'd have to say to the other staff that you've got four children, and things. You don't seem to see them counting out the children, and letting others know where they're going … They're quite free to sort of go, aren't they?

Ensuring children's safety, as well as protection from the weather, was a key consideration for the English practitioners in thinking about taking children out of the nursery. Two practitioners explained that one adult taking a group of children out put them all at risk:

> A: Because one of them fell off and hurt himself, and she obviously had to comfort that child … and, like, if he hurt his leg and couldn't walk, how far away is she? … You would have thought she'd have another member of staff, just in case.
>
> B: Or had a telephone or something to call, if anything happened.

Having said this, workers from one of the English nurseries represented said they went out almost every day with small groups of children. But in the other nursery, there was never a good time to take children out as a group which may in part have to do with the short hours of attendance of some children.

A third practical consideration was that getting ready to go out took time, which appeared to be built into the expectations of the day in the Danish and Hungarian examples, but was not in England. The Hungarian informants saw that the Danish practitioners put emphasis on encouraging the children to put on their own outdoor clothes, just as they did:

> This (watching children get ready for the garden) is something they do the same way as us ... the encouragement, saying 'you can do it', 'just try it, you will do it'. There's time for them to do it themselves, so it is done virtually the same way as here, before we go out to the garden. This is what I spoke of, that they give extraordinary encouragement, that they can do it alone, or if not, take my hand and I will help. What we missed in the other (English) film, you get here completely. (Korintus et al., 2004: 16)

The response from the English practitioners was to admire the practice, but to acknowledge that it was: 'quicker to put their shoes on. Because otherwise you've got to sit there patiently for half an hour waiting for your child to put their socks and shoes on. And the laces and stuff.'

The practical matters discussed above speak of an underlying concern with safety and protection about whether, in England, leaving the setting was a manageable proposition. But the English practitioners also thought 'being able to go out in nature' offered 'a lot of learning through the environment ... they must have got so much from, like, that ... walk, and having that opportunity to sort of explore' (Cameron and Clark, 2004: 22). This is not quite the same strength of expression as the Danish ideas about freedom to roam, but indicates a value attached to learning and exploring outdoors.

Danish study informants commented that outdoor life represented both a space for playing and an environment for learning. As one member of the expert group said, 'When they are outside in the Danish film, there is some instruction too. They go fishing after snails' (Jensen, 2004: 25). One girl was seen going very close to the edge of the stream. A worker quietly told her to mind the edge. Asked by the researcher if she was being strict, she replied: 'No, I am not, I tell her "I do not think you should go any further out". And I think she feels it too. I am not telling her off...' (Jensen, 2004: 25). Jensen comments (2004: 25):

> the girls should learn about the limitations on their own. The pedagogue's tone of voice is only a little dictating. She expressed equality and respect for the child through her statement: 'I do not think you should go further out'. She did not say: 'do not go further out', and thus she appealed to the child's judgement in a situation in which she may fall into the water.

This example shows how a freedom to roam approach is not necessarily a lack of care, but a finely tuned appeal to judgement (of both child and worker) in a risky situation.

Jensen (2011: 153) refers to the Danish practice of going outdoors as expressing a value that 'children must look and feel part of the wider world, and the world should see them'. Being seen outdoors is part of children's integration into society. Another Danish value of being outdoors is that this space offers a 'haven' for children where the role of adults is less obviously 'in charge'. The Danish expert group thought that in the English film:

the adults participate when they go outside, compared with Denmark. Here they unwind and the children are on their own to sort things out. [In the English film] the adults participate just as much in the outdoor and indoor activities. There is no haven as applied by the Danish institutions. (Jensen, 2004: 25)

The idea of a 'haven' outdoors is arguably another dimension to the idea of freedom to roam as self-directed learning.

Bringing the outdoors in and taking the indoors out

Some activities were noted for transcending traditional outdoor/indoor divisions. In the English film, children took tea party equipment and books outside. A member of the English expert group applauded this: it was 'nicely done, the children have the chance to move things inside and outside', and with a member of staff 'actually sitting on the floor with the children', where she 'seemed very relaxed'. One respondent saw an implicit distinction between the 'learning thing we're going to do and now we're just going to play. So, in the morning when … we're doing the printing, this is just the activity for the day, and this is more like a kind of relax. And it actually felt much more natural'. They also praised the practitioners for tipping a container of sand onto the floor indoors, describing it as a 'bold move'. There were no examples of similar transcending of indoors and outdoors in the Danish and Hungarian videos. In fact, some of the study informants in Denmark were puzzled by the practice of taking the indoors outside and vice versa. One member of the expert group described the practice in the English nursery as 'upside down'. She referred to the worker, who said:

'I have now opened the gate'. But the things they experience inside could easily have taken place outside, the sand for example. It is really turned upside down. The environment may matter, the get-together with the tea could easily have taken place outside. That would change the situation somewhat. I could not see any greenery or any grass tickling their toes. They would get some fresh air, they would get outside.

In her view, the purpose of outdoor life in the English film is to get fresh air, whereas the Danish self-understanding sees a number of purposes. One of the practitioner respondents said 'sometimes we go outside to give the children more space. They went outside to get fresh air. Their playing was almost identical but it just took place outside. We go outside to use our energy' (Jensen, 2004: 26).

Data in this study showed two main lines of thinking about being outdoors: one was a safety and care-oriented approach, the other a freedom to roam approach, where self-directed learning was uppermost. It would be unfair to characterize the care-oriented approach as uninterested in learning, but the discourse was much more hesitant about the learning opportunities as overriding possible risks to safety and care. Having suggested that these two ways of thinking about being outdoors in ECEC practice map onto two perspectives of ECEC in general – pre-primary being linked to a care-oriented approach, and the Nordics linked to a freedom to learn approach – what are the implications for gender roles and recruiting male workers?

Implications for professional gender roles in ECEC and recruiting male workers

Studies of gendered professional roles find few differences in professionals' practice by gender (Cameron et al., 1999). Brandes and colleagues' (2012) observation study of male and female professionals in a controlled ECEC setting found no gendered differences in the practice dimensions of expressing empathy, challenging children and dialogical communication. In Harris and Barnes' (2009) study of 4-year-olds' perceptions of male and female staff in South Australian kindergartens, few differences were noted. Male teachers were noted by children as being good at sports and outdoor games; boys in particular saw value in forging a relationship with male members of staff. But there was so little difference in having a male member of staff that Harris and Barnes questioned whether employing male workers would have any impact at all on children's understandings of gender equity. Rather, they considered that the connection between being male and being good at sports might reinforce gender stereotypes. This study adds weight to the idea that being male and being outdoors are linked but not by any means exclusively. The OECD (2006) report on Australian ECEC suggests that the orientation to practice is dominated by a 'care' philosophy which may influence how being outdoors is conceptualized.

From a Dutch perspective, Timmerman and Schreuder's (2008) survey of ECEC students found little evidence to support the idea of gendered professional roles: 86% of respondents considered male workers to be just as suitable as female. Treating children equally, having eyes in the back of one's head and good discipline were considered very important professional traits. In terms of activities, the two considered most important were letting off steam outside and reading aloud, singing and games. These were not associated with gender-stereotyped professional roles. Moreover, there was no preference for calm, ordered play over noisy play: children's enjoyment and using energy outside was very important to workers. The authors attribute these findings to a pedagogical or learning orientation to practice, and a professional shift away from seeing ECEC as 'care'. They state: 'nowhere in this study [did] we [find] evidence to support the idea of a stereotypical female professional image within the childcare sector' (Timmerman and Schreuder, 2008: 13).

By contrast, Emilsen and Koch (2010) argue that, on the basis of studies of ECEC workers in Norwegian outdoor and ordinary pre-schools, and Austrian ECEC students and kindergarten workers, male workers who work in settings with opportunities to go outdoors 'feel more freedom to work with children in their own way, without the tradition of caring in a "mother's home". As we see it, outdoor pre-schools are a new area that fits more in a masculine image, both in Norway and Austria' (2010: 551) and many men are more comfortable working outdoors. Norway is one of very few countries where there has been considerable attention paid in national policy to recruiting male workers, and, as noted, great value is attached to being outdoors in pre-schools (OECD, 2006; Owen et al., 1998). Yet, despite the policy efforts, the proportion of male workers remains at 9%, although it is higher

(19%) in specialist outdoor pre-schools (Emilsen and Koch, 2010). The tradition of outdoor ECEC work has therefore been largely built on the efforts of a female workforce working in an example of a Nordics/pedagogic approach that prioritizes children's self-expression, risk taking and physical development. Austria, on the other hand, is more safety, care or mother-like in its orientation to practice, and although there has been a recent shift towards seeing ECEC as 'education', the proportion of male workers is under 1% and there is no tradition of outdoor pre-schools (Emilsen and Koch, 2010).

For more male workers to be recruited, it would perhaps be necessary to ensure a shift not just to a higher value placed on being outdoors in ECEC, but also to valuing children's 'freedom to roam', while attending ECEC services. Currently, this would seem to be most clearly in place in those ECEC systems described by Bennett (2006) as 'the Nordics'. But, on its own, this is unlikely to be a sufficient condition. In Denmark, which, as we have seen, has a clear pedagogic orientation and places a high value on being outdoors, only 2% of pedagogues working with children under 3 are male. While around 25% of pedagogue students are male, they prefer older age groups and different settings (such as residential care, youth work) when it comes to employment, and employers often select unqualified young men to fill positions in ECEC settings (Jensen, 2010). On the other hand, in the UK, there is largely a pre-primary and care orientation and a limited value placed on being outdoors (DfE, 2012) but specialized recruitment campaigns have shown that numbers of male ECEC workers can increase quite substantially (Spence, personal communication, 2011).

Final thoughts

This chapter has argued that being outdoors and being male do not have to connect in early childhood education and care. In the study data presented, two lines of thinking about being outdoors could be found. One was about concerns around safety, protection and practical matters; and the other emphasized freedom to roam. I linked these two lines of thinking to orientations to practice: care and pedagogy, which map onto established categories in international comparisons of ECEC. Both lines of thinking value children's enjoyment of being outdoors, but the care orientation discusses more barriers to being outdoors. Recent studies of professional gender roles and early childhood practice find more similarities than differences. Gendered practice is more likely to be visible and articulated in relation to a 'care' orientation to practice. Where a care orientation is in place, this is likely to view ECEC as 'mother-like', and to be associated with gender stereotypical practices, within which male presence offers a stark contrast. In these circumstances, perhaps male workers need to be outdoors to have a clear identity. But, in the absence of a pedagogic approach, male workers are likely to reinforce gender stereotypes, not challenge them.

Summary

1. One possible way to increase the number of male ECEC workers is to put more emphasis on being outdoors. This chapter considers this argument using data from the Care Work in Europe study, using practitioner and expert responses to filmed ECEC practice, including being outdoors in three countries: Denmark, England and Hungary.
2. There were two kinds of response to being outdoors: a care orientation to practice that emphasized safety matters and a pedagogic orientation that was characterized as valuing 'freedom to roam'.
3. Being male and gendered practice was not discussed to any great extent by the study participants. There was little to link being male with being outdoors specifically. Being outdoors and being male do not have to connect but appeared more likely where there was a pedagogic orientation to practice.
4. Alongside a pedagogic approach that values freedom to roam, recruiting male workers is more likely to require specific policy and practical effort directed at training, mentoring and support, as well as attention to the content of practice.

Questions for discussion

1. What, if any, differences are there in the ways male and female workers practise in ECEC settings?
2. Do you agree with the distinction between a care orientation and a pedagogic orientation in working outdoors in ECEC services? If so, how can ECEC settings move away from a care and safety orientation and towards a learning and pedagogic orientation to practice?
3. In your experience, are there any connections between being male and outdoor practice? Can you cite one or more examples from your own experience/practice? (*Higher-level question*)

Further reading

Levels 5 and 6

Roberts-Holmes, G. and Brownhill, S. (2011) Where are the men? A critical discussion of male absence in the early years. In: L. Miller and C. Cable (eds) *Professionalization, Leadership and Management in the Early Years*. London: SAGE, pp. 119–132.
This is an introduction to the issue of male workers in ECEC.

Waller, T. (2010) 'Let's throw that big stick in the river': an exploration of gender in the construction of shared narratives around outdoor spaces. *European Early Childhood
Education Research Journal*, 18(4): 527–542.
Using photographs, video and observation, this study of 3- and 4-year-old girls and boys
investigates how children interact with their natural surroundings, the effect of these experiences on their levels of well-being and the evolving outdoor pedagogy. The research found
that children's play outdoors was rather similar, did not follow gender stereotypes and that
girls were as active as boys.

Levels 6 and 7

Cameron, C., Moss, P. and Owen, C. (1999) *Men in the Nursery: Gender and Caring Work*.
London: Paul Chapman Publishing.
One of the first and most comprehensive studies of male workers in ECEC in England, this
is a primary reference point for the field. Data sources are extensive interviews with 21 male
and female workers in settings focused on children under 3 years of age, and 77 interviews
with parents of children attending these settings.

Emilsen, K. and Koch, B. (2010) Men and women in outdoor play: changing the concepts of
caring findings from Norwegian and Austrian research projects. *European Early Childhood
Education Research Journal*, 18(4): 543–553.
The contrasting approaches to male workers and outdoor activities in ECEC in Austria and
Norway are discussed here. The conclusion is that men with the opportunity to stay outdoors
feel more freedom to work with children in their own way, without the tradition of caring in
a 'mother's home'.

Websites

http://www.koordination-maennerinkitas.de/en/home-page/
The German government has funded widespread recruitment of male early childhood work-
ers. This website hosts information about current projects and networks and the latest
European research.

http://www.meninchildcare.co.uk/index.htm
Hosted in Scotland, this is the most comprehensive UK-based website about male workers in
childcare services, including opportunities for training, conference presentations and current
projects.

Notes

1. ECEC in England is highly diverse and particularly so at the time of the fieldwork.
   Selecting a 'typical' setting was not possible; instead the aim was to select a
   setting where the criteria of (a) offering full day care and (b) typical qualifications
   of staff for the country, were met.
2. The study was inspired by Tobin, Wu and Davidson's (1989) *Pre-school in
   Three Cultures*, and a full account of the method is available in Hansen and
   Jensen (2004).

3. In England, children aged 0–4 attending day nursery do so, on average, for 18 hours per week (Huskinson et al., 2013).
4. Summaries are unpublished: no page numbers are given for quotations.

References

Aasen, W., Grindheim, L. and Waters, J. (2009) The outdoor environment as a site for children's participation, meaning-making and democratic learning: examples from Norwegian kindergartens. *Education 3–13: International Journal of Primary, Elementary and Early Years Education,* 27(1): 5–13.

Austin, R. (ed.) (2007) *Letting the Outside in: Developing Teaching and Learning Beyond the Early Years Classroom.* Stoke on Trent: Trentham Books.

Bennett, J. (2006) 'Schoolifying' early childhood education and care: accompanying pre-school into education. Paper presented at the Contesting Early Childhood conference, Institute of Education, University of London, 10 May.

Brandes, H., Andrae, M. and Roeseler, W. (2012) Does gender make a difference? First results of the German tandem-study about pedagogy. Paper presented at the 22nd EECERA annual conference, Porto, Portugal, 31 August.

Cameron, C. (2012) Neu betrachtet: Männer und Professionalität in der Kinderbetreunng. In: M. Cremers, S. Hoyng, J. Krabel and T. Rohrmann (eds) *Männer in Kitas.* Berlin: Barbara Budrich, pp. 329–348.

Cameron, C. and Clark, A. (2004) Video Observation Study of Centre-based Services for Young Children. UK national report (unpublished national report for Care Work in Europe).

Cameron, C. and Moss, P. (2007) *Care Work in Europe: Current Understandings and Future Directions.* Abingdon: Routledge.

Cameron, C., Moss, P. and Owen, C. (1999) *Men in the Nursery: Gender and Caring Work.* London: Paul Chapman Publishing.

Department for Education (DfE) (2012) Statutory Framework for the Early Years Foundation Stage. Available at: http://media.education.gov.uk/assets/files/pdf/eyfs%20statutory%20framework%20march%202012.pdf

Emilsen, K. and Koch, B. (2010) Men and women in outdoor play: changing the concepts of caring findings from Norwegian and Austrian research projects. *European Early Childhood Education Research Journal,* 18(4): 543–553.

Hansen, H. and Jensen, J. (2004) A Study of Understandings in Care and Pedagogical Practice: Experiences using the Sophos Model in Cross-national Studies: Consolidated Report. Unpublished national report for Care Work in Europe.

Harris, K. and Barnes, S. (2009) Male teacher, female teacher: exploring children's perspectives of teachers' roles in kindergartens. *Early Child Development and Care,* 179(2): 167–181.

Huskinson, T., Pye, J., Medien, K., Dobie, S., Ferguson, C., Gardner, C., et al. (2013) Childcare and Early Years Survey of Parents SFR08/2013. Available at: https://www.gov.uk/government/uploads/system/uploads/attachment_data/file/167890/sfr08-2013.pdf.pdf (accessed 2 July 2013).

Jensen, J.J. (2004) A Study of Pedagogical Practice in Centre Based Services for Young Children: Experiences Using the Sophos Model – The Danish National Report. Unpublished national report for Care Work in Europe.

Jensen, J.J. (2010) The Danish Pedagogue Education: A Case Study – Competence Requirements in Early Childhood Education and Care. A study for the European Commission Directorate General for Education and Culture (unpublished report).

Jensen, J.J. (2011) Understandings of Danish pedagogical practice. In: C. Cameron and P. Moss (eds) *Social Pedagogy and Working with Children and Young People: Where Care and Education Meet.* London: Jessica Kingsley, pp. 141–158.

Kernan, M. and Devine, D. (2010) Being confined within? Constructions of the good childhood and outdoor play in early childhood education and care settings in Ireland. *Children & Society*, 24(5): 371–385.

Korintus, M., Vajda, G. and Török, Z. (2004) Workpackage 10: Video Observation Study of Childcare Work – Hungarian National Report. Unpublished report for Care Work in Europe.

Little, H. and Wyver, S. (2007) Outdoor Play: Does Avoiding the Risks Reduce the Benefits? Available at: http://www.earlychildhoodaustralia.org.au/australian_journal_of_early_childhood/ajec_index_abstracts/outdoor_play_does_avoiding_the_risks_reduce_the_benefits.html (accessed 8 February 2013).

Mooney, A., Candappa, M., Cameron, C., McQuail, S., Moss, P. and Petrie, P. (2003) *Early Years and Childcare International Evidence Project: A Summary*. London: DfES.

Organisation for Economic Co-operation and Development (OECD) (2006) *Starting Strong II: Early Childhood Education and Care*. Paris: OECD.

Organisation for Economic Co-operation and Development (OECD) (2012) *Encouraging Quality in Early Childhood Education and Care (ECEC): International Comparisons – Minimum Standards*. Available at: http://www.oecd.org/edu/preschoolandschool/48483436.pdf.

Owen, C., Cameron, C. and Moss, P. (eds) (1998) Men as Workers in Services for Young Children: Issues of a Mixed Gender Workforce. Bedford Way Papers. Institute for Education, University of London.

Roberts-Holmes, G. and Brownhill, S. (2011) Where are the men? A critical discussion of male absence in the early years. In: L. Miller and C. Cable (eds) *Professionalization, Leadership and Management in the Early Years*. London: SAGE, pp. 119–132.

Taguma, M., Litjens, I. and Makowiecki, K. (2012) Quality Matters in Early Childhood Education and Care, New Zealand, OECD. Available at: http://www.oecd.org/newzealand/NEW%20ZEALAND%20policy%20profile%20-%20published%203-8-2012.pdf (accessed 15 February 2013).

Timmerman, G. and Schreuder, P. (2008) Pedagogical professionalism and gender in daycare. *Gender and Education*, 20(1): 1–14.

Tobin, J., Wu, D.Y. and Davidson, D.H. (1989) *Pre-school in Three Cultures*. New Haven, CT: Yale University Press.

Waller, T. (2010) 'Let's throw that big stick in the river': an exploration of gender in the construction of shared narratives around outdoor spaces. *European Early Childhood Education Research Journal*, 18(4): 527–542.

CHAPTER 10

AGENCY AND CHILDREN'S WELL-BEING

Roger Hancock, Ann Cameron and Ayshe Talay-Ongan

Overview

This chapter draws on a study of children's 'thriving' carried out by an international team of researchers. In that study, seven young girls from seven countries were filmed for a day in their lives, in order to understand how families promote children's thriving. The chapter begins with a brief examination of the concept of 'well-being' and relates this to our 'A Day in the Life' research. Referring to our published findings, we suggest that there is much in our data that helps us understand children's well-being in families. We highlight, in particular, the significance of the 'culture of play' in which our seven young children appear immersed; and, moreover, the importance of promoting their personal agency in order that these children come to know what is truly in their interest. Through four illustrative examples from Peru, Turkey, the USA and the UK, respectively, we examine the subtle ways in which children's agency is promoted jointly by caregivers and the children

(Continued)

(Continued)

themselves. We conclude with a plea that early educationalists, and especially those working in schools, do all they can to promote children's personal agency and thus their well-being.

'Wilkes continued to oversee Polly's education, pouring vast amounts of time, effort and money into her well-being' (Curator's wall text linked to the painting 'John Wilkes and his daughter Mary (Polly)' by Johan Zoffany). (Royal Academy, London, 21 May 2012)

The concept of well-being

'Well-being' is a ubiquitous concept increasingly used in policy, professional and everyday contexts. There is, for instance, the Well-being Institute of Australia, a Well-being and Human Development MSc at Bath University in the UK, employer policies in many countries to enable 'well-being at work', and well-being for sale in high streets from 'beauty and well-being salons' – thus placing it as a commercialized commodity.

Edelman (1964), in his analysis of American political discourse and the symbolic effect of language, suggests that words and phrases can serve to distil emotions and feelings. These, he terms, 'condensation symbols'. Vincent (1996), moving this argument into educational policy and practice, believes that words like 'participation', 'partnership', 'community' and 'citizenship' evoke specific emotions and this can result in a lack of clear definition and scrutiny of their use. Vincent (1996: 12) suggests such terms can take on 'a warm and humane gloss', resulting in them carrying a high impact in everyday discourse and professional debate.

'Well-being', it would seem, qualifies as an example of a condensation symbol. All would agree that it has a positive connotation but it is a diffuse concept often drawing on a very wide array of ideas relating to health, welfare, security, quality of life and happiness. Ereaut and Whiting (2008), in their enquiry into the use of the term, saw it as a cultural construct with a shifting set of meanings linked to the idea of a 'good life'. They note its frequent use in UK educational policy and guidance documents (from 1997 to 2010) and the way it is ambiguously referred to in many government publications during this period, and also that the term was not well understood by many parents and children (and probably teachers too, we would add).

Objective measures and indexes of well-being have proliferated. For instance, attending to a whole country's well-being, the Canadian Index of Well-being (CIW, 2012) highlights the following broad themes: living standards, community vitality, democratic engagement, education, healthy populations, environment, time use, leisure and culture.

In Scotland, well-being for children is conceptualized in terms of eight outcomes – healthy, safe, achieving, nurtured, active, respected, responsible and included (Scottish Executive, 2005). Such indexes serve both to provide a sense of the extensiveness of the concept but also demonstrate the breadth and pervasiveness of their use.

Save the Children's 12th annual 'mothers' index' of well-being of mothers and children (in 164 countries) placed Norway, Australia and Iceland in the highest rankings. These countries attained very high scores for mothers' and children's health, education and economic status. The UK was ranked 13th (Save the Children, 2011) and Justin Forsyth (Save the Children's chief executive) commented on the effect of the UK government's cuts in childcare support and, in particular, the impact of benefit cuts on economically poor families (see Coughlan, 2011). Such policy changes serve to remind us that well-being is not a static concept. Indeed, both adults and children may experience some of its core elements as momentary and precarious and these can be depleted, or even lost, during times of financial restraint.

When examining well-being, it is important to consider both its objective and subjective dimensions. It can be regarded as something that is provided to children by their families, early years settings, schools and the state. Economic affluence affects all of these, of course. It may also be seen more subjectively, as something brought about by individuals themselves through their personal action and the day-to-day life choices they make. If the latter is important, and we believe it is, then children can be encouraged, through their own agency, to choose what is in the interests of their well-being. John Wilkes, in our opening quote, could possibly be doing a little too much as a father to bring about well-being for his daughter Mary. Maybe she could be helped to do more for her own well-being. We pick up on this theme and, specifically, the fostering of children's agency, later in this chapter.

In summary, 'well-being' is a complex concept defined and operationalized in many ways. Explanations of its meaning may include, and lay different emphases on, personal and psychological extents but also environmental, social and economic considerations.

A Day in the Life

In our research into the development of 2-year-old girls living with their families in seven countries – Peru, Thailand, Italy, Canada, Turkey, the USA and the UK – we focus on the nature of their 'thriving' and their personal 'strength' (Gillen and Cameron, 2010; Sameroff, 2010) as they interacted with all that surrounded them. We have sometimes used the term well-being in our project writings but it was not a core concept for us. Arguably, however, concepts like thriving (for us, being well and doing well within a family context), resilience (the ability to cope with challenges and difficulties) and being strong (physically but also psychologically) feed well into the notion of well-being and well-being feeds into them.

Through visiting each of the seven families and filming them for the child's 'waking' day, we gathered a total of 50 hours of video data. We also interviewed parents about their children and, with parental assistance plus our own observations, compiled detailed field notes related to each family setting. Using a 'constructivist grounded analysis' approach (Charmaz, 2006; Glaser and Strauss, 1967), our writing focused on themes that appear to us to be related to children's thriving. Within our seven families, we examined 'emotional security' (Cameron et al., 2010), 'eating and family meals' (Gillen and Hancock, 2006), 'child–adult play collaborations' (Cameron et al., 2011), 'family notational systems' (Pinto et al., 2009), 'musicality' (Young and Gillen, 2007), 'secure domestic bases' (Cameron et al., 2006), 'safe play spaces' (Hancock and Gillen, 2007), 'humour' (Cameron et al., 2008) and 'joint book reading' (Cameron and Pinto, 2009). We revisited and extended a number of these themes in Gillen and Cameron (2010).

Resisting the temptation to start out with a definition of young children's 'thriving' or 'strength' and then look for exemplars in our data to feed into this, we examined our video data in a naturalistic way. In discussion with parents, we were able to put together a compilation tape for each child, lasting around 30 minutes, that aimed to show selected examples of a child's interactions and activities throughout the day. This compilation was then shared with families and gave rise to further understandings to enable theory grounded in the data.

On reflection, we believe we have addressed themes that are relevant to well-being too. The multi-national composition of our research team – with researchers situated across the globe – meant there was not only discussion about the various ways in which children were thriving in each of the seven families, but also about whether identified instances and sequences were, in fact, relevant to thriving in a particular cultural location (see Chapter 8).

The themes highlighted in our published works may not, at first glance, seem to be immediately linked to children thriving. However, it was the way in which the children interacted that decided for us that such data exemplified their thriving. For instance, when studying eating and family meals (Gillen and Hancock, 2006), we examine how, when required by parents to be involved in a formal meal, children in five countries (Peru, Canada, Thailand, Italy and the UK) looked for opportunities to integrate their explorations and play. The children wanted to live in and enjoy the moment (in their own way) whereas adults (in their way) sought a focus on nutrition and the progress of a meal. The children, we suggest, were 'strategic actors' (James and Prout, 1996: 47) and were often successful in extending these family occasions in certain ways for themselves. Parents, for their part, generally wanted the 'business' of the meal to progress but, nevertheless, were persuaded to go along, to some extent, with what the children wanted. Such mealtime negotiations and compromises were supportive of children's wider interests, achievements and enjoyment. Eating, an important element of thriving and well-being, thus proceeded while the children sought to integrate other dimensions of well-being through their personal interests.

Play and agency

In our scrutiny of many hours of video data and listening to what caregivers had to say about their children, we were surprised by the extent to which play features in all our children's days. Before we embarked on our research, as researchers and educationalists (and as parents too), we thought we understood that children, especially young children, like to play and learn from play (see Chapter 4). The data suggest that we had underestimated how important play was to the seven studied girls. How would these children describe what they spontaneously wanted to do through most of their waking days? How did they feel when family members interrupted them to get them to do something they, the adults, wanted them to do?

We didn't ask the children directly, and given the level of their linguistic and communicative skills, and their understandable tentativeness about engaging with relative strangers, they might not have been able to tell us explicitly about their deeply felt urge. This is not to say such a question should not be asked of very young children. It's more a comment on the limitations of our researcher interviewing skills and methodologies.

What we saw in the children is best described as a 'way of life' and a 'complete way of being in the world'. The term 'play' seems not to capture the comprehensiveness of how they wished to be. It was the intensity of this quest and the completeness of children's involvement that caught our attention as researchers and, as we have said, caused us to think more than we had to date about the meaning of play in children's day-to-day lives.

To suggest that play is child's work, as does Paley (2004), seems to us to be a partial acknowledgement of what play meant to our children. Winnicott (1972: 63) captures the completeness and intensity of what we observed when he writes of play as 'the search for self' involving the whole personality. James et al. (1998: 81) get close to what we observed in our children when they describe 'play as a childhood culture'. In all our publications to date, play features strongly. We thus see play and thriving as inextricably linked, and so, by association, are play and well-being (see also Chapters 3 and 4).

Agency and well-being

When observing the seven girls, we noted the extent to which they appeared to know, most of the time, what they wanted to do – sometimes this was achieved, or negotiated, alongside other family members but also when alone. Not, of course, that what they wanted to do was always appropriate or, indeed, safe for them, so adult judgements were applied; when the girls played by themselves, personal agency was readily apparent. At these times, the children seemed in charge and made ongoing decisions about the nature of their play and how it would be progressed. They appeared to be exploring what might be in their best interests. When playing with others, especially adults, there was a sense in which agency needed to be established, even 'won', given the intrinsic power of adults and their tendency to make decisions and do things for young children.

In our writings (many of which are indicated above), the importance of children's personal agency in association with their play is often highlighted. Hancock and Gillen (2007) noted how three of our children established and equipped specific places in their homes – a gate (Peru), a corridor (USA) and a balcony (Italy). These were all 'play places' that enabled them to explore something that held meaning for them. Parents sometimes facilitated or influenced this in some way but in each of these examples children took a leading role. Cameron et al. (2010) found that five of the children used humorous interactions that arose from their language play and actions. Further, they used humorous gambits to negotiate achieving their personal goals. In addition, the children drew, even inducted, adult family members into their play and humour, thus, arguably, supporting adult fun-making, thriving and well-being.

In all A Day in the Life publications, we note the way in which children's agency, as with play, albeit in varying degrees, enters into all the analysed themes. The consistency of this theme suggests that the development of personal agency is of central importance for children's well-being within their respective families, and, moreover, that it supports their developing abilities to choose for themselves what is in their interests and thus their well-being.

Roberts (2007) provides support to our emphasis on the connection between agency and well-being. In her research into the 'resilient well-being' of children from birth to 3 within the UK, she conducted interviews with 100 mothers and carried out case studies of 10 families, which included some video data. From her findings, she proposed four constructs of 'resilient well-being' which prioritize agency – agency, belonging and boundaries, communication and the physical world.

Enabling agency: four examples

The study data provides ample evidence of how each family instinctively promoted the child's well-being. Here we provide four examples, and, in so doing, argue that these examples provide suggestions for early childhood practice in supporting children's agency. The four selected data sequences come from the families in Peru, Turkey, the USA and the UK respectively. This selection is based on two factors. First, it enables the reader to obtain a sense of the differences that existed between our seven children; and second, it is guided by the situated professionals (i.e. we three authors) who were experienced in interpreting the relevant culturally located data.

Example 1: Peru – 'Plates and counters' (1 min 50 secs)

It's 10.05 am and Juanita is dressed and standing on the bed with two balloons. Her 6-year-old cousin, Ana, enters the room and handles a number of toys that are on the bed. She sits on the bed and Juanita tries to hit her on the head with a balloon but Ana gives a shriek and holds her hands up to prevent this. Ana picks up a pile of red plastic plates, puts a white counter on one plate and places it on the bed near where Juanita is standing. Juanita becomes interested and sits down still holding a balloon. Ana picks up another plate, puts a counter on it and places that near Juanita. Meanwhile, Juanita turns to put the balloon on a pillow. She then re-engages with Ana and the plates and gives her a white counter that Ana puts on the third plate. Both girls start to put more counters onto one of the plates. Juanita picks up a plate with a counter on it, removes the counter and puts that on the plate with the most counters. She keeps the empty plate and puts it in her lap. She picks up another plate with its counter and places that onthe plate in her lap. She then puts both plates on the bed and Ana places these (upside-down) to cover the plate containing many counters. Juanita finally picks up the whole pile of plates and shakes them to hear the sound of the counters rattling within. Ana watches her.

Researcher comment

We noted the empathic and subtle way in which Ana engaged Juanita in jointly playing with the plates and counters. Each child makes moves that serve to develop joint playing and, moreover, the 'moves' surrounding this game-like activity. Ana, however, discreetly supports Juanita's interest and involvement at all times. Ana, a young child herself, seems to intuitively adjust her role to enable participation and enjoyment by her younger cousin. Juanita, for her part, rises to the occasion in her matching responses and adaptations.

Example 2: Turkey – 'Blackboard game' (4 mins 3 secs)

It's early evening. Selin and her twin sister, her mother, father and adult cousin are all on the terrace. The adults are interacting and playing with the children. There are green plums on a table and a number of objects and toys including books, musical instruments, a playpen and a small blackboard with chalks. Father has drawn a horse's head on the blackboard and Selin and her sister are looking at it and drawing on the board. Selin's attention moves towards a small drain lid on the floor of the terrace. Father starts to draw a car logo (BMW) on the blackboard and invites both daughters to guess what it is. While Selin is examining it, he draws another – a VW logo. Then he draws a FIAT logo next to the horse's head. Selin is unsure about responding and uses a finger to smudge two of the logos. Father then starts to wipe the board with a piece of cloth. Selin takes over and finishes the wiping task. Father writes 'NISSAN' with Selin's sister close by. Selin is now a little away from the board, eating plums. After father has written 'FIAT' and said the word, Selin returns to his side. He then writes 'VOLVO' and Selin says 'VOLVO'. Father claps, waves his arms and kisses her on the cheek in approval. Selin moves away and climbs on a chair to eat plums. Father continues the guessing game with her twin sister but also encourages Selin to join in. Selin, still on the chair, looks away from the board, eats a plum and listens to a barking dog. Father writes her sister's name and invites Selin to respond. She says her sister's name and father claps. However, although she can be coaxed to participate in this way, her body language suggests she isn't really interested in the game. She gets down from the chair, walks across the terrace and offers a plum to her adult cousin.

Researcher comment

Selin's father seeks to involve his daughters in a guessing game. One daughter wants to play the game. Selin, however, although not disinterested, is never wholly involved and progressively reveals this. Her curiosity for a drain lid, her occasional movement away from the blackboard, the eating of plums and the attention given to a barking dog are signs of disengagement. We noted the adaptations that the father makes to the game to maintain both daughters' interest. Many parents (and teachers) learn to do this but it isn't an easy skill, especially if children are not fully interested. At no time does he show impatience with Selin, appearing to accept her wish not to join in and to seek out other interests. This seems respectful of her individuality and agency.

Example 3: USA – 'Pineapple trick' (15 mins 22 secs)

It's lunchtime and mother, father, brother James (aged 6) and Katy are sitting around a table. Katy is given a bowl of pineapple chunks. 'Pineapple', she says five times, seemingly enjoying the word and almost singing it. She reaches into the bowl, touches a chunk and then tastes her fingers. Her father gives her a toothpick. She uses it to pierce chunks and put them in her mouth. She holds up a chunk saying, 'Look it.' Her mother comments, 'You got a pineapple?' Katy says, 'I'm gonna eat it.' Thus begins Katy's lunch, the physical play with pineapple chunks and the language play while eating them. With one chunk, she hesitates, pushing it in and out of her mouth, spinning it around on the toothpick and savouring it. Mother and father are talking to James and having exchanges about what lies ahead in the day. Katy finally eats the chunk and selects others that she eats. While trying to eat one chunk, it accidentally falls onto the table and Katy says, 'I popped it into my mouth, and do a trick.' 'You popped it into your mouth and did a trick?' says her mother. Katy does it again, spitting it out onto the table this time. Her mother says, 'Oh, that's disgusting, Katy. You need a new pineapple?' Her mother puts more chunks into the bowl. Katy pierces one and spins it on its stick. Her mother says, 'I tricked you', as though to repeat a known family phrase and to encourage the idea of doing a trick. Katy continues to manipulate the chunks playfully. At one point, while gently rubbing one against her face, she says, 'This is an ice-cube.' Her mother breaks momentarily from her conversation with her husband to say, 'Um, a pineapple ice-cube.' A chunk falls from Katy's mouth and she says, 'Let me do it again.' She then flips the cube off its stick onto the table and it then bounces onto the floor. She pierces another and practises putting it into her mouth and letting it fall onto the table. Meanwhile, there's family conversation which sometimes draws Katy in while she continues to play with pineapple chunks. Again, when she successfully gets one to fall onto the table, she says to all, 'That was a trick.' But the rest of the family are not taking much notice and father just repeats Katy's words with a tone of growing disinterest. At one point, after Katy has spat out yet another chunk, and claimed another trick, father says, 'I don't think that's a very good trick.' Her mother then brings an end to the pineapple tricks by saying, 'Mind if I put it away, are you all done?'

Researcher comment

We note the way in which mother, father and brother accept that Katy wishes to play with pineapple chunks during lunch and to practise, what she regards as, her trick. In the interests of Katy's age and agency, they tolerate the repetition of the trick for a while but there's a point at which mother and father feel it has usefully served its purpose. For young children, the learning of tricks and humour that might please others is a subtle affair. It helps a child to establish when something they're doing is no longer funny to an audience – to push the boundary in the interests of self-knowledge. This family appeared to accept such pushing in this instance and that it seemed in the interests of Katy's understanding, and she acquiesces at the point when her parents call a halt to the fun.

Example 4: UK – 'Shoes and socks' (3 mins 13 secs)

'What happened to your socks?' Jessica's mother says. 'She pulled them off,' comments grandfather. 'Take your shoes to grandpa,' says mother, and he remarks encouragingly, 'Come on Jessica, let's put your shoes and socks on.' They both go into the sitting room; grandfather has Jessica's socks and Jessica has her shoes. He sits and stretches both hands towards her to urge her to come to him, saying 'Jessica, Jessica.' She looks the other way but mother also calls out that she needs her shoes on. Grandmother holds Jessica momentarily but she breaks away and sits on the carpet near her grandfather. He kneels down and starts to put her socks on, saying, 'I told you, you would need to put them on when you took them off.' She remains still as he does this but when he says, 'Now the sandals,' she doesn't want him to help her but she and Matthew (her brother) get their sandals mixed up and tugging ensues. Grandfather is accepting of her need to be independent and says, 'Well, you try then.' She has difficulty unfastening the buckle and grandfather offers his help but she wants to do it herself. Matthew is close by doing his own sandals. Grandmother suggests that grandfather helps Michael. He also rejects help and grandfather accepts this saying, 'No, he wants to try.' Grandfather tries to provide some help to Jessica by loosening the buckle but she wishes to do it all herself. She has difficulty with the buckle and her grandfather becomes slightly impatient with her, saying, 'Jessica, we want to get these sandals on.' Meanwhile, both grandmother and mother are watching what is happening. Matthew has progressed things a little further and he allows his grandmother to help him to fasten the first sandal. There's yet another attempt by grandfather to help Jessica but she resists and he says, holding back, 'You put it on this foot then.' At one point, she seeks to put the strap back into the buckle and grandfather says, with some frustration, 'No, don't put it back in; we want to get these sandals on.' 'I do it self,' says Jessica. 'Alright,' he says, 'You do it yourself,' seemingly exhausted by events.

Researcher comment

We noted the role of the grandfather in this episode. He clearly wanted to progress the putting on of shoes and socks – not least because the family were getting ready to go to a children's farm. However, despite this, he was prepared to drop back from over-helping and, at times, didn't help Jessica at all with her task. Although making the occasional comment to indicate a degree of frustration, he respected Jessica's wish to independently put on her own socks and shoes. In short, he showed a great deal of patience and regard for her agency, and she created, and took full advantage of, all opportunities to be agentive.

Final thoughts

The four children in this chapter will soon move out from their families to experience care and education set within a wider local community. They will, increasingly, be expected to engage with learning that is specified by governments and professionals and organized and taught by adults (see Chapter 3 for further discussion). Given our argument that personal agency is central to children's ability to thrive and their well-being, what would we highlight, more specifically, as important for those education professionals who work with them?

First, we would want them to provide these four children with the kind of personal respect and individual regard that they receive from their family members. Second, we would consider it essential that the children's preferred way of being, i.e. playing, is valued and afforded time and places where they can freely develop their explorations and spontaneous imaginings. Third, we would hope that they have scope for decision making and the selection of what most engages them.

Our knowledge of early care and education in Peru, Turkey, the USA and the UK enables us to feel some confidence that the above aspects would be addressed in each of these countries, albeit in various ways and to various extents. However, having immersed ourselves in a day in the lives of these four girls, we do feel concern that they might experience a loss of what they have been experiencing at home – certainly in the areas of opportunities to play (as they wish) and opportunities to express themselves in ways that are not stipulated by adults.

Education policy, in many countries, suggests that children in the early years should be consulted. However, early years professionals are increasingly required to implement centrally prescribed curricula in systematic and accountable ways. This has doubtless had an impact on the time that can be given to discussions and nego-tiations with children. So, our four Day in the Life children are unlikely to be given the level of personal agency experienced within their families. There could thus be a reduction in this core aspect of their well-being. That's not to say these children won't be able to relate to and enjoy much that is arranged for them.

When our studied children begin school, however, we expect the loss of personal agency to be even greater. In schools, it is invariably adults who lead and children who follow. One only has to spend a day in a school with the eye of an observer to note the extent to which children are often being told what to do and when to do it. It is especially in schools, therefore, that we would encourage professionals to look for ways of offering children more choice and more say in what happens to them. The selected data sequences above suggest that even small interpersonal exchanges can enable children to feel their agency is respected. This, we believe, can powerfully promote and enable their well-being.

Summary

This chapter:

- critically examines the concept of 'well-being' and notes the way in which it has entered political and educational discourse
- provides an overview of the Day in the Life project, a video study of seven young girls from seven countries, which examines the nature of their 'thriving' (and thus well-being) within their respective families
- emphasizes how the seven girls' wish to play entered into much of their waking hours
- suggests a strong connection between children's play, personal agency and well-being
- illustrates, through four case studies from families in Peru, Turkey, the UK and the USA, how family members foster, in a fine-grained way, the girls' personal agency
- concludes that if they are to promote children's well-being, early education settings and schools need to take note of this family practice and look for ways of ensuring children's agency in their professional practice.

Questions for discussion

1. How can early education settings extend personal choice and agency to children for the benefit of their well-being?
2. Given the formal structure and organization of schools, to what extent can they truly offer pupils opportunities for decision making and personal agency?
3. How can play, fun and playfulness be incorporated into the curriculum beyond early years settings? (*Higher-level question*)

Further reading

Levels 5 and 6

Hancock, R. and Gillen, J. (2007) Safe places in domestic spaces: two-year-olds at play in their homes. *Children's Geographies*, 5(4): 337–351.

This article focuses on children's explorations, play and well-being within the domestic spaces of their homes, i.e. a family grocery shop in Peru, the upstairs rooms of a house in America and the balcony of an apartment in Italy.

White, J. (2011) *Exploring Well-Being in Schools: A Guide to Making Children's Lives More Fulfilling*. London: Routledge. (See the Introduction, Chapters 1 and 2.)

This book adopts a philosophical stance on the concept of well-being and considers how schools might place well-being at the heart of their work with children.

Levels 6 and 7

Cameron, C.A., Tapanya, S. and Gillen, J. (2006) Swings, hammocks, and rocking chairs as secure bases during a day in the life in diverse cultures. *Child and Youth Care Forum*, 35(3): 231–247.

This article explores the importance of 'secure bases' for the well-being of five young girls in Thailand, Canada, Peru, Italy and the UK.

McAuley, C., Morgan, R. and Rose, W. (2010) Children's views on child well-being. In: C. McAuley and W. Rose (eds) *Child Well-being: Understanding Children's Lives*. London: Jessica Kingsley.

This chapter reviews studies that enable us to know more about how children understand the concept of well-being. The views of children from different family types and circumstances are considered, including disabled children and those in care.

Websites

The Children's Society (2011) Promoting Positive Well-being for Children. Available at: http://www.childrenssociety.org.uk/what-we-do/research/well-being/promoting-positive-well-being-children (accessed 13 August 2012).

This is research which found that a significant minority of UK children have low levels of well-being. The report recommends six priorities for children's well-being.

UNICEF (2007) An Overview of Child Well-being in Rich Countries: A Comprehensive Assessment of the Lives and Well-being of Children and Adolescents in the Economically Advanced Nations. Innocenti Report Card 7. Available at: http://www.unicef-irc.org/publications/pdf/rc7_eng.pdf

This provides a comprehensive assessment of the lives and well-being of children and young people in 21 nations of the industrialized world. Its purpose is to encourage monitoring, permit comparison and stimulate discussion.

UNICEF (2011) Children's Well-being in the UK, Sweden and Spain: The Role of Inequality and Materialism. Available at: http://www.unicef.org.uk/Documents/Publications/IPSOS_UNICEF_ChildWellBeingreport.pdf (accessed 14 August 2012).

This research pays particular attention to the role of materialism and inequality in children's well-being. Materialism is thought to be a cause, as well as an effect, of negative well-being, and countries that have higher levels of inequality are known to score lower on subjective well-being indicators.

References

Cameron, C.A. and Pinto, G. (2009) A Day in the Life: secure interludes with joint book reading. *Journal of Research in Childhood Education*, 23(4): 437–449.

Cameron, C.A., Pinto, G., Accorti Gamannossi, B., Hancock, R. and Tapanya, S. (2011) Domestic play collaborations in diverse family contexts. *Australasian Journal of Early Childhood*, 36(4): 78–86.

Cameron, C.A., Talay-Ongan, A., Hancock, R. and Tapanya, S. (2010) Emotional security. In: J. Gillen and C.A. Cameron (eds) *International Perspectives on Early Childhood Research: A Day in the Life*. London: Palgrave Macmillan.

Cameron, C.A., Tapanya, S. and Gillen, J. (2006) Swings, hammocks, and rocking chairs as secure bases during a day in the life in diverse cultures. *Child and Youth Care Forum*, 35(3): 231–247.

Cameron, E.L., Kennedy, K. and Cameron, C.A. (2008) 'Let me show you a trick!': a toddler's use of humor to explore, interpret, and negotiate her familial environment during a Day in the Life. *Journal of Research in Childhood Education*, 23: 5–18.

Canadian Index of Wellbeing (CIW) (2012) How are Canadians *Really* Doing? Highlights: Canadian Index of Wellbeing 1.0. Waterloo, ON: Canadian Index of Wellbeing and University of Waterloo. Available at: http://uwaterloo.ca/canadian-index-wellbeing/sites/ca.canadian-index-wellbeing/files/uploads/files/HowareCanadiansreallydoing_CIWnationalreport2012.pdf (accessed 17 June 2012).

Charmaz, K. (2006) *Constructing Grounded Theory: A Practical Guide through Qualitative Analysis*. London: SAGE.

Coughlan, S. (2011) UK lags in children's well-being rankings. BBC News: Education and Family, 1 May. Available at: http://www.bbc.co.uk/news/education-13268306 (accessed 17 June 2012).

Edelman, M. (1964) *The Symbolic Uses of Politics*. Urbana, IL: University of Illinois Press.

Ereaut, G. and Whiting, R. (2008) What Do We Mean by 'Wellbeing'? And Why Might it Matter? Government Research Report No. DCSF-RW073. Available at: https://www.education.gov.uk/publications/eOrderingDownload/DCSF-RW073.pdf (accessed 20 June 2012).

Gillen, J. and Cameron, C.A. (eds) (2010) *International Perspectives on Early Childhood Research: A Day in the Life*. London: Palgrave Macmillan.

Gillen, J. and Hancock, R. (2006) 'A Day in the Life': exploring eating events involving two-year-old girls and their families in diverse communities. *Australian Journal of Early Childhood*, 31(4): 23–29.

Glaser, B. and Strauss, A. (1967) *The Discovery of Grounded Theory: Strategies for Qualitative Research*. Chicago, IL: Aldine.

Hancock, R. and Gillen, J. (2007) Safe places in domestic spaces: two-year-olds at play in their homes. *Children's Geographies*, 5(4): 337–351.

James, A. and Prout, A. (1996) Strategies and structures: towards a new perspective on children's experience of family life. In: J. Brennen and M. O'Brien (eds) *Children in Families: Research and Policy*. London: Falmer Press, pp. 41–52.

James, A., Jenks, C. and Prout, A. (1998) *Theorizing Childhood*. Cambridge: Polity Press.

Paley, V.G. (2004) *A Child's Work: The Importance of Fantasy Play*. Chicago: University of Chicago Press.

Pinto, G., Accorti Gamannossi, B. and Cameron, C.A. (2009) From scribbles to meanings: social interaction in different cultures and the emergence of young children's early drawing. *Early Child Development and Care*, 179(8): 1–19.

Roberts, R. (2007) Companionable Learning: The Development of Resilient Wellbeing from Birth to Three. Unpublished PhD thesis, University of Worcester.

Sameroff, A. (2010) A unified theory of development: a dialectic integration of nature and nurture. *Child Development*, 81(1): 6–22.

Save the Children (2011) State of the World's Mothers 2011. Available at: http://www.savethechildren.org.uk/sites/default/files/docs/State_of_the_Worlds_Mothers_2011_1.pdf (accessed 17 June 2012).

Scottish Executive (2005) Getting it Right for Every Child: Proposals for Action. Edinburgh: The Scottish Executive. Available at: http://www.scotland.gov.uk/Publications/2005/06/20135608/56098 (accessed 17 June 2012).

Vincent, C. (1996) *Parents and Teachers: Power and Participation*. London: RoutledgeFalmer.

Young, S. and Gillen, J. (2007) Toward a revised understanding of young children's musical activities: reflections from the 'Day in the Life' project. *Current Musicology*, 84: 7–27.

Winnicott, D. (1972) *Playing and Reality*. Harmondsworth: Penguin Books.

CHAPTER 11

INTERNATIONAL PERSPECTIVES: USING THE LENS OF 'OTHER' TO CONSIDER WHAT WE LEARN

Claire Cameron and Linda Miller

Introduction: What do we learn from international perspectives?

Interest in learning about early childhood education and care (ECEC) in other countries has perhaps never been greater. There has been a burgeoning of comparisons, investigations and inquiries in recent years, from country reports on whole systems such as Starting Strong (OECD, 2001, 2006) to thematic inquiries such as international reviews of curriculum and assessment frameworks (Bertram and Pascal, 2002), the contribution of ECEC to social inclusion policies and practices (Children in Scotland, 2011) and investigations into the competences held by ECEC practitioners (CoRE, 2011). International studies can be highly influential. An international enquiry reviewing research evidence about the social benefits of ECEC (NESSE, 2009) concluded that high quality ECEC benefits all children, especially those from poor and migrant backgrounds. Prior to this, the EU's perspective on ECEC was largely driven by the Barcelona Targets, set in 2002, which supported the development of a greater quantity of places, in order to support women's employment in the labour market. But the evidence of particular benefits for disadvantaged children from high quality ECEC services contributed to the publication, in 2011, of a Communiqué, *Providing All Our Children with the Best Start for the World of Tomorrow*, which stated:

> High quality early childhood education and care can make a strong contribution – through enabling and empowering all children to realize their potential – to achieving two of the Europe 2020 headline targets in particular: reducing early school leaving to below 10%, and lifting at least 20 million people out of the risk of poverty and social exclusion. (EC, 2011: 2)

This recognition of the highly important role of ECEC in achieving the EU's economic, social and educational goals was also, in this Communiqué, an impetus for further research and policy development within the EU.

However, there are different ways of using international evidence. One response to international rankings of countries on specific measures, such as the OECD's Programme for International Student Assessment (PISA) measure of 15-year-olds' achievements in reading, mathematics and science, is to enable participant countries to measure their position against others and perhaps help them to rethink national policies and practices and track progress towards success in these measures. Another is to seek to understand a different system and the combination of factors that contribute to its success with a view to replication or rejection, depending on the degree of match with one's own system. Third, it is possible to use international evidence on a particular theme to stimulate review of one's own policies and practices, perhaps where goals and values are mutually held. For example, the Welsh Minister for Children, Education, Lifelong Learning and Skills stated that the Welsh early childhood policy drew on 'best international practice from countries such as Denmark, New Zealand and Italy' in introducing the Welsh Foundation Phase (Hutt, 2007: n.p.). Wales could have selected other countries to examine 'best' practice, but found shared values and goals among those they did select.

Fourth, it is possible to use international evidence and examples as a source of inspiration, from which we might learn in different ways. Rather than decontextualized comparison on particular benchmarks, which are assumed to be universal but may well not be, or wholesale rejection or adoption of particular methods or systems, it is more effective, and more respectful of cultural traditions and local social and political issues, to use international evidence as stimuli for self-questioning, provoking debate and identifying values and goals to work towards. As Oberhuemer argues in Chapter 2: 'it is highly questionable, if not impossible, to take policies and particularly educational approaches, which are always strongly values-based, from one cultural context to another' (p. 26).

Instead of advocating imposition, this book provides inspiration for its readers. By providing examples of very different ways of constructing and providing ECEC in Europe and beyond, we are opening up readers' imaginations to other possibilities. There is a strong tendency, in examining international examples of practice, to absorb the different into what we are familiar with, to make everyone the same. Dahlberg and Moss (2005: 13) argue that ethical early childhood practice requires conscious thought about how to respect 'otherness' that does not 'grasp the Other and make them into the Same'. By introducing research evidence, practice examples and policy comparison from across western and eastern Europe, the Americas and beyond, we have invited our readers to delight in difference, be self-critical in reflection and become motivated to learn more in such a way as to contribute to advancing high quality ECEC for the children of today and tomorrow.

From many themes in the chapters of this book, we have selected three for discussion that resonate with wider debates. The first is the relationship between ECEC and formal education, the second is the idea of new spaces for childhood within ECEC settings, and the third considers bridging the space between public and private worlds.

The relationship between ECEC and formal education

The dominant vision of ECEC services, children and childhood that countries choose to embrace through their policies and practices shapes and frames the experiences of young children and the spaces they occupy. In Chapters 2 and 3, Pamela Oberhuemer and Yoshie Kaga noted a growing (and worrying) trend towards a narrower and more goal-oriented curricula across many countries, partly influenced by international comparisons of educational achievement, such as the OECD PISA measures mentioned above. This is happening to some extent even in countries such as Sweden, which has been regarded as embracing more child-centred and holistic early childhood approaches. Such changes negatively impact on the roles and practices of those who work with young children, contributing to the 'schoolification' of early childhood settings, and so affect the experiences of the children they care for and educate. This trend towards the 'schoolification' of ECEC raises questions within the countries concerned about the nature of children and childhood, for example about what children are expected to 'become' (i.e. pupils), what they are expected to learn ('basic skills' and subject content) and which pedagogical practices are privileged (formal teaching versus holistic learning). As Bennett (2006: n.p.) notes, 'schoolifying' denotes 'taking over early childhood in a colonizing manner' and stems from historic structures and practices whereby early education was absorbed by primary education, despite there being strong advocates of holistic early education and care (see Miller and Pound, 2011).

As noted above, a key factor in the relationship between ECEC and formal education is the way in which both the 'child' and the 'setting' are conceptualized. This relationship is not confined to what children might learn but also covers how they are expected to behave in these different contexts. Jones et al. (2012: 174) researched children's experiences in their first 18 months of formal schooling in four English primary schools, focusing on the processes whereby children are required to learn to 'act properly' in such settings. They found that 'children must not only act appropriately, but must be recognized as having done so'; and also that 'schooling demands that children behave in ways that are normal as dictated by the discourses of the "regular" classroom' (Jones et al., 2012: 175).

Jones et al. (2012) pose the question of how things might be different; this is an issue addressed by a number of chapters in this book.

In Roger Hancock, Ann Cameron and Ayshe Talay-Ongan's account of their research with young children and families across seven countries, in Chapter 10, we see how easily and enjoyably children can learn and develop in the context of their own homes, in familiar spaces and with familiar adults, raising questions about how this might be replicated in ECEC settings, thus enabling smoother transitions while also investigating and respecting children's agency and well-being.

Tullia Musatti and her co-workers offered a fresh perspective on the definition of curricula for ECEC in Chapter 4, emphasizing the 'how' and 'why' rather than the 'what' of learning, and focusing on co-constructing learning through 'elementary activities', reflective dialogue and the involvement of families. This is made possible when early childhood educators are working within 'guideline' documentation which devolves decision making and the implementation of the curriculum to practitioners who are trusted by governments, rather than within national curricula externally imposed and regulated by governments (Bennett, 2006). Musatti and colleagues demonstrated what is possible at a 'micro' level without these external constraints and through thoughtful reflection and a common philosophy. As they say, 'we provided the children with a map' and eventually some 'pathways to reflection' of various durations and complexities emerged.

While examples of curricular innovation can be inspiring and enabling, Pamela Oberhuemer's warning, in Chapter 2, about the dangers of 'policy borrowing' and 'policy lending' in addressing a country's particular concerns leads us to suggest that we should focus rather on how it is possible to use international evidence and examples as sources which we might learn from and perhaps use in different ways. An example of drawing on other curricular approaches is documented by Maynard and Chicken (2012) who explored Reggio Emilia practice with early years teachers in five primary schools in a Welsh context. The aim of the project was not to 'transplant' the approach but to use it as a lens for critical reflection and as a means of making visible the teachers' existing thinking and practice, in a context 'dominated by prescribed and subject related outcomes' (Maynard and Chicken, 2012: 221).

At a 'macro' level, Yoshie Kaga in Chapter 3 addressed the issue of 'schoolification' by proposing a 'strong and equal partnership' model where the two sectors of primary education and ECEC work together in a relationship where they are equal partners, each building on the strengths of the other. Kaga proposed ways to promote this model including: developing meeting places, actionable strategies and policies; identifying differences and common heritage and developing shared visions and understandings; and building up the ECE sector. However, as Bennett (2006) notes, such a move requires ECEC services to be seen as a public good and as the *foundation* stage of the education process. He argues for a recognition of the diverse perspective of the two sectors, for a more unified approach to learning and smoother transitions for children.

New spaces for childhood

A new literature is emerging about spaces for childhood within ECEC. By 'spaces', we are referring to the metaphoric sense of space in which ECEC settings are seen as 'environments of many possibilities – cultural and social, but also economic, political, ethical, aesthetic, physical – some predetermined, others not, some initiated by adults, others by children … public places for children to live their childhoods' (Moss and Petrie, 2002: 9). Spaces are places where children's identities and expertise are seen as actively contributing to the education and care on offer within a setting. From this perspective, children are not (only) seen as passive recipients of 'instruction' given by adults, but are 'experts in their own lives', that is, they are 'skilful communicators, active participants, meaning makers, researchers and explorers' (Clark, 2010: 116). In this understanding, 'space' refers to a site for developing, through interaction or alone, meanings, memories and reference points on which children's expertise and participation can build. They become, or are, citizens of their setting, with rights and responsibilities. The term 'spaces' also refers to the physical locations or environments in which interaction and learning can take place. In one sense, high quality ECEC provides a 'haven' or protected space, a nurturing environment for the expression of children's expertise. Kernan and Loyzaga (Chapter 7) draw attention to this idea of the ECEC environment: 'early years settings can provide a "safe haven" for children to play, to learn, to engage in peer culture and to nurture their resilience' (p. 98). Other chapters in this volume have highlighted different aspects of space for childhood. One of these is ECEC as a space for dialogue where children, practitioners and parents can come together on issues or themes and collectively contribute their expertise.

In Musatti et al.'s chapter on constructing a curriculum in Italian centres for very young children, the starting point was an acceptance that everyday life was a shared life for practitioners and children. The practitioners aimed to develop and extend the children's experience of continuity and learning while at the same time closely analysing what children did with the 'bait' the practitioners offered. The actions of the practitioners deliberately encouraged a sense of shared space and peer solidarity, through involving children in many everyday tasks. The practitioners' observations and analysis of children's actions and interactions were called 'pathways to reflection'. They involved parents through sharing information, requests to supply materials and inviting their direct participation. The focus on developing a curriculum that foregrounds shared space, in dialogue, over time, has the potential to generate important social bonds between participants, and, indeed, social competences that will nurture children's learning in different environments. It is quite different to the English ECEC curricula, as set out in the national government's 17 Early Learning Goals, which is:

> the statutory framework that sets the standards that all early years providers must meet to ensure that children learn and develop well and are kept healthy and safe. It promotes teaching and learning to ensure children are ready for school and gives children the broad range of knowledge and skills that provide the right foundation for good future progress through school and life', a statement that suggests 'top-down' knowledge imparted by adults. (DfE, 2013: n.p.)

Musatti et al.'s chapter was very much focused on the everyday within an ECEC setting. Several of the chapters invited reflection on the relation between the setting and its physical context. Nimmo (2008) argues that formal early childhood settings are in danger of excluding children from access to what he calls 'real life', or the activities of adults in community or employment arenas, through being risk-averse, and instead containing them in a protected space. Bronwen Cohen and Wenche Rønning's chapter on place-based learning was an example of a direct challenge to such thinking. Drawing on Norway and Scotland, Cohen and Rønning argue that while outdoor education, including forest kindergartens, is the main manifestation of place-based learning, extensive use is made, especially in Norway, of 'real life' in 'art galleries, museums, fish farms or other kinds of local industry' (p. 115). The intention in this work is to educate children in local history, culture and traditions, including minority linguistic traditions, such as Gaelic in Scotland and Sami in Norway. Place-based learning, therefore, is an important interface between the ECEC setting as a 'haven' and place for citizenship and the integration of children into communities, generating the memories, reference points and constructed meanings that build ECEC into community economic and social life. One of the implications of place-based learning in rural areas is that children's childhood experiences tie them to their local communities, and may encourage them to return to their home areas once they are educated adults, contributing to the economic life of the area.

Kernan and Loyzaga's chapter extends the idea of ECEC's bridge with 'real life'. Their description of the work of an NGO, Melel Xojobal, in a very poor urban region of Mexico, illustrates how the ECEC setting does not have universally recognizable characteristics but is an expression of culturally, socially and economically relevant provision to support children's childhoods. In the Melel case, this includes supporting children's work, by taking the 'setting' to areas of the city where children are working as vendors, spreading a sheet on the ground to symbolize the early childhood 'space' and running games and activities that bring participants together as children. ECEC practitioners reinforce the notion of the city as a childhood space by stimulating debates with working children about who the city belongs to and invoking ideas of their membership of the city.

All three of these chapters focus, in different ways, on aspects of developing a sense of belonging through valorized participation in, and relationships developed within, ECEC spaces. Another 'new' space for childhood is that of physical exploration, both through designated settings, such as Forest Schools, and through employment of the outdoors in the curriculum. There is a growing recognition of the importance of physical exploration, not just for 'letting off steam' but also for sheer enjoyment, exercise of the imagination and being away, albeit temporarily, from the supervision of adults in ECEC settings (Clark, 2010; Jensen, 2011). In addition, physical exploration facilitates children's physical development, and this in turn is highly connected to the development of personal, social and emotional capacities and communicative abilities (Tickell, 2011).

Forest Schools began to be developed in Britain in the mid-1990s, building on the tradition in Norway, and other Scandinavian countries, of valorizing the outdoors and encouraging a love of nature for exploration and physical challenge among children (Blackwell and Pound, 2011). By 2004, there were about 140 Forest Schools in the UK, and growing interest in giving children a Forest School-type experience by spending a day a week in the woods (O'Brien and Murray, 2006). Research on the impact of attending Forest Schools in England highlighted benefits such as confidence developed through having the freedom, time and space to learn and show independence, social skills through sharing tools and team games, extending language development and communication skills, motivation and concentration on the fascination of the woodland, development of physical stamina, and greater knowledge and understanding of the natural environment (O'Brien and Murray, 2006).

The outdoors as a childhood space in ECEC settings is highlighted in Chapter 7, where Claire Cameron picks out two main ways of conceptualizing key early childhood stakeholders' perceptions of the use of outdoor space in three countries. The distinction was between a 'freedom to roam' approach, that was associated with the practice in Denmark, and valued by practitioners and early childhood experts, and a 'safety' oriented approach, that was more common among the English and Hungarian stakeholders. Any link between the gender of the practitioner and valuing being outdoors was very limited or non-existent. This data highlighted the need, if the benefits of using the outdoors are to be fully realized, to pay much more attention to this childhood space in English regulations of ECEC.

The chapters identifying 'new' spaces for childhood have benefited not only from the international 'lens' but also from a refreshing combination of disciplinary sources, drawing not just on 'care' and 'education' literature but also on new geographies of childhood, environmental planning, rural and urban studies and economic regeneration. This multidisciplinary thread continues in the third theme on which we have elected to focus, namely the ECEC role in bridging the space between public and private worlds.

Bridging the space between public and private worlds

A bridge can be an object of architectural beauty, a lifeline to safety, a means of accessing places that might otherwise be unreachable; we talk about 'bridging relationships' and politicians worldwide use phrases such as 'bridging the gap' between the 'haves' and 'have nots'. In ECEC services, there is a body of literature on bridging the gap between home and school. In the context of this book, ECEC services can be seen as a bridge between the public world of the services they encompass and the private world of family and community. As Bennett (2006) notes, ECEC services have both a social and a learning function and countries have responded by providing both universal and targeted services. Bridges between such services and communities are important, in particular for families who are socially isolated through economic circumstance, culture or ethnicity, as chapters in this book discuss.

In Chapter 4, we saw that constructing a suitable curriculum for children of this age means also building a bridge between this micro-culture and that of the broader society in which they are growing up; involving families is key to this process.

Belonging and participation are themes underpinning Chapters 5, 6 and 8. Anne-Marie Doucet-Dahlgren, in Chapter 5, described the 'Folk University' initiative as a specific form of early intervention, organized within the wider framework of the Service de Protection Maternelle et Infantile (PMI) in France. She reported how the Folk University became a vehicle for reducing the isolation of parents through opportunities to participate in group situations which bridged the gap between institutional stakeholders such as ECEC services, to share mutual understanding about issues of concern to parents such as child upbringing, care and education. Thus, parents were supported and enabled to find a 'voice' and a community presence.

Chapter 6 provided a disturbing account of the 'separateness' of the Roma population in the countries studied in the Roma Early Childhood Inclusion (RECI) Project. John Bennett documented how, in their daily lives, Romani people face 'discrimination and social exclusion, based on racial prejudice and stereotyping, and, as a consequence, are confronted by profoundly negative attitudes, frequently articulated by populist politicians, ultra-nationalist political parties and the mass media' (p. 79). In many cases, it would seem that ECEC services, far from providing a bridge for the Roma population to ECEC, act as a barrier and exclude them by not being accessible or meeting their needs. In Chapter 3, Yoshie Kaga argued for an accessible model of ECEC (the 'ready school' model) that stresses the school's (or ECEC setting's) adaptation to the child's characteristics and needs. Bennett argues further that in certain circumstances, and in particular in relation to the youngest Roma children, services need to be brought to the people rather than the people to the services.

An example of ECEC's bridge with 'real life' is offered in Chapter 7, and noted earlier in this chapter, in Kernan and Loyzaga's account of the work of an NGO, Melel Xojobal, in Mexico, where the 'setting' is taken to areas of the city where children are working, thus reducing barriers to access of services. In a second centre-based programme, *Arrumacos* (meaning 'nurturing hugs'), for children from birth to 4 years, the authors described how great importance is given to fostering a positive identity and sense of belonging. One way in which this takes place is through creative workshops involving drawing, photography, story and activities and discussions with the children which reflect 'family, their home, and the street where they live'. The use of cultural artefacts including local fabrics, traditional 'rebozo' or 'chal' (shawls or baby-carrying cloths) and 'masa *de tortilla*' (dough) provides a bridge between the centre and the community it serves.

The isolation of schools from family and community and the failure to make use of children's experiences is highlighted in Chapter 8, where Bronwen Cohen and Wenche Rønning recounted their experiences in Norway and Scotland. They advocate 'place-based learning' as an approach that creates awareness of, and links to, the unique history, culture and tradition of communities. In Norway, examples included children in schools and kindergartens undertaking activities such as spinning and dying wool, making and using traditional tools and cooking traditional dishes, sometimes involving grandparents or other older people living in the area. In the far north of Scotland, in the Shetland Islands, the cultural strategy makes strong links between the islands' environment, history and cultural traditions, and economic and social regeneration. The educational strategy includes promoting interest in local dialects, place names, literature and traditional crafts. The authors describe ways in which this was effectively harnessed to build a bridge between what happens in ECEC settings and schools and the wider community, developing awareness of local and national identities.

The chapters in this book have drawn attention to the ECEC role in bridging the internal world of the setting and the external world. ECEC settings can act as a site for addressing disadvantage, poverty, social cohesion and social exclusion, building bridges with families and communities and developing a sense of belonging and connectedness.

Final thoughts

In this chapter, we have argued that there is a growing international interest in ECEC and that high quality services and provision can make a strong contribution to children's care, education and well-being, and address social disadvantage. We have said that although we can learn from looking at what other countries do, there is more than one way of using international evidence. These other ways include: measuring what we do against the progress of others; seeking to understand a different system and take what we deem useful from this; and using international research to stimulate a rethinking of policy and to seek inspiration. We have however noted the dangers of 'policy lending' and 'policy borrowing' in considering other policies and approaches. From the chapters in this book, we have extracted what we consider to be the three key themes:

1. The relationship between ECEC and formal education, referred to as the 'schoolification' of early childhood, is, we believe, an ongoing theme. It is under considerable debate in England at the time of writing, where concerns are being expressed about the increased formalization of the primary school curriculum, arguably resulting in inappropriate pressure on young children to achieve and be 'ready' for school.
2. The idea of 'new' spaces for childhood recognizes children as active contributors to, and participants in, the life of the ECEC setting which is a public place for childhood. Chapters have shown that physical locations and environments can be spaces in which children explore and learn, are protected and claim the right to inhabit, belong and participate.
3. If ECEC settings are to act as a bridge between public and private worlds, as chapters in this book have demonstrated, then they need to reflect on, learn from and reach out to the communities and cultures they serve.

☐ **Summary**

- In this chapter, we have made a case for considering international perspectives in order to 'shine a light' on established practice in the UK and consider how to improve the ways in which ECEC services are developed and implemented.
- We have advocated using international evidence as a vehicle for questioning existing practice and policies, to provoke debate and to consider what values and goals we might share and work towards.
- We have highlighted the importance of learning from a range of disciplines when considering ECEC in an international context, from geographies, and sociology of childhood to studies of parenting as well as education – all may offer sources of inspiration that extend our understanding of young children's lives in ECEC settings.
- We discussed three themes of the book: the relationship between ECEC and formal education, the opening up of new spaces for childhood, and ECEC as a bridge between public and private worlds, and in all these themes a foundation value was the idea of the child's experience, in the here and now, being important in any assessment of the quality of the service on offer. All the chapters in the book, in their different ways, seek to promote the child as an expert in their own life, with rights to self-expression, citizenship and a sense of belonging in ECEC.

Questions for discussion

1. In your view, how accessible is ECEC to children most at risk of social exclusion?
2. What do you understand by the term 'new spaces' for childhood? What implications might this notion have for your practice or the practice in a setting you are familiar with?
3. How might the terms 'policy lending' and 'policy borrowing' be useful in learning from an international context? (*Higher-level question*)

Further reading 📖

Levels 5 and 6

Brooker, L. and Woodhead, M. (eds) (2008) *Developing Positive Identities: Diversity and Young Children*. Milton Keynes: The Open University/The Hague: Bernard van Leer Foundation. This book, from the Early Childhood in Focus Series (M. Woodhead and J. Oates, Series Editors), provides a clear and accessible account of research, information and analysis relating to the fundamental right of every child to develop a positive identity.

Maynard, T. and Chicken, S. (2012) Through a different lens: exploring Reggio Emilia in a Welsh context. In: L. Miller, R. Drury and C. Cable (eds) *Extending Professional Practice in the Early Years*. London: SAGE/The Open University, pp. 211–222.

In this chapter, Maynard and Chicken explore how the philosophy and practice of Reggio Emilia can be used to assist practitioners to look at their practice with a different lens, as an aid to critical reflection.

Levels 6 and 7

Dahlberg, G. and Moss, P. (2005) *Ethics and Politics in Early Childhood Education*. Abingdon: RoutledgeFalmer.

Drawing on the Italian 'Reggio Emilia approach' and others, this book explores the ethical and political dimensions of early childhood services and argues for the importance of these dimensions at a time when they are often reduced to technical and managerial projects, without informed consideration of what is best for the child. The authors make complex material accessible and invite reflection on questions of assuming universal truths such as 'best practice' in ECEC.

Georgeson, J. and Payler, J. (2013) *International Perspectives on Early Childhood Education and Care*. Buckingham: Open University Press.

This book examines both key influential approaches to ECEC and some less well-known international examples. It aims to inform those studying early years about perspectives in other countries, encourage critical thinking about issues, influences and the complexities of early years provision around the world and promote critical reflection on systems with which the reader is familiar.

Websites

http://www.forestschools.com

This organization aims to encourage and inspire individuals through positive outdoor experiences and offers training to forest school leaders.

http://www.oecd.org/edu/school/startingstrongiiearlychildhoodeducationandcare.htm

Starting Strong remains the most comprehensive international analysis of ECEC systems. In two volumes of country reports and a 'toolkit' for policy makers, the material is thorough, with research conducted by many of the leading figures in ECEC worldwide.

References

Bennett, J. (2006) 'Schoolifying' early childhood education and care: accompanying pre-school into education. Paper presented at the Contesting Early Childhood and Opening for Change conference, Institute of Education, University of London, 10 May.

Bertram, T. and Pascal, C. (2002) *Early Years Education: An International Perspective*. London: QCA.

Blackwell, S. and Pound, L. (2011) Forest Schools in the early years. In: L. Miller and L. Pound (eds) *Theories and Approaches to Learning in the Early Years*. London: SAGE, pp. 133–149.

Children in Scotland (2011) Working for Inclusion: Final Report. Available at: http://www.children-inscotland.org.uk/docs/pubs/WFIFINALOVERVIEWREPORTA4.pdf

Clark, A. (2010) Young children as protagonists and the role of participatory, visual methods in engaging multiple perspectives. *American Journal of Community Psychology*, 46(1–2): 115–123.

CoRE (2011) Competence Requirements in Early Childhood: A Study for the European Commission Directorate-General for Education and Culture. Available at: http://ec.europa.eu/education/more-information/doc/2011/core_en.pdf

Dahlberg, G. and Moss, P. (2005) *Ethics and Politics in Early Childhood Education.* London: RoutledgeFalmer.

Department for Education (DfE) (2013) Early Years Foundation Stage. Available at: http://www.education.gov.uk/schools/teachingandlearning/curriculum/a0068102/early-years-foundation-stage-eyfs (accessed 22 March 2013).

European Commission (EC) (2011) *Early Childhood Education and Care: Providing All Our Children with the Best Start for the World of Tomorrow,* COM (2011) 66 final, Brussels. Available at: http://eur-lex.europa.eu/LexUriServ/LexUriServ.do?uri=COM:2011:0066:FIN:EN:PDF (accessed 21 March 2013).

Hutt, J. (2007) Wales Kids Will Learn through Playing. Available at: http://www.newswales.co.uk/index.cfm?section=Education&F=1&id=15025 (accessed 22 March 2013).

Jensen, J.J. (2011) Understandings of Danish pedagogical practice. In: C. Cameron and P. Moss (eds) *Social Pedagogy and Working with Children and Young People: Where Care and Education Meet.* London: Jessica Kingsley, pp. 141–158.

Jones, L., Holmes, R., MacRae, C. and MacLure, M. (2012) Improper children. In: L. Miller, R. Drury and C. Cable (eds) *Extending Professional Practice in the Early Years.* London: SAGE/The Open University, pp. 173–183.

Maynard, T. and Chicken, S. (2012) Through a different lens: exploring Reggio Emilia in a Welsh context. In: L. Miller, R. Drury and C. Cable (eds) *Extending Professional Practice in the Early Years.* London: SAGE/The Open University, pp. 211–222.

Miller, L. and Pound, L. (eds) (2011) *Theories and Approaches to Learning in the Early Years.* London: SAGE.

Moss, P. and Petrie, P. (2002) *From Children's Services to Children's Spaces: Public Policy, Children and Childhood.* London: RoutledgeFalmer.

Network of Experts in Social Sciences Education and Training (NESSE) (2009) *Early Childhood Education and Care: Lessons from Research for Policy Makers.* Available at: http://www.nesse.fr/nesse/activities/reports (accessed 22 March 2013).

Nimmo, J. (2008) Young children's access to real life: an examination of the growing boundaries between children in child care and adults in the community. *Contemporary Issues in Early Childhood,* 9: 3–13.

O'Brien, L. and Murray, R. (2006) A Marvellous Opportunity for Children to Learn: A Participatory Evaluation of Forest School in England and Wales. Forest Research, Farnham. Available at: http://www.forestresearch.gov.uk/fr/INFD-5Z3JVZ (accessed 22 March 2013).

Organisation for Economic Co-operation and Development (OECD) (2001) *Starting Strong I: Early Childhood Education and Care.* Paris: OECD.

Organisation for Economic Co-operation and Development (OECD) (2006) *Starting Strong II: Early Childhood Education and Care.* Paris: OECD.

Tickell, C. (2011) *The Early Years: Foundations for Life, Health and Learning.* An independent report on the Early Years Foundation Stage to Her Majesty's Government. London: The Stationery Office.

INDEX

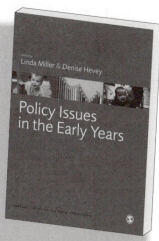

PROFESSIONALIZATION, LEADERSHIP AND MANAGEMENT IN THE EARLY YEARS

Edited by **Linda Miller** and **Carrie Cable** both at *The Open University*

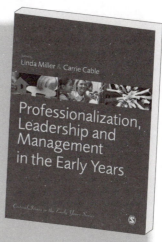

With the rapid change experienced by the Early Years Workforce over recent times, this book considers what constitutes professionalization in the sector, and what this means in practice. Bringing a critical perspective to the developing knowledge and understanding of early years practitioners at various stages of their professional development, it draws attention to key themes and issues.

Chapters are written by leading authorities, and provide case studies, question and discussion points to facilitate critical thinking.

Topics covered include:

- constructions of professional identities
- men in the early years
- multi-disciplinary working in the early years
- professionalization in the nursery
- early childhood leadership and policy.

Written in an accessible style and relevant to all levels of early years courses, the book is highly relevant to those studying at Masters level, and has staggered levels of Further Reading, that encourage reflection and progression.

CRITICAL ISSUES IN THE EARLY YEARS
November 2010 • 184 pages
Paperback: (978-1-84920-554-2) • £24.99
Hardback: (978-1-84920-553-5) • £74.00

ALSO FROM SAGE